Fascists, Fabricators and Fantasists

Fascists, Fabricators and Fantasists
Antisemitism in South Africa from 1948 to the present

Milton Shain

First published by Jacana Media (Pty) Ltd in 2023
10 Orange Street
Sunnyside
Auckland Park 2092
South Africa
+2711 628 3200
www.jacana.co.za

© Milton Shain, 2023
© Cover photo: Alexander Joe/Getty Images

All rights reserved.

ISBN 978-1-4314-3358-2

Cover design by publicide
Editing by Russel Martin
Proofreading by Lara Jacob
Indexing by Rita Sephton
Set in Ehrhardt MT Std 10.5/14pt
Job no. 004013

See a complete list of Jacana titles at www.jacana.co.za

For Millie

Rather than conceive anti-Semitism as a virus, we will do better to think of it as a deep reservoir of stereotypes and narratives, one which is replenished over time and that can be dipped into with ease.
David Feldman, *Haaretz*, 27 November 2019

Praise for *Fascists, Fabricators and Fantasists: Antisemitism in South Africa from 1948 to the present*

'This is a very fine book. As with the earlier two volumes covering the history of antisemitism in South Africa, Milton Shain shows a mastery of the subject matter, taking the chronology from the early days of apartheid through to its dismantlement and then the early decades of the twenty-first century. There is a subtle and persuasive balance in which traditions of antisemitism that cut across racial and religious divides are meticulously documented, but also allowing for the limitations, especially in the political sphere, of how it has been articulated. Written fluently with wit and wisdom throughout, Milton Shain concludes his definitive study of the complex beast that is South African antisemitism.'
Professor Tony Kushner, James Parkes Professor of Jewish/non-Jewish relations, University of Southampton

'Milton Shain gives exceptional service to South Africa by detailing the existence of the scourge of antisemitism, and even more because of his talent for transforming meticulous research and level-headed thinking into a readable text. This third volume of a historical trilogy is especially valuable because it covers both the antisemitism of the apartheid era and its carryover into the democracy of the present. Also the future: Prof. Shain warns about "a burgeoning anti-Zionism, which for some provides a fig-leaf for simple Jew-hatred". As he notes, the nature of antisemitism and its chief perpetrators have changed, but the evil remains a menace both to Jews and to the country's health and stability.'
Benjamin Pogrund, deputy editor of former *Rand Daily Mail*, author of *How Can Man Die Better: Robert Mangaliso Sobukwe*

With Fascists, Fabricators and Fantasists: Antisemitism in South Africa from 1948 to the present, *Milton Shain has completed one of the most thorough and intelligent histories of anti-Jewish sentiment and actions of a single national state* yet written. As the final volume of his trilogy, Shain turns to a South Africa initially suspended between European antisemitic fascism and the global politics of the 1940s and '50s. That he is attuned to how internal political debates are shaped by (and may also shape) external debates about the status of the stereotypical "Jews", moves the politics of South Africa onto the global post-war stage. That there was a disparity in a political world shaping apartheid between the lived experience of Jews in the nation-state and their image is not surprising. How this helped move all towards 1994 and majority rule is, however, new. Shain completes the volume by again looking at the nation-state – now defined by the ANC – and its complex relationship to Zionism as a surrogate for the "Jews". And how Jews as South African citizens in this new political environment are dealing with this aspect of global politics. A brilliant, well-written, well-documented, and often prescient study of the past as shaping our NOW.'

Professor Sander L. Gilman, author of *"I Know Who Caused COVID-19": Xenophobia and Pandemics*

'Shain's succinct and stimulating study of antisemitism in South Africa over the past seventy years demonstrates the tenacity of ideas, especially the most pernicious ones: those rooted in fantasy and falsehood. Superbly researched and elegantly written, this book shines a light on the commonalities between reactionary white right-wingers and self-styled progressive leftists in their depiction, at different historical junctures, of Jews. Timely, accessible and engaging, Shain's deft treatment of these themes should resonate with an international readership.'

Dr Michael Cardo, Member of Parliament of South Africa

'Milton Shain is generally regarded today in South Africa and abroad as the doyen of South African Jewish history, and this for very good reason, both for the quality of his scholarship and his ability to communicate it in a lively and accessible way. His new book is testimony to this. The third in a trilogy of work on the origins and evolution of antisemitism in South Africa, it breaks new ground like its two critically acclaimed predecessors. Taking up the story with the victory of the National Party in 1948, it shows both how antisemitism in South Africa subsided in some quarters but revived and emerged in others in virulent forms. The book is a fitting cap to Milton Shain's career both as an acclaimed historian and as a highly respected and engaged public intellectual.'

Professor Richard Mendelsohn, Emeritus Professor of Historical Studies, University of Cape Town

Contents

About the Author	xi
Acknowledgements	xiii
Preface	xvii
Introduction	1
1 Subversive Outsiders: 1940s to 1960s	15
2 Neo-Nazis, Fantasists and Conspiracists: 1940s to 1960s	49
3 The Resurgence of Exclusivism and Neo-Nazism: 1970s to 1980s	85
4 Into the 'New' South Africa: 1990 to the Present	119
Afterthoughts	155
Notes	169
Index	219

About the Author

Milton Shain is Emeritus Professor of Historical Studies at the University of Cape Town. He has written, co-authored and co-edited over a dozen books on South African Jewish history, South African politics and the history of antisemitism, including *The Roots of Antisemitism in South Africa*; *Antisemitism*; *The Jews in South Africa: An Illustrated History* (co-authored with Richard Mendelsohn); *Holocaust Scholarship: Personal Trajectories and Professional Interpretations* (co-edited with Christopher Browning, Susannah Heschel and Michael Marrus) and *A Perfect Storm: Antisemitism in South Africa, 1930–1948*.

The Roots of Antisemitism in South Africa was awarded the University of Cape Town book prize in 1996 and *A Perfect Storm: Antisemitism in South Africa, 1930–1948* won Media 24's Recht Malan Prize for Non-Fiction in 2016.

In 2014 he was elected a Fellow of the Royal Society of South Africa.

Acknowledgements

In attempting to trace and understand the persistence of antisemitism in South Africa since 1948, I have been assisted by numerous colleagues and friends to whom I am most grateful. Benjamin Pogrund, Richard Mendelsohn and Michael Cardo read drafts of the manuscript, while earlier incarnations of sections were read by Shlomo Avineri, Adam Mendelsohn and Gideon Shimoni. I particularly want to thank Millie Pimstone, whose editorial eye brings order to disorder. She perceptively read and reread the entire manuscript, tirelessly clarifying ambiguous prose and weakness of argument, while challenging fanciful claims and infelicities. I am also grateful to David Welsh, who willingly acted as a sounding board and provided wise counsel and encouragement, and to Tony Kushner and Lesley Klaff who were helpful with material from the United Kingdom, as well as Alex Myers, who traced some hidden web material. My thanks also to Russell Martin who, with his usual professionalism, contributed his unmatched editorial skills on behalf of the publishers.

Over the last few years, I have been fortunate to present aspects of my research and benefit from the insight of scholars in academic conference settings: the Hebrew University of Jerusalem, under the auspices of the Vidal Sassoon International Center for the Study of Antisemitism, in 2014; the Institute for the Study of Contemporary Antisemitism, Indiana University, Bloomington, in 2016; the Pears

Institute for the Study of Antisemitism, Birkbeck, University of London, in 2017 and the Institute of Jewish Studies, University College London, in association with the Isaac and Jessie Kaplan Centre for Jewish Studies and Research, University of Cape Town, in 2020.

In the final analysis, however, it was my dialogue with the printed word, housed in a range of libraries and archives, that enabled me to reach the conclusions presented in this study. I wish therefore to extend my thanks and appreciation to the following institutions: Special Collections and Archives, Jagger Library, University of Cape Town; Government Publications Department and Interlibrary Loans Department, Chancellor Oppenheimer Library, University of Cape Town; Archives for Contemporary Affairs, University of the Free State, Bloemfontein; National Archives of South Africa, Pretoria; National Library of South Africa, Pretoria; National Library of South Africa, Cape Town; Special Collections, National Library of South Africa, Cape Town; National Dutch Reformed Church in South Africa Archive, Stellenbosch; Nederduitsch Hervormde Kerk van Afrika: Archives, Pretoria; DF Malan Collection, Manuscript Section, JS Gericke Library, University of Stellenbosch; Historical Papers Research Archives, South African Institute of Race Relations, University of the Witwatersrand, Johannesburg; OB Archive, North West University, Potchefstroom; Jewish Studies Library, Isaac and Jessie Kaplan Centre for Jewish Studies and Research, University of Cape Town; Wiener Library, London; Jacob Gitlin Library, Cape Town; and the SA Rochlin Archives, South African Jewish Board of Deputies, Johannesburg.

A great number of individuals in the foregoing institutions generously assisted. In particular I would like to thank David Saks and Gwynne Robins of the South African Jewish Board of Deputies, who diligently answered questions and supplied information on request. I am also grateful to the following professionals for their time and efforts: Roni Mikel Arieli, Marietta Buys, Lynn Fourie, Melanie Geustyn, Najwa Hendrickse, Clive Kirkwood, Andrew Kok, Glynnis Lawrence, Huibre Lombard, Eric Mathobo, Joshua Mendelsohn, Naomi Musiker, Mandy Noble, Busi Khangala, Allegra Louw, Chelsea O'Regan, Isaac Ntabankulu, Maryna Rankin, Jacqui Rogers, Roseanne

Acknowledgements

Rosen, Laureen Rushby, Nándor Sarkady, Tanya Schaffer, Christine Schmidt, Michal Singer, Rosie Watson and Russel Williams. I have also worked with three research assistants: Orrie Staschen devoted many hours to chasing documents and locating newspapers, a particularly brave and difficult task at a time of Covid-19, while David Patrick and Dawid Mouton assisted me in the Archives for Contemporary Affairs, University of the Free State, and the National Archives and Record Service of South Africa, Pretoria, respectively.

I also want to acknowledge financial assistance from the National Research Foundation, South Africa; the University Research Committee at the University of Cape Town; and the Isaac and Jessie Kaplan Centre for Jewish Studies and Research at the University of Cape Town. Colleen Peterson of the Department of Historical Studies, University of Cape Town, carefully and professionally managed these funds, while Ryan Mitchell White, Janine Blumberg and Benjamin Vigne of the Kaplan Centre provided technical support when needed. The Centre itself has provided an environment for reflection and engagement. Here I wish to thank its director, Adam Mendelsohn, for his support and advice, which went beyond the call of duty. Finally, my thanks to Bridget Impey, Maggie Davey and the Jacana team for their generous and dedicated guidance.

Preface

History teaches us that even the most tenuous phantoms can come to life if objective circumstances change. The fantasies of one generation can provide the mental furniture, even the life-blood, of another.
HR Trevor-Roper, 'The Phenomenon of Fascism', 1981

Hugh Trevor-Roper's elegant insight into the staying power of ideas, and the way in which the 'fantasies of one generation can provide the mental furniture, even the life-blood, of another', largely informs this study – the third volume in a trilogy on the history of antisemitism in South Africa.[1] Its focus is an examination of the anti-Jewish ideas and tropes that survived South Africa's 'Jewish question' in the 1930s and early 1940s. While these never threatened to transform 'private' or 'ideational' antisemitism into 'public' or 'programmatic' action, their survival reveals the deep roots of anti-Jewish hatred dating back to the late nineteenth and early twentieth centuries.[2]

Since the Second World War anti-Jewish fantasies have mutated in fascinating and complex ways, always sensitive to prevailing socio-cultural patterns and political issues, but never posing a serious threat to Jewish well-being. This is not to say that things cannot change. As Trevor-Roper warns, fantasies and phantoms can 'come to life if objective circumstances change'.³ We saw this in South Africa in the 1930s and early 1940s, when specific contingencies transformed widespread anti-Jewish prejudice and stereotyping into a politicised 'Jewish question'. Economic, social and political instability, coupled with an ascendant *völkisch* Afrikaner nationalism, the likelihood of a Jewish refugee influx from Germany, and an upwardly mobile Jewish community, ensured the utilisation of anti-Jewish canards for political agendas.[4]

Although hostility waned rapidly from the late 1940s, 'the Jew' still loomed large in reactionary and conservative circles, which were often connected to global networks. Focus was on Jewish and Zionist conspiracies and subversion; but these charges had little impact beyond a relatively small group of white English- and Afrikaans-speaking fanatics. Importantly, the upward mobility of Afrikaners and their growing power meant the utilisation of 'the Jew' for political purposes (as had been the case for ethnic mobilisation in the 1930s) was unnecessary. From the 1970s, however, classic Jew-hatred gained some momentum as white reactionaries sought to reclaim their diminishing status and blamed the erosion of pristine apartheid on the Jew. On the other hand, the 'progressive' left increasingly characterised Israel – the collective Jew – as a locus of global evil and a supporter of apartheid, as manifest in the Pretoria–Jerusalem axis. Politicised young Muslims, especially, were informed by an Islamist literature that targeted Zionism, secularism, capitalism and communism. Here they shared much with the radical white right and its characterisation of malevolent 'political Zionism'.

In an unequal society like South Africa, the search for scapegoats to explain societal problems remains an ever-present possibility. The scapegoats, of course, do not have to be Jewish and, given the protracted struggle for human rights in South Africa and the opposition to 'racial' discrimination manifest in the first democratic constitution, it is unlikely that Jews as an ethnic group will be targeted – at least in the foreseeable future.[5] In fact, Jews today are far more integrated into society than they were in the interwar years when a perfect storm had generated the 'Jewish question'. There is, moreover, acknowledgement and celebration of diversity in the South African Constitution, which has the potential to blunt distinctiveness. But history moves in strange ways. The tenacity of antisemitism and its ability to mutate and survive cannot be underestimated. Latent hatreds can become manifest, especially in the age of the internet and social media where, in the words of the historian Richard Evans, 'anyone can put out their views into the public sphere, no matter how bizarre they might be'.[6]

It is, however, not the intention of this book to be alarmist, neither for South African society in general nor for Jews in particular, who today constitute a tiny minority of less than 50,000 or 0.08 per cent of the population.[7] Essentially it aims to investigate, trace and unpack hostile attitudes towards Jews and irrational fantasies about them in apartheid and post-apartheid South Africa.[8] Rather than an exhaustive description of every instance of Jew-hatred since 1948, the focus is on the evolution, survival and resurfacing of anti-Jewish ideas and the ways in which these intersect with one another in diverse ways.[9] Its most recent manifestation is in the form of 'progressive' anti-Zionism where we see an uncanny convergence with the white radical right. This is not to suggest all anti-Zionism is synonymous with antisemitism. The connections are more complex; but the tropes employed by both the radical left and right are often alike. To be sure, it is no coincidence that both share an obsession with the veracity of the Holocaust and peddle *The Protocols of the Elders of Zion*, a foundational text of modern antisemitism. Clearly, for some, hatred of the Jew is the true motivation for anti-Zionism.[10]

South Africa is a country divided not only along racial, but also class and ethnic, lines. Race, however, remains the cardinal divide. A history of slavery, colonialism, segregation and apartheid has ensured this. A great amount of scholarly attention has justifiably been devoted to this legacy. Less well-known, however, is the country's lengthy history of antisemitism that persists to the present day. Through a series of essay-like chapters, broadly respectful of chronology but also attentive to thematic coherence, this book attempts to capture this history within cultural and religious patterns, as well as changing political and economic frameworks.

Introduction

Thought precedes action as lightning does thunder.
Heinrich Heine, 'On the History of Religion and Philosophy in Germany', 1834

The 'Jewish Question' before 1948

Ideas have consequences. They inform and influence how we see and understand the world. But ideas do not operate in a social vacuum. They evolve, take shape, and resonate within specific contexts. Ideas are also not autonomous. In the words of the historian Richard Hofstadter, changes in the structure of ideas 'wait on general changes in economic and political life'. Whether ideas are accepted, maintains Hofstadter, depends less on truth and logic 'than suitability to the intellectual needs and preconceptions of social interests'.[1] Looking at the merging of ideas into a meaningful narrative or ideology, Mark Lilla puts it another way: 'if an ideology endures this means that it is capturing something important in social reality'.[2]

We certainly see this in the transformation of anti-Jewish ideas in South Africa from the late nineteenth century into a 'Jewish question' in the 1930s.[3] Political turmoil, social and economic instability, and 'poor white' (mainly Afrikaner) unemployment, coupled with the upward mobility of Jews and the prospect of more Jewish immigrants, all at a time of rising *völkisch* Afrikaner nationalism, ensured that anti-Jewish ideas were injected into party-political life.[4] Only in this context did eugenicist and nativist concerns (already evident in the 1920s and manifest in the Quota Act of 1930, which effectively precluded the influx of eastern European Jews) generate formal and public calls for Jewish exclusion and marginalisation.[5] Radical white rightists, influenced by European fascism and Nazism, increasingly introduced a conspiratorial discourse that threatened Jewish well-being. Although largely unknown and for the most part poorly educated, these extremists, obsessed with dark and demonic fantasies, demanded attention and attracted a community of believers. More importantly, they succeeded in shifting the 'Jewish question' from the political margins of South African public life to its centre. A diverse Jewish community was transformed by them into a uniform and menacing monolith.[6]

By 1936 Daniël François Malan, the leader of the opposition Gesuiwerde Nasionale Party (Purified National Party, or GNP), which had broken away from the National Party in 1934, was imitating the rhetoric of the radical right. He successfully pressured the government to introduce an Aliens Act in early 1937, which employed notions of 'unassimilability' and succeeded in blocking the influx of German-Jewish refugees, hitherto exempt from the provisions of the 1930 Quota Act. Driven by an influential Afrikaner think tank, the Broederbond (Band of Brothers), the GNP subsequently pushed for Jewish occupational and professional quotas, their propaganda underpinned by an insistence on the threat of Jewish domination in business and the professions. At the same time, attention was drawn to leftist Jewish activists who undermined *völkisch* ambitions by threatening to divide Afrikaners along class lines and to act in alliance with a restive black African proletariat.[7] Ethnic entrepreneurs now mobilised 'poor white' Afrikaners, many of whom were hopelessly unsuited to the urban challenges.

By the time South Africa joined the Commonwealth war effort against Nazi Germany in late 1939, the GNP – now bolstered by an exclusivist paramilitary cultural organisation, the Ossewabrandwag (Ox-wagon Sentinel, or OB) – made it quite clear that it envisaged no place in South Africa for the 'unassimilable' Jew.[8] This was much the same for the Herenigde Nasionale of Volksparty (Reunited National or People's Party, or HNP), an alliance forged in early 1940 between Malan and Hertzog, who had opposed South Africa's entry into the war. Its publications – partly informed by the German-educated Oswald Pirow's pro-Nazi Nuwe Orde (or New Order), a National-Socialist pressure group within the HNP – now demonstrated the formative influence of Mussolini and Hitler on the nature of *völkisch* Afrikaner nationalism.[9]

Evidently the 'alien' Jew appeared to challenge an emerging sense of 'South Africanness' among white English and Afrikaans speakers, who were considered South Africa's founding immigrants. Grappling with nativist categories and manipulating notions of 'Nordicism' that flourished internationally in the 1920s, these white South Africans were *ad idem* when it came to concerns about Jews, believing that yet another racial group was being added to the already problematic Indian, Coloured and black African mix.[10] Because of their perceived difference, Jews were considered immutably unassimilable, thus posing a threat to 'the delicate balance between the black and white populations of the Union' and indeed contaminating 'the body of the nation itself'.[11]

While the ruling United Party believed that a limited number of Jews could be absorbed, Malan's GNP (and thereafter the HNP) saw Jews as a race apart – a consequence of a *völkisch* mindset, informed by a neo-Kuyperianism that viewed individuals primarily as members of organic communities.[12] Here we have hints of a paradigm that would subsequently inform Nationalist thought about culture and ethnicity in general. Indeed, it was this same cast of mind that underpinned the apartheid project in its aim to safeguard the values and standards of 'white civilisation'.[13] In this sense, the 'Jewish question', and ways of dealing with it, paralleled – and even to some extent presaged – apartheid ideology as it evolved from the mid-1930s.[14]

It would be wrong, however, to suggest that there was a widespread consensus on the 'Jewish question'. Many individual Jews enjoyed respect at the highest level and attained prominence in diverse fields including public life. Few confronted naked antisemitism as opposed to social snobbery. But across the party and language divide there remained an essentialist understanding of 'the Jew'. Even the liberal South African Party member of parliament for Johannesburg North, Jan Hofmeyr, who was a champion of the Jews, had maintained at the time of the 1930 Quota Act that the entry of eastern European Jews into the country would be advisable only if they were part of a wider immigration stream of the 'stock of people from whom we have sprung'.[15] At the same time, however, relatively few South Africans shared an affinity with the extreme conspiracism of the radical white right – most evident in the peddling of *The Protocols of the Elders of Zion* – and many felt a distinct discomfort with vulgar Jew-baiting. Electoral contests too showed little support for the radical white right. Yet it needs to be noted that the GNP imported much of its rhetoric from that quarter and welcomed anti-Jewish extremists into its fold in the late 1930s.[16]

For all that, the 'Jewish question' lost steam, especially once the tide of war turned against the Axis Powers in late 1942. In the 1943 general election campaign, it was far less visible than in the campaign five years earlier when the Jew had been employed as a stick with which to beat the United Party.[17] In fact, in the build-up to the 1948 general election, Malan had refused to kowtow to his antisemitic lieutenant, Eric Louw, who persisted with Jew-baiting and did his best to pressure the HNP to maintain its anti-Jewish policies.[18] Apart from some anti-Jewish pamphlets circulating early in the election campaign and brisk sales for a new edition of *The Protocols of the Elders of Zion*, it was only Louw who, in a letter to *Die Burger*, bothered to articulate and affirm his party's policies towards the Jews.[19] Other Nationalists were largely silent. Indeed, less than two weeks before the polls, 'Karl Lemeer' (the pen name for Henry Katzew) reported in his regular *Zionist Record* column that 'not a single Nationalist paper has given a line of publicity to any anti-Semitic utterances or statements generally unfriendly to Jews'. The Jewish question, he asserted, 'is a dead letter'.[20] Only very occasionally was 'the Jew' employed for political purposes. More than that, many individual Nationalists took pains to reassure the Jewish community that the party had turned its back on its past hostility.[21] The reason was clear: it was more rewarding for the National Party not to play the Jewish card and to concentrate instead on other matters. There were more important wedge issues and hence little need for Malan (a political opportunist par excellence) to mobilise support around the potentially divisive 'Jewish question'.[22] In any event, the Holocaust and the creation of the State of Israel had ended the prospect of large-scale Jewish immigration to South Africa. This, however, did not prevent the OB from harping on the possibility of Jewish immigrants streaming into the country.[23]

Malan, on the other hand, lost no opportunity to focus his 1948 election campaign on pressing social and economic issues as well as vague promises of territorial separation between the races. South Africa, he told an increasingly colour-conscious electorate, would remain a 'white man's country' and a bulwark against the communist threat linked by Nationalists to the 'black peril'. Although the HNP's race policies had yet to be clearly defined, the slogan 'apartheid' (which would later evolve into 'separate development') had a visceral appeal, especially among recently urbanised working-class Afrikaners who saw the growing presence of black Africans in the cities as a threat to their livelihood.[24] Apartheid promised Afrikaner survival and served as the glue that held together various interest groups. Taking a different approach, Jan Smuts, leader of the United Party, called for large-scale white immigration to ensure 'Western civilisation', an approach seen by Malan as a ploy to dilute Afrikaner numbers.[25]

In a weighted constituency system that favoured rural areas, Smuts and his allies won just over 53 per cent of the popular vote but lost the election, despite only a 41 per cent vote for Malan and his ally Nicolaas ('Klasie') Havenga, leader of the Afrikaner Party. In the final tally Malan obtained 70 seats, Havenga 9, Smuts 65 and his ally, the Labour Party, 6. Three years later the HNP merged with the Afrikaner Party under the name of National Party.

Terms of Engagement

'An arrangement allowing peoples or groups of people who have different opinions or beliefs to work or live together' is how the *Cambridge English Dictionary* defines 'modus vivendi'. It is an apt description of the accord reached by South African Jewish leaders with Malan following clandestine meetings held shortly before and after the HNP came to power in 1948.[26] After they had been characterised for nearly two decades as an economic threat, dangerously subversive, unassimilable and an additional race problem in an already deeply divided society, Jewish fears were, at least in part, assuaged by Malan's wish to relegate the 'Jewish question' to the past. It was time for a fresh start, maintained the newly elected prime minister. His government stood 'for a policy of non-discrimination against any section of the European population in South Africa'.[27] Faithful to his word, Malan assured Jews in October 1948 that blood relatives of Jews in South Africa would be admitted on humanitarian grounds, and there would be 'no stumbling-blocks in the way of providing for the cultural and religious requirements of the Jewish community'. Notably, the 'Jewish question' was absent during the 1949 provincial elections campaign.[28]

Indicative of the new mood, the government bowed to a request from the South African Jewish Board of Deputies (hereafter the Board), the representative voice of the Jewish community, to reject the planned immigration of James Larratt Battersby, a British fascist who had come to South Africa shortly after the election and had unsuccessfully tried to set up a number of so-called Hitler memorial institutes.[29] A few years later Malan even praised Jews for maintaining a distinctive 'racial' identity while contributing significantly to the society at large. In a preface to *The Birth of a Community* by Chief Rabbi Israel Abrahams, Malan wrote that Jews could serve as a model for a complex 'multi-racial country' like South Africa.[30] Jewish communal longevity, in other words, could serve as a prototype for the Afrikaner, who was existentially threatened in a decolonising world. Grand apartheid – the National Party's putative solution to South Africa's racial problems – can thus be seen as a substitute for the Jewish spiritual fortress.

Notwithstanding Malan's about-turn, the approximately 104,000 Jews in South Africa (4.36 per cent of the white population or less than 1 per cent of the total population) remained uneasy.[31] Despite rapid acculturation, upward mobility and public success, they remained outsiders to a greater or lesser extent. The philosemitic Jan Hofmeyr (albeit with approbation) had even referred to Jewish 'distinctiveness' and 'otherness' when delivering the first Hoernlé Memorial Lecture in 1945 for the Institute of Race Relations, a liberal think tank. 'The Jew', he said, 'is different from the rest of us – we are conscious of that fact – and for all too many people the consciousness of difference acts as a seed-bed of intolerance.'³²

Such essentialism was de rigueur in mid-twentieth-century South African thought. Afrikaners, especially, conflated culture with nation, a nexus that inevitably informed a strong desire for separation that manifested itself in republicanism and a powerful sense of religious mission. This mission had been neatly expressed in 1944 by JC van Rooy, chairman of the Broederbond:

> In every People in the world is embodied a Divine Idea and the task of each People is to build upon that idea and to perfect it. So God created the Afrikaner People with a unique language, a unique philosophy of life, and their own history and tradition in order that they might fulfil a particular calling and destiny here in the southern corner of Africa. We must stand guard on all that is peculiar to us and build upon it. We must believe that God has called us to be servants of his righteousness in this place. We must walk the way of obedience to faith.³³

Unsurprisingly, these Christian impulses, coupled with a God-given sense of destiny, had served to sharpen perceptions of the Jew as alien. They were *bloedvreemdelinge* (foreigners by blood), explained Potchefstroom University's Hendrik Stoker, one of the *volk*'s key neo-Calvinist intellectuals, and should not enjoy full rights in an Afrikaner republic.³⁴ Tellingly, a draft constitution drawn up in 1942 by leading Afrikaner organisations opposed to the government included the following article: 'The propagation of any State policy and the existence of any political organization which is in strife with the fulfilling of this Christian National vocation of the life of the people is forbidden.'³⁵ When in power, however, the National Party turned away from such exclusivity and instead fashioned a race-based authoritarian society in which English- and Afrikaans-speaking whites were dominant and in which Jews – as whites – shared all privileges. Indeed, the Sauer Commission of 1947, which was established to shape a race policy, made no mention of Jews when identifying 'population groups', which provided the rationale for what would become the apartheid template: a far cry indeed from the 1930s and early 1940s when Jews had invariably been identified as a distinctive racial group, and certainly from the early twentieth century when bureaucratic forms included the racial category 'Hebrew' alongside 'European' and other racial groups.[36]

There were, of course, historical divisions between white English and Afrikaans speakers, but these increasingly narrowed as apartheid unfolded and Afrikaners ascended the ladder of economic success. In the final analysis most whites wished to avoid majority rule and, for Afrikaners especially, white survival was paramount. They would set the tone and define society's templates. Importantly, Malan's modus vivendi with the Jews anticipated – albeit subtly – appropriate behaviour from Jewish citizens, who would be keenly watched. Subversion was to be avoided and loyalty (undefined) was expected. Acceptance of Jews, in other words, was somewhat conditional – akin to the 'bargain' or 'contract' that defined Jewish status at the time of Jewish emancipation in France in 1791.[37] In the South African case, however, it was appropriate behaviour and not, as in France, assimilation that required. On the contrary, in a race- and ethnicity-obsessed society (or what historian Yuri Slezkine in another context calls 'chronic ethnophilia'), endogamy was welcomed, and ethnic barriers encouraged.[38] But this was not multiculturalism *avant la lettre* or, at least, as we have come to understand the term in recent decades. The shape and intellectual framework that would define the new order would be in the hands of an Afrikaner elite, informed at that time by a powerful religiosity that harboured an abiding fear of liberalism and communism. It is not without significance that Sheila Patterson's *The Last Trek* (1957) and Gwendolen Carter's magisterial *The Politics of Inequality* (1958) stressed – more than later scholars – the conservative Christian impulses driving the apartheid project in its formative years.[39] Conducting their research in the 1950s, both Patterson and Carter sensed the ideological mood underpinning Afrikaner Christian Nationalism and the formative power of the three Dutch Reformed Churches – the original and largest Dutch Reformed Church (the Nederduitse Gereformeerde Kerk, or NGK), and its two offshoots, the Nederduitsch Hervormde Kerk and the more fundamentalist Gereformeerde (Reformed or Dopper) Kerk. Exclusivist or *völkisch* organisations, with origins dating back to the 1920s and 1930s, made every effort 'to create out of nationalistic Afrikanerdom an integrated whole', writes Carter.[40] The Broederbond, the Federasie van Afrikaner Kultuurverenigings (Federation of Afrikaner Cultural Organisations, or FAK), the Reddingsdaadbond (Rescue Act Alliance, or RDB), the South African Bureau of Racial Affairs (SABRA) and the Instituut vir Christelik-Nasionale Onderwys (Institute for Christian National Education, or ICNO) all provided intellectual ballast for an evolving racial project that was primarily at the service of Afrikaner interests, and secondly in the interest of non-Afrikaner whites. Informed for many years by the Broederbond, the South African Broadcasting Corporation (SABC) added to the conservative voice and the shaping of intellectual debate.[41] White advantage, opportunities and survival would be protected. Jews were part of the privileged white minority who had nothing to fear, wrote the government mouthpiece, *Die Burger*, in the wake of Malan's 1948 electoral victory, and were indeed encouraged to support the new ruling party even though they were precluded from membership of the Transvaal National Party at this time. In its view, Jewish leaders had mistakenly done their best to tarnish the policies of the National Party at the hustings and had not prepared their own community for Smuts's defeat. Now, gloated *Die Burger*, Jews were hoping that they had been 'misled by their leaders'.[42]

It would take more than pious *Schadenfreude* on the part of *Die Burger* to convince Jews that they had nothing to fear. The feisty Gustav Saron, secretary general of the Board, made this quite clear when he warned the Nationalists that the onus was on the new government 'to prove that it had learned the lessons of history' – a direct reminder of the National Party's Nazi sympathies during the war.[43] Similar concerns were shared by the *Zionist Record*. Arguing that Malan had not sufficiently repudiated his rabidly antisemitic colleague Eric Louw, it warned that his party still harboured concerns about Jewish immigration.[44] Indeed, the National Party gave cause for concern when, within months of its election victory, it released from custody Erik Holm, a pro-Nazi South African version of Lord Haw-Haw.[45] Robey Leibbrandt, arrested in 1941 for plotting the overthrow of the Smuts government, was also freed and was once again actively promoting Jew-hatred,[46] while the vulgar antisemitic 'Hoggenheimer' cartoon caricature that personified the power of Jewish finance continued to be published.[47] In parliament, the newly elected United Party MP for Kimberley City, Harry Oppenheimer, was conveniently characterised as 'Hoggenheimer' by turncoat JH Loock, the National Party MP for Vereeniging, who ominously told the House that the young Anglo American managing director represented '*geldmag*' (money power), a sinister throwback to antisemitic accusations of the 1930s.[48] More significantly, Jews continued to be precluded from joining the Transvaal National Party, a rule that would only be lifted in 1951.[49] In fact, just one year earlier, the Transvaal leader of the National Party, JG ('Hans') Strijdom, had turned down a request from the Board to discuss Jewish exclusion by stressing the party's desire to develop 'our national life along Christian national lines'.[50]

For all that, Jews appreciated the absence of public Jew-baiting (especially notable in the 1953 general election) and the toning down of anti-Jewish rhetoric, while at the same time recognising their outsider status rooted in historical constructions over decades in an essentialist discourse. Notwithstanding the modus vivendi, Jews remained rarities (or at least religious deviants), operating in a dominantly neo-Calvinist culture that was in the process of reshaping a political agenda. Afrikaners were attempting to inculcate a dour, repressive and God-fearing conservatism that was infused with scriptural justification and dominated by racial categories and territorial separation. Religious sentiments were constantly exploited and, as non-Protestants and English speakers, Jews were marginalised. Like other non-Protestants, but even more so, they would also have to navigate Christian National Education (CNE), a doctrinaire manifestation of a neo-Calvinist ethos and ethic.

CNE had its philosophical antecedents in the nineteenth-century Boer Republics and, before the National Party came to power, had been promoted by ICNO, an outfit sponsored by the FAK, the cultural arm of *völkisch* Afrikaner nationalism. It sought to ensure that the education of Afrikaner children was both Christian and national, rooted in the Holy Scriptures and 'formulated in the articles of faith of our three Afrikaans churches'.[51] Phyllis Lewsen, a University of the Witwatersrand historian, asserted at the time that Jewish children would be unable to fit into Christian-Nationalist schools. Furthermore, she warned that an education scheme 'in which the Jew can find no place – outside the Ghetto – is one which threatens the intellectual and spiritual freedom of all sections equally'.[52]

Notwithstanding its potential divisiveness, the programme went ahead, much to the chagrin of the Education League, which was founded in 1948 to oppose racial exclusiveness in education. 'Fanatical, fundamentalist and doctrinaire' was the way the League defined CNE in its pamphlet *Blueprint for Blackout*.[53] But it had little impact. CNE was rapidly approved by the executive committee of ICNO, as well as the Afrikaans Teachers' Association in all four provinces and the Union Congress of the Afrikaans Teachers' Association in March 1949. It was also accepted by the FAK and the Dutch Reformed Churches.[54] Essentially, schools were to inculcate loyalty to the 'fatherland' and a substantial premium was placed on Christian religious instruction and prayer at school.[55] It was anticipated that teachers would be expected to give religious instruction unless formally exempted from such an obligation.

Whereas Christian-National philosophy – driven by teachers steeped in conservative attitudes – had hitherto operated as a lobby and had penetrated schooling in an informal way, it was now policy. For Jews, the implementation of CNE was, in the words of the historian Gideon Shimoni, 'yet another reactionary, and therefore potentially anti-Jewish, expression of Afrikaner Nationalism'.[56] Their concern was eloquently captured by Adolf Davis, a Jewish MP for Pretoria City:

> if there is one thing which causes a great deal of suspicion and anxiety in my mind, it is the use of the words 'Christian National'. I know that in Germany the Christian Nationalists were responsible for the murder of six million Jews, and when I see that term introduced in South Africa, after a conclusion of a war which was waged in order to determine the right of people to think and worship and act as they like within the four corners of the law, then I say, I am entitled to an explanation, and a detailed explanation as to whether the Minister is prepared to repudiate the principles which have resulted in misery and suffering to so large a sector of humanity.[57]

In practice, however, the impact of CNE on English-medium schools (far removed from the NGK) was negligible; but CNE did marginalise Jewish (and, to a lesser extent, Roman Catholic) pupils and wilfully ignored the tapestry of a multicultural society and its premise of secularism.[58] Twenty years after the National Party came to power, the question of CNE was still a subject of debate. It was a necessity, insisted the minister of education, Cornelius ('Connie') Mulder, during the debate on the National Education Policy Act of 1967. 'Dare we ask for anything else?' he asked rhetorically when addressing the House:

> Dare we for a single moment desire to ban the Christian idea from our education or dare we object to that idea if we consider the history and the past of our nation step by step? After Vegkop and after Bloedrivier, dare we, if we accept that we have been planted here as a nation with a task and a calling in Africa, and if we look at the future, hesitate for a single moment to speak out for the Christian standpoint of a nation that has been planted here from the Western civilisation of previous centuries on Europe?

Mulder was fully aware that there were many who opposed CNE but considered it foolish to 'change the entire nation's character' for the sake of 'a few people'. 'We demand that our education must have a Christian character and as a Christian people who believe in religious freedom, we give children the choice to absent themselves from periods of religious instruction if they have any conscientious objections thereto.'[59]

Another and related concern for Jews was persistent talk of removing the 'conscience clause' in tertiary education which ensured that no test of religious belief could be imposed on any university teacher or student.[60] The clause had long-standing currency in South Africa, but had been challenged in 1932 when the Reverend Marthinus Fick (MP for Potchefstroom) in a private member's bill on behalf of the Potchefstroomse Universiteitskollege vir Christelike Hoër Onderwys (Potchefstroom University College for Christian Higher Education) objected to the clause because it undermined the college's Calvinist principles. Although the initiative was defeated, the issue was resurrected with some success in 1950 when it was agreed that the University Council had to ensure 'that the Christian historical character of the university shall be maintained'.[61] A year earlier, the University College of the Orange Free State had also done its best to scrap the conscience clause when motivating its incorporation as a university. Although unsuccessful, the idea survived, and in 1966 the NGK requested the government 'to accept it as policy that universities that choose to replace the Conscience Clause by a positive Protestant-Christian provision, shall have the right to do so'. Such a policy, argued the NGK, 'will be in agreement with the principle of sovereignty in its own area and guarantees freedom of conscience, while the Conscience Clause protects the liberalist lecturer to the detriment of the Christian student'.[62]

Two years later, an anxious Board had talks with the incoming rector of the Rand Afrikaans University (RAU), Gerrit Viljoen, who made it clear that all students were welcome at RAU without any religious tests. In appointments, however, the university reserved its Afrikaans and religious character that had been set out in the preamble of the RAU Act; but this did not exclude the possibility of appointing non-Afrikaners and non-Protestants.[63]

Only in 1974 did the Van Wyk De Vries Commission into universities finally put an end to the idea of restricting religious freedom, albeit with the caveat that 'a university shall be free to determine its own character and direction'.[64] But this was not a sign that Christian views no longer held sway among conservative Afrikaners. As late as 1981, the creation of an advisory President's Council that was not restricted to Christians aroused the ire of conservatives. 'If we are prepared to share power with the Muslim, who is on the path of darkness, then I don't know any more,' commented Ada Claassen (wife of the iconic rugby player and administrator Johan Claassen) on the anticipated absence of reference to Jesus Christ in the new body. 'There is no doubt in my mind that the Jews and the Muslims and other non-Christians cannot be part of the true belief and we must try to bring them to the path of light. You can see that the heart of the Lord is no longer in the National Party and you cannot rule a country without HIM.'[65]

The Church, then, was a primary focus of guidance in apartheid South Africa, with God's authority all-pervasive. In the countryside

– the base of the National Party – the *predikant* (clergyman) and the teacher provided a cultural compass and backbone. Thus it was that Church and school, as well as Afrikaans-medium 'white' universities, provided the intellectual rationale for an unfolding racial order. Cultural norms and social mores were firmly in the hands of Afrikaners. Jews, who were tied historically to the English-speaking community and branded for decades as cosmopolitans, liberals, parvenus and communist subversives, had good reason to be anxious. After all, sixteen years before the National Party came to power in 1948, a chilling warning had been sounded by the Reverend Marthinus Fick when he introduced his bill to remove the conscience clause at Potchefstroom University College. Taking exception to Jewish opposition to the bill, he made it quite clear that South Africa was a Christian country. 'If the Jew has that suspicion of us, then we on our side also have a suspicion of him,' he said. 'If the Jew wishes to harm us thereby, he must bear in mind that by doing so he will get the worst of it in the matter. He must not touch that tender chord with the Afrikaner by saying that he is afraid of the word "Christian".'[66]

ONE

Subversive Outsiders: 1940s to 1960s

'... we have liberalism which believes in ... freedom of the individual and which discerns in nationalism ... an impediment to the individual... On the other hand, we have nationalism that sees in every nation ... a destiny to fulfil...'
Dr Nico Diederichs, *Hansard*, 19 August 1948

'We associate ourselves with the anti-Communist countries ... because we regard the communist doctrine to be a danger ... but if there is one country in which it is a greater danger than in other countries, it is for us here in South Africa with our large non-European population...'
DF Malan, *Hansard*, 1 September 1948

'My good wishes go to the Jewish community... on the occasion of the Jewish New Year 5724... More than ever before are we called upon to stand together in loyalty and both by word and deed to protect our country against subversion from within and aggression from without.'
State President, CR Swart, *Star*, 14 September 1963.

'Labour and Socialism is the movement of protest. That is why Jews abound in Socialist and Leftist politics.'
Barnett Potter, *The Fault, Black Man*, 1970

'South Africa Belongs to Us Once More'

Twenty years after the National Party's accession to power in 1948, and despite rapid integration and upward mobility, Jews remained edgy and sensitive. There were still ripples of fear following an alarming speech by Prime Minister Balthazar Johannes Vorster's newly appointed minister of police and the interior, Lourens Muller, in which he focused on the predominance of Jews among student activists at the University of Cape Town (UCT) and the University of the Witwatersrand (Wits). When speaking in Potchefstroom in the wake of student protests against the government's refusal to allow a black African social anthropologist, Archibald ('Archie') Mafeje, to take up an appointment at UCT, Muller drew attention to a list of names to illustrate the disproportionate Jewish presence 'among those who committed acts of sabotage' and among the leadership of the National Union of South African Students (NUSAS), a liberal and essentially English-speaking student organisation opposed to apartheid policies. But Muller went even further and appealed to Jewish leaders 'to use their influence with their young people to respect authority and not to disrupt it'.[1]

The Jewish Board of Deputies issued a formal condemnation of Muller's speech, but the tone of its media statement betrayed an uneasiness reminiscent of the 1930s and early 1940s when Jews had good reason to feel beleaguered and afraid. 'To fasten responsibility on the Jewish community for actions of its individual members inevitably furthers anti-Semitism, albeit unwittingly,' claimed the Board. These students, it contended, acted as individuals, 'and it is as individuals that they are answerable for their conduct'. Nevertheless, the Board was aware that notice had been served on the Jewish community – and not for the first time. Subversion, commonly associated with liberalism and communism in the mind of *völkisch* nationalists, had long featured on the agenda of the National Party, and menacingly so, for Jews were historically associated with both these ideologies and were indeed prominent among student and other anti-apartheid activists.[2]

Muller's attack on the Jewish students – in effect an assault on liberalism – recalls a similar assault made by the reactionary Austrian diplomat and politician Prince Metternich in the post-Napoleonic years. Like the apartheid leaders, Metternich had decried liberals and warned against subversive actions which, for the most part, were led by secret student fraternities at German universities – the so-called *Burschenschaften*. NUSAS in that sense was a modern incarnation. So, in fact, Muller was treading a well-worn path laid in the early nineteenth century that became even more entrenched in the face of European anarchism and communism. In what had been a year of European-wide student protests, Muller may have sensed the need to clamp down on activism before things spiralled out of control and may even have been emboldened by the Warsaw Pact's invasion of Czechoslovakia only eight days earlier.

Whatever his motivation, the script is well known. In attempting to control all aspects of society, authoritarian states do not look kindly upon deviance of any sort, and the National Party was no exception. As already noted, the party was determined to fashion a new society shaped by strict neo-Calvinist values and informed by notions of 'distinct peoples, distinct languages, nations and cultures' – as Nico Diederichs, a leading Afrikaner intellectual, had told parliament three months after the National Party came to power.[3] A raft of legislation dedicated to ethnic and racial separation was launched with great vigour and purpose. Building on a legacy of colonialism and formal segregation, a new order was being engineered, whose aim was to ensure white survival and Afrikaner hegemony. English speakers, dominant in South Africa for decades, had now effectively lost political power. 'South Africa belongs to us once more,' exclaimed DF Malan at the time of electoral victory in 1948.[4]

Driven by a sense of mission that was underpinned by a deep-seated conservatism grounded in religious confession and guided by the NGK, the National Party rapidly consolidated Afrikaner power. Race was of supreme importance; but, as we have seen, culture and religion also informed policy. A 'Christian National Spirit' spelled out by the Broederbond and a myriad of other institutions defined its *Weltanschauung*.[5] God's authority was pervasive. A lengthy statement defining the Christian state, which was adopted by the Federal Council of the NGK in 1951, elucidated this. Communism, National Socialism and 'revolutionary democracy' were rejected as displeasing to God.

Government obtained its mandate from God and not the people, and the franchise was a privilege exercised with responsibility towards God rather than an automatic right. 'Non-whites' as well as those who 'openly rebel against God', such as communists, were excluded. Allegiance to Christianity was essential in a Christian state, concluded the resolution, and no adherents of an anti-Christian philosophy were to be allowed to form political parties.[6]

While the NGK resolution provided a set of guiding principles, church, school and university would ultimately provide the cultural compass and intellectual rationale for an unfolding racial order. This, as noted earlier, was evident in debates around Christian National Education (CNE) and the 'conscience clause'. Both confirmed the Christian character of South African society as well as the marginality of non-Afrikaners, including not only Roman Catholics, but especially Jews, who were not only religious deviants but also politically suspect. Thus, when he highlighted Jewish involvement in NUSAS in the 1968 speech, Lourens Muller was tapping into deep-seated fears and long-established stereotypes.

It is not without significance, however, that Muller was happy to tell his critics that he had not wilfully intended to disparage Jews. In fact, he indicated that he agreed with the statement issued by the Board and regretted that the press had distorted his words. 'What I said about Jews and Jewish students this week has been grossly misunderstood and wrongly interpreted,' he told the *Sunday Express*.[7] Furthermore, Muller professed a high regard for the Jewish community and said he could count hundreds of Jews among his friends. His words, however, failed to stop opposition commentators from accusing him of ugly politicking.[8] But the Nationalist press supported him: *Beeld* considered his comments perfectly reasonable given the disproportionate number of activist Jewish students on the list, adding that Jews formed 23 per cent of the first ten pages of listed communists, a high proportion given that Jews composed a mere 0.66 per cent of the total population.[9] The National Party, however, had no wish to ignite the flame of antisemitism, or to undermine its own modus vivendi with the Jewish community, which for two decades had operated, for the most part, with quiet success.[10]

Muller's assault was therefore neither a harbinger of Jew-baiting nor a return to the 1930s; but his intemperate comments were a stark reminder that Jews remained suspect. Lingering prejudice saw them barred from several prestigious sporting and recreational clubs and, for some, they remained outsiders, a curiosity on the fringes of society.[11] Nonetheless, the Jewish community continued to prosper. Jewish institutions were strengthened, and many Jews climbed the ladder of business and professional success. A few even attained prominence in public life.[12] But for some whites, especially fantasists, Jews remained suspect, their loyalty questioned and their imagined global machinations a source of concern. Most importantly, Jews personified the reviled ideologies of liberalism and communism, both of which challenged the apartheid order. These ideologies were often conflated by Nationalists. As DF Malan put it: 'Liberalism is almost the same as the ideal of Communism [because it] disintegrates all nations, states, cultures into one world nation.'[13] Dirk Richard, editor of *Dagbreek en Sondagnuus* (the most widely read Afrikaans newspaper), outlined the challenge both these ideologies posed to stability, order and the national project:

> In our country liberalist and communist are regarded as cart horses harnessed together, the one will cry out if you touch the other. He is thus one who puts himself out to change or to destroy the existing order. He may even have an aversion for subversion and bomb throwing, but he does not want the South Africa of today, but an integrated country which does not consist of various population groups, but simply of so many people White, Black, Yellow and Brown all mixed up. His struggle against the prevailing authority will become all the more intense, or the more fanatical: he is forced to seek spiritual allies, and this communism readily offers … The true liberal believes in the doctrine of international equality. He is the enemy of nationalism which gives a community its own identity. He wishes to destroy a person's feeling of belonging and the patriotism which provides his spiritual strength.[14]

Not a New Phenomenon

Both liberalism and communism had long preoccupied *völkisch* intellectuals. During the 1930s and 1940s, scepticism of 'British-Jewish-liberal' democracy had been a mantra of the radical right, and it was an easy transition in the post-war years to associate Jews with the liberal English-speaking opposition. Jewish upward mobility from the inner cities of Cape Town and Johannesburg to the leafy suburbs and their use of English as the language of choice certainly bolstered this perception. Few supported the National Party (most had admired Jan Smuts) and a disproportionate number – especially among the youth – were critical of apartheid. Ideologically, Jews challenged the notion of 'spiritual nationalism' advocated by *völkisch* thinkers who conflated race and culture and gave pride of place to Calvinist notions of diversity. In essence, this meant Afrikaner separation coupled with a belief in a religious mission.[15] Ignoring racial and 'national' divisions would, they argued, doom Afrikanerdom.[16] 'Every person can only attain his highest freedom and fullest self-realization within the unit of the nation,' explained Nico Diederichs. Liberal individualism, he claimed, sought 'to remove the boundaries between nations and races and cultures until it lapses into a hopeless international unnational mass of individuals who may be separated from each other historically but who apart from that have no dividing line in respect of race and colour.'[17] Liberalism, in other words, was a corrosive force, alien to the spirit and tradition of the Afrikaner.

Communism and its perceived influence on black Africans also posed a threat to the *völkisch* agenda, and it too was linked to Jews.[18] Here it is instructive to go back to the early twentieth century when eastern European Jewish immigrants were commonly associated with trade unionism and radical activism, exemplified in the creation of the Yiddish-speaking branch of the International Socialist League in 1915, which was the forerunner of the Communist Party of South Africa (CPSA), founded in 1921.[19] Jewish links with radicalism were further evident after the overthrow of the Tsarist regime in 1917 when immigrant Russian or 'Bolshevik' Jews celebrated in the streets of Johannesburg's cosmopolitan neighbourhoods.[20] Five years later 'Bolshevik Jews' were accused of instigating white workers against mine owners during the Rand Rebellion.[21] By then the stereotype of the subversive Jew was well entrenched. In the 1930s, radical Jewish trade unionists such as Solomon (Solly) Emil Sachs, general secretary of the Garment Workers' Union, were accused of subversion and of turning Afrikaner working women away from the *volk* (some had even enjoyed sponsored visits to the Soviet Union and returned with great enthusiasm for what they had seen), as well as propagating notions of racial equality and inspiring black insurrection.[22] This was of particular concern to the NGK, which believed that it had to 'act as a vanguard to shield the Afrikaner people from the "Red Peril" and its offshoots'.[23] A special commission to examine communist activities in the unions was established by the NGK in 1937. Its report, published two years later, revealed the main themes of its anti-communist rhetoric – summed up by the historian Aletta Norval as 'a concern with the communist focus on class differences at the expense of "national" differences; a complete rejection of the "equalization" between white and black propagated by communists, as well as a demonization of communist "agitators" working in black communities'.[24]

One year before the NGK report appeared, the threat of specifically Jewish agitators had been highlighted with startling clarity by DF Malan when addressing the GNP's Free State congress in Bloemfontein:

> Behind Communism and Liberalism there was a power which had grown tremendously of late – a power that made itself felt during the last elections. That power was Jewry. The Jews were in the minority in all countries, but they understood the art of attracting to themselves a great deal more than was due to them in proportion to their numbers. The means they employed were not only their economic power, but, directly or indirectly, they always preached the doctrine of Liberalism, or, where it suited their purposes better, the doctrine of Communism. They disseminated and propagated these doctrines of equality because they wanted no race or colour discriminations. Jews did not always support Communism or Liberalism on the political merits of these creeds, but because they were a means of protecting Jews.[25]

Shortly after Russia entered the war on the side of the Allies in the summer of 1941, Malan, in yet another anti-Jewish salvo, warned that a German defeat would result in Bolshevism, under Jewish leadership, flooding Europe:

> Bolshevism is a destroyer of the foundations of civilisation and of everything the Christian nations deem to be holy. If this is the case in other countries, we in South Africa have a hundred more reasons to detest and to fear Bolshevism... It wants to initiate a Bolshevist revolution here and therefore seeks its support mostly with the non-white elements. Under the leadership of Communist Jews, it has nestled itself into a number of our trade unions. It does not acknowledge the colour bar in any sphere, and where it is legally possible, it agitates tirelessly – with the vehement incitement of the non-whites – to remove it. It does not know any patriotism. It is the sworn enemy of all religion, not least of Christianity. In short, Bolshevism is the negation of everything Afrikanerdom has stood for and fought for, suffered for and died for, for generations.[26]

Malan's tirade was typical of radical right responses throughout the war years.[27] 'Godless communism' was perceived as a largely Jewish evil, hell-bent on a proletarian revolution at the behest of the black population.[28] Fear indeed ran deep and would persist for decades, nourished by the Cold War, the advance of decolonisation in Africa, and the ever-present prospect of South Africa's black majority falling under the seductive sway of communist (often Jewish) agitators. It mattered little that Malan, when raising the Jewish bogey, had grossly exaggerated the situation and that, in reality, only a small minority of South Africa's Jews were on the radical left. This meant nothing to those comfortable with simplistic labelling. After all, Russian-Jewish immigrants were prominent among the members of the CPSA and active among the Friends of the Soviet Union, while the activities of the Yiddish-speaking Afrikaner Gezerd, a movement which assisted land settlement and industrialisation of Jews in the USSR, were known to many. The activities of the Yiddisher Arbeter-klub (Jewish Workers' Club) in Johannesburg, with its links to various left-wing groups such as the CPSA, Friends of the Soviet Union and the Left Book Club, were also well known. It was easy to evoke the 'Jew-Bolshevik' threat.[29]

Thus Malan's anti-Jewish outbursts captured a visceral paranoia that was widely shared among Nationalist colleagues. In particular, the Ossewabrandwag (OB) had identified a nexus between Jews and communism during the war years. Except for the chief secretary of the Communist Party, all the other Bolshevik leaders were Jews, claimed its mouthpiece, *Die OB*.[30] Unsurprisingly, a 1942 agreement signed by the government to establish consular relations with the Soviet Union had 'provoked hysteria' among the white right of South African politics.[31] Eric Louw implored the House to close the Russian Consulate, while JG Strijdom (a future prime minister) accused Smuts of embracing Stalin.[32] Louw's booklet, *The Communist Danger in South Africa*, offered an unadulterated glimpse into Nationalist fears.[33] Towards the end of the war, Karl Bremer (a man who had showed little love for Jews in the 1930s) warned parliament about the possibility of a 'bloody revolution'. Communism, he asserted, threatened the very existence of South Africa and had the potential to surpass the 'barbarism of the native'.[34]

Such scaremongering now framed National Party propaganda. Within months of the end of the war, Malan called on South Africans to stand together as a 'white bloc against the menace of communism' – a menace that threatened 'the white race and everything South Africans held dear'.[35] 'Too long have Jewish Communists been allowed a free home in our country,' fulminated Louw when advocating the closure of communist newspapers in August 1946.[36] A few months later, building on several anti-communist conferences and symposia that had been convened under the auspices of the Afrikaner churches during the war years, an Anti-Kommunistiese Aksiekommissie (Anti-communist Action Committee, known as Antikom) was established by the NGK.[37] Designed specifically to withstand both the communist and liberal danger, Antikom (and its newsletter *Antikom*) sought to promote Christian-nationalist trade unionism among the 'white' workers of South Africa and to ensure that black workers shared a Christian-nationalist worldview that included support for racial apartheid.[38]

Reverend Jacobus Daniël ('Koot') Vorster. Courtesy: National Dutch Reformed Church in South Africa Archive, Stellenbosch

Among those present at the founding of Antikom was the Reverend Jacobus Daniël ('Koot') Vorster, brother of the future prime minister BJ Vorster. A highly regarded NGK minister, Koot Vorster had grown up on the farm 'Predikantskop' near the small, eastern Cape hamlet of Jamestown where he and his brother developed an acute sense of identity and culture, a fierce pride in Afrikaner nationalism, and an abiding hostility to communism. Vorster devoted substantial energy to the study of Marxism as an ideology and concluded that it was a diabolical enemy.[39] Both he and his brother had opposed South Africa's entry into the war in 1939 and supported the pro-Nazi OB, establishing a branch of the movement in Cape Town. Koot Vorster's far-right politics were vividly on display when he told students in Cape Town in September 1940 that Hitler's *Mein Kampf* had shown 'the way to greatness – the path of South Africa'. The Nazi leader, he asserted, has given 'the Germans a calling. He gave them a fanaticism which causes them to stand back for no one. We must follow his example because only by such holy fanaticism can the Afrikaner nation achieve its calling.' Significantly, Vorster anticipated a new Great Trek, but, instead of Afrikaners, it would now consist 'of Jingos and Jews'.[40] Soon after his speech, he was arrested for passing information to the enemy about military installations in Simon's Town and was subsequently interned.[41]

At the time of Koot Vorster's incarceration, the 'Jewish question' was raging within Afrikaner circles: too many Jews appeared to be challenging racial segregation. Jewish activism at English-speaking universities (notably Wits and UCT) was of particular concern.[42] Already in 1938, *Die Transvaler* had complained about the preponderance of Jews on the Student Representative Council (SRC) at Wits, while an Afrikaans-language Wits student newspaper, *Spore*, denounced the 'Jewish negrophilists' in student politics.[43] In 1943 a commission set up by the NGK (although far from widely accepted) associated Jews with secret societies, communism and domination.[44] The same fears informed perceptions of the Springbok Legion, a short-lived anti-racist war veterans' association founded in 1941 (led by a Jew, Jock Isacowitz, a one-time socialist Zionist, later a communist, and still later a leading member of the anti-apartheid Liberal Party) to safeguard the interests of discharged servicemen. Committed to the principles of liberty, equality and fraternity, the Legion was essentially a left-leaning movement dominated by communists in leadership positions. It found itself condemned in the most scurrilous terms at an anti-communist congress organised by Malan's HNP in September 1945.[45]

Riddled with communists was *Die OB*'s assessment of the Springbok Legion,[46] while Hans van Rensburg, the leader of the OB, described its members as 'spiritual fellow travellers' of the Communist Party.[47] Some years later, the minister of justice, Charles Robberts ('Blackie') Swart, went further, characterising the Legion as 'a military branch of the Communist Party'.[48] Only a few days before the opening of the congress, *Die Burger* endorsed a Free State NGK commission which had concluded that Jewish communists stood at the head of the anti-European agitation.[49]

The burgeoning influx of politicised black African workers into the cities during the war years exacerbated the anti-communist mood and intensified fear among jobless and unskilled Afrikaners. Keen to minimise competition and establish a firm foothold in the economy, an emergent Afrikaner bourgeoisie joined the fray. Nationalists chose as their bogeyman the liberal politician and cabinet minister Jan Hofmeyr, predicting that his inclusive franchise policy would ultimately result in the collapse of 'white civilisation'. Malan sensed the unfolding political opportunities and linked the 'black peril' to the communist threat during the 1948 general election campaign.[50]

Old Ideas Never Die

Ideas have an ability to survive through time. They may be modified, and patterns of action may change, but beliefs persist and connect limpet-like to new ideas.[51] In an emerging Cold War atmosphere, a decades-old hostility to liberalism and communism would solidify, as would perceptions of the subversive Jew. Indeed, soon after the National Party came to power in 1948, Albert Robinson, the United Party MP for Langlaagte, told the House that his Jewish parliamentary colleagues were being targeted as communists by 'members of the Government benches'. Tellingly, however, Robinson added that this was not the case for those sitting on ministerial benches.[52] Malan's modus vivendi with the Jewish community was evidently accepted by senior Nationalists. A 'Jewish question' per se never emerged. But it was hardly necessary to mention the identity of heavyweights like Sam Kahn, a Cape Town-born Jewish communist.[53] Kahn was elected a Native Representative in the House in 1949 but expelled from parliament three years later after the CPSA had been declared illegal in 1950.

National Party parliamentarians were fully aware that Jews were prominent in radical politics.[54] They needed no reminding of this during debates on the Suppression of Communism Act of 1950, which outlawed communism, and in debates on the Riotous Assemblies and Suppression of Communism (Amendment) Bill, finally passed in 1954.[55] Although not identified as such, the names of Jews were frequently mentioned deprecatingly in the House.[56] Nationalists also knew that many of those who spoke in defence of liberal values and opposed the Riotous Assemblies Bill were Jewish. Among them were Bernard Friedman (MP for Hillbrow), Hyman Davidoff (MP for Edendale and then Johannesburg City), Alex Hepple (MP for Rosettenville), Leo Lovell (MP for Benoni) and Morris Kentridge (MP for Troyeville). No Nationalist could have missed a report tabled in the House at the time of the debate (based on a police investigation carried out under the Smuts government) in which Jewish names were prominently cited for involvement in communist subversion. A presumably intercepted letter included in a report from Michael Harmel, a communist Jew, to the executive council of the Communist Party (dated 7 March 1945) went so far as to claim that the CPSA was in control of the South African Jewish Board of Deputies.[57] Although patently absurd and officially denied by the Board, the accusation stuck for decades and was periodically aired on public platforms and resuscitated in the far-right media and in 'Cold War' publications.[58] Importantly, during exchanges on the Riotous Assemblies and Suppression of Communism (Amendment) Bill, one-time Eastern Province Greyshirt leader, Johannes von Strauss von Moltke – always on hand to attack Jews – reminded critics of the bill (whom he obviously identified as Jewish) of debates that had taken place in the 1930s on the Riotous Assemblies Bill which was intended to outlaw the radical right. At that time the Board had been fully behind that draconian bill, noted von Moltke; a classic case, he suggested, of double standards.[59] He returned to condemnations of the Board's devious activities a few years later during a debate on the Entertainment and Publications Bill.[60]

So, at least for some, the 'Jewish question' had not entirely abated. Jewish behaviour was being monitored. *Die Burger*, for example, looked askance at the liberal Bernard Friedman (identified in parliament by a Nationalist member as the 'Voice of Moscow') whose aspersions on the integrity of the minister of finance, Klasie Havenga, were considered an offence to Afrikaner nationalism. 'By doing so, he was not doing his people any good,' warned the Nationalist daily. 'We hope that the Jewish community will stand aloof from Dr Friedman's utterances.'[61] One year later, a police list of members of the South African Communist Party, or SACP (the renamed CPSA), in the Johannesburg District showed that of the 65 members, 23 were Jewish.[62]

One cannot underestimate the fear of subversive communists and liberals, allegedly acting at the behest of Moscow. One sees this vividly in the observations of Frederick Metrowich, a contemporary Cold War commentator, who claimed that Africa was ripe for a communist takeover and that liberals supported these efforts in nefarious ways.[63] Of course, the 'red peril' did provide a useful opportunity to corral all whites into the laager.[64] The National Party could tar all oppositional groups with a 'communist' or 'liberalist' brush, including the Torch Commando, a movement established in 1951 to fight initiatives to remove Coloureds from the common voters' roll. Both communism and liberalism were equally reprehensible, explained Johannes Schoonbee, MP for Pretoria District. The 'cloak of liberalism under which some of the people are trying to shield is only another name for Communism', he told the House, while insisting that the Afrikaner 'can never and will never countenance liberalism or Communism or call it what you like'.[65] In similar fashion, the National Party MP for Mossel Bay, Petrus van Nierop, warned the House that 'certain people are propagating certain things in the name of liberalism, things which are absolutely communistic'.[66] This conflation of liberalism and communism is well illustrated in a 1954 memorandum to the justice minister, CR Swart, from security policeman Captain E Buys regarding the Springbok Legion's Jock Isacowitz: '[He] is a very strong Liberalist and staunch supporter of the Liberal ideology. He is a self-confessed Communist. The Liberal Party is sponsoring the Congress of the People which is known to consist of Communists and fellow travellers. Isacowitz admits his close association with the Springbok Legion and must therefore be aware that the Legion was the Military Branch of the Communist Party of South Africa.'[67]

Subversive Outsiders: 1940s to 1960s

SED Brown. Courtesy: Special Collections, National Library of South Africa, Cape Town

Such thinking graphically expressed the mood among far-rightists, readily given to stereotypes of Jewish disloyalty and subversion. An illustration (made more explicit, as we shall see, in a personal communication) was a 31-page booklet issued by the Sons of South Africa, a nativist movement founded in 1946 by the English-speaking Sydney Eustace Denys Brown to bridge the divide between white English and Afrikaans speakers.[68] The child of an English immigrant father and an Afrikaner mother, Brown was born in Vryheid, Natal, in 1910. He had grown up in Pietermaritzburg where he matriculated at Maritzburg College at the age of sixteen and then joined the League of Gentiles, a fringe antisemitic movement founded in the mid-1920s. At the age of twenty, he enlisted in the British South Africa Police in Rhodesia and in 1939 joined the Intelligence Corps of the

South African armed forces, but was discharged because he refused to serve outside Africa.[69] Brown's private communication with Ernest George Jansen, a senior Nationalist, future governor-general of South Africa, and editor of the *New Era* (a short-lived Nationalist English-language mouthpiece), whom he invited to become a member of the organisation's provisional council, lifts a lid on the Sons of South Africa and provides a taste of his politics, which would evolve over decades in the *South African Observer*, a monthly Brown founded in 1955 and edited for over thirty years. Liberals were described as part of the 'Russian column in South Africa' (together with trade unions, labour parties and municipalities), while 'English jingoes' and Jews were characterised as disloyal. But it was the 'Jewish question' and 'political Zionism' that remained a primary concern for Brown.[70] Quite astonishingly, in a letter to Jansen written in 1946, he recommended that Jews be formally segregated from the wider society and that membership of his Sons of South Africa be open only to those born in South Africa or those South African in the 'full cultural sense'.[71] The meaning was obvious.

Hardly visible in its first few years, Brown's Sons of South Africa gained attention in 1950 when the organisation was welcomed and praised by *Die Transvaler* for its hostility to liberalism and the United Party English jingo-press.[72] An editorial in *Die Vaderland* also commended the *South African Observer*, while in parliament the minister of Bantu administration and development and Bantu education, Michel Christiaan de Wet Nel, praised the monthly, saying, 'It is only a person who does not mean well by South Africa who would say anything derogatory about that journal.'[73] Ultimately, however, the *South African Observer* made little impact, but its views were echoed by some mainstream Afrikaner commentators who shared hatred of the 'jingo' English press and expressed concerns about the preponderance of Jews among anti-Nationalist activists. One of *Die Transvaler*'s most prominent columnists, Neels Natte, for example, specifically noted the high proportion of 'foreign names in the liberalistic left-wing' of the United Party in the Transvaal. Woolf, Miller, Bielski, Weiss, Nestadt, Einstein, Emdin, Taurog, Kowarsky, Myer, Eppel, Fisher and Sive were identified, presumably as symbols of disloyalty and subversion.[74] Letters to the press reinforced Natte's observations, with one correspondent warning Jews that their liberal behaviour was being watched:

> We as Afrikaners would very much like to learn why the Jews work so conspicuously in every sphere against the Government's apartheid policy, because their names appear most prominently as advocates for all agitation movements ... What do they aim at with their liberalistic policy of mingling between White and non-White? ... Our Jewish friends work against apartheid in every field by indecent commiseration with the native, encouragement of intermingling, support of integration and advocacy of social levelling in city councils and Parliament. We see this everywhere in their dwellings and in their private cars, in which they do not scruple to travel together [with non-Whites] ... Why has not one of the leaders of the Jewish community yet openly stepped into the breach in support of the Government's apartheid policy? We wish to bring to our Jewish friends' attention that these actions will not be observed without consequences by South Africans as a whole.[75]

Other anti-Jewish missives echoed this warning:

> That the support of the Jews is readily granted to the powers which aim at the downfall of the Boer must be deduced from the behaviour of the Jews. When photographs appear in newspapers of resistance processions, or of joint singing and dancing with 'Africans', or of the 'Black Sash's' slander tableaux, the Jewish facial type is in the majority. When a book is published on the 'bad conditions' in South Africa, the writer is ten to one a Jew. Under petitions protesting against the Boer's policy there always appear numbers of Jewish names. Jewish professors, lecturers, doctors, rabbis and lawyers fall over one another in order to be able to sign. Behind tables in the street collecting signatures against the Boer's policy a Jewish lady is usually enthroned ... The patience of the Boer must one day become exhausted.[76]

Evidently, Jews were widely perceived as disloyal and subversive aliens, even by some Afrikaner intellectuals. For instance, in his review of *The Jews of South Africa: A History* (co-edited by Gus Saron and Louis Hotz), the historian and assistant editor of *Die Transvaler*,

Gert Daniël Scholtz – a tenacious critic of liberalism – linked Jews to British imperialism, the age-old enemy of the Afrikaner. Scholtz also informed readers that 'it was chiefly certain Jews who came to preach all sorts of foreign political ideologies in South Africa', by which he was unmistakably referring to liberalism and communism.[77] Similar sentiments were expressed by Professor CJ Uys, a historian at the University of the Orange Free State, who, during a symposium on the Saron and Hotz book, urged Jews to find salvation in the Bible and the synagogue, and not in capitalism or liberalism or communism, the last-mentioned being, in Uys's view, 'essentially a Jewish conception'.[78]

Changing the Guard

In late 1954 Malan was replaced as prime minister by the 61-year-old JG Strijdom, the so-called Lion of the North. Well known for his conservative views as well as his determined opposition to Jews becoming members of the National Party,[79] Strijdom was patently concerned about Jewish activism. Indeed, soon after his inauguration he met with the Jewish Board of Deputies and, foreshadowing Lourens Muller's speech (discussed at the start of this chapter) by thirteen years, suggested that Jewish university students 'were challenging the things fundamental not only to the Afrikaner's way of life but of the whole white population in this country'.[80]

At this time, domestic and urban protests, as well as anti-apartheid boycotts, had taken on greater militancy. After the banning of the CPSA in 1950, many left-wing radicals migrated to various trade unions where they provided an important cadre of leadership. A nationwide passive resistance campaign in the early 1950s against unjust laws – known as the Defiance Campaign – added to government concerns, as did widespread popular stirrings against apartheid legislation. Even an increased majority in the 1953 general election at the expense of the United Party was of little comfort to the National Party. Anxiety mounted in June 1955 when the Congress of the People – an alliance of the African National Congress (ANC), the South African Indian Congress, the South African Coloured People's Organisation, the South African Congress of Trade Unions, and the (white) Congress of Democrats – met at Kliptown outside Johannesburg to launch the

Freedom Charter, which was dedicated to a vision of a democratic South Africa.

Viewing the Freedom Charter (in the words of the historian David Welsh) as 'a blueprint for a Marxist-Leninist state', the government responded in December 1956 by arresting 156 people linked to the Congress Alliance on the charge of high treason.[81] Of the 23 whites charged, 15 were Jews. While the arrests were splashed across the media, this over-representation of Jews among the trialists was somewhat surprisingly ignored in the immediate aftermath of the round up. Even Brown's S*outh African Observer*, characterised from its inception by grand conspiracy theories and the denigration of 'liberals' and 'political Zionists', did not initially focus on the number of Jews among those charged. Instead, it emphasised in broad terms the communist onslaught faced by South Africa, which was being driven by the 'propagation of Marxist Leninist theories'.[82] However, the disproportionate involvement of Jews associated with subversion and wider political challenges to the state was deeply etched and would later be noted. Two years after the Treason Trial, Dr Christiaan Fick Albertyn, the general manager of Nasionale Pers, the powerful publishing company closely allied to the National Party, warned Jews against the incitement of the 'Native against the White man', which could endanger the whole Jewish population in South Africa.[83]

Fear-mongering was now commonplace in a highly charged Cold War atmosphere in which the Soviet leader Nikita Khrushchev spoke of inevitable African decolonisation and radical economic and political transformation. In these circumstances, even a mainstream liberal Jew like Helen Suzman, the MP for Houghton for the United Party and later the Progressive Party (a liberal breakaway from the former, subsequently renamed the Progressive Federal Party, or PFP, in 1977) was targeted as a subversive threat, and was subjected to regular antisemitic slurs from across the benches.[84] Indeed, in what was referred to by the *Natal Witness* as the worst case of antisemitism since the Second World War, Suzman and her colleague Boris Wilson, MP for Hospital, were the subjects of outrageous anti-Jewish comments during a debate on malpractices against black African workers by white farmers. Essentially, the two Jewish MPs were told that they had no right to criticise farmers for their treatment of black African workers because several Jewish farmers faced court action for such felonies.[85]

White angst grew with accelerated decolonisation across Africa and especially with British Prime Minister Harold Macmillan's 'winds of change' speech to South African parliamentarians in February 1960, which acknowledged the need for universal rights. The killing of 69 black Africans in Sharpeville outside Johannesburg six weeks later, followed by a domestic financial crisis and the reported chaos accompanying the hasty Belgian withdrawal from the Congo, exacerbated the gloom and strengthened the voice of pro-apartheid and anti-communist hardliners. In his autobiography, Frederik Willem de Klerk recalls the newspapers being 'full of horror stories brought back by white refugees from the Congo and other newly independent territories, where the hasty transfer of power to former revolutionaries had led in many instances to the collapse of effective government and law and order'. Like most whites at that time, De Klerk was 'deeply concerned about the influence of the South African Communist Party on the ANC'.[86]

None of these developments diverted the National Party from its political goals. In 1961 South Africa's withdrawal from the Commonwealth provided clear evidence that the *völkisch* project was on track: republicanism had always been a National Party objective. Challenges to the state, however, were mounting. Sensing the hopelessness of peaceful change following its banning in 1960, the ANC established a military wing, Umkhonto we Sizwe (Spear of the Nation, or MK), in 1961. Poqo, a military offshoot of the Pan Africanist Congress (PAC), which had broken from the ANC in 1959, also began a campaign of violence, as did the (almost all-white) African Resistance Movement (ARM), which came to prominence when one of its members planted a bomb at the Johannesburg railway station. Inspired by on-going guerrilla wars in Vietnam, Cuba and Algeria, many opponents of apartheid, it seems, saw violence as the only option. Although NUSAS condemned acts of sabotage, some of its ex-leaders (among them a number of Jews) were involved in the ARM, further focusing government attention on the student movement, which was described by the minister of justice, BJ Vorster, as 'a cancer in the life of South Africa' and a 'mouthpiece of the liberals and tinged with communism'.[87]

Two months prior to Vorster's outburst against NUSAS, Nelson Mandela and ten of his comrades had been arrested and charged with sabotage following a raid at Lilliesleaf, a smallholding in Rivonia outside Johannesburg.[88] Five of the eleven defendants in what became known as the Rivonia Trial were Jews, the only whites among those charged.[89] Initially the press, including the *South African Observer*, did not identify specifically Jewish involvement,[90] but the tone changed when two of the white defendants, Harold Wolpe and Arthur Goldreich, escaped from a Johannesburg gaol in August 1963. To be sure, shortly after the escape, General Hendrik van den Bergh, South Africa's deputy commissioner of police and head of the Security Branch, told the Afrikaanse Nasionale Kultuurraad (Afrikaner National Cultural Council) that Jews were behind radicalism.[91] Although the lanky Van den Bergh (closely connected to the South African-born British antisemite Arthur Kenneth Chesterton, and by all accounts a Jew-hater) clarified his comments after a minor media storm, the dominance of Jews among white activists was patently obvious.[92] This was demonstrated in newspaper columns, letters to the press, and parliamentary comments.[93] The matter had to be faced by the Jewish community, wrote 'Grensboer' in his column 'Political Horizon' in *Die Oosterlig*,[94] while behind the scenes a representative of *Dagbreek en Sondagnuus* told the Board of Deputies that the weekly had received correspondence on the subject that it did not wish to publish for the sake of harmonious group relations; but it asked the Board to reply to the following questions:

1. How is it that such a high percentage of white persons detained under the 90-Day Clause of the General Law Amendment Act are Jews?
2. Is this an indication that Jews are not happy in South Africa, or is it the consequence of their strong freedom urge?
3. What is the official Jewish standpoint about the actions of people like Goldreich and Wolpe?

Here was an outright affirmation that in the public mind, the subversive

Jew was considered a source of concern.⁹⁵ The Board responded that 'the actions of individuals of any section are their own responsibility, and no section of the community can or should be asked to accept responsibility. If individuals transgress the law, they expose themselves to the penalty of the law.' This reply would not pacify those concerned about Jewish loyalty, warned Saron, who told the executive of the Board that many people of influence, especially Afrikaners, 'were expecting the Jewish community to dissociate itself in some official manner from the alleged subversive activities of certain individual Jews'.⁹⁶

Saron undoubtedly sensed the extent to which Jews were now targeted as subversive liberals and communists. A well-known member of the South African Medical Association, Dr GFC Troskie of Kroonstad, even spoke of dangerous liberalism dating back to 'the Zionist Conference held in 1895 [*sic*] in Switzerland'. At that meeting, reported Troskie, the plans – found in *The Protocols of the Elders of Zion* to enable liberalism to conquer the world – were hatched.⁹⁷ Cas Greyling, MP for Ventersdorp, put it differently: 'English and Afrikaners were not responsible for the Liberal Party,' he told the House in 1963. 'Just look at the people who have been banned, note the names. Those leaders are a small number of intellectuals among one particular group in South Africa.'⁹⁸ Seasoned journalist Schalk Pienaar certainly understood the inference that 'the liberalistic trouble-makers came mostly from the Jewish ranks'.⁹⁹

Could it have been accidental that in his Jewish New Year message that was delivered soon after the escape of Wolpe and Goldreich, State President Swart called upon all 'to stand together in loyalty and both by word and deed to protect our country against subversion from within and aggression from without'?¹⁰⁰

A Spike in the Anti-Communist Temperature

A few months after South Africa's state president had delivered his 1963 Jewish New Year message, Antikom hosted another *volkskongres* (people's congress) in Pretoria. Attended by 2,428 delegates, it focused on the theme of 'Christian Civilisation against Communism'. Despite known Jew-haters such as SED Brown and the journalist Ivor Benson (who represented the SABC) serving on the conference planning committee, the presentations were – much to the chagrin of special guest AK Chesterton – McCarthyite in tone rather than antisemitic. Koot Vorster did, however, use the occasion to lambast liberals of all persuasions. 'Liberal Christians, liberal Jews and liberal-minded universities have, down the years, rendered the greatest assistance to the Communists and have furnished the largest number of fifth columnists,' he told the gathering.[101] Emphasis, however, was on communism's global challenge to Christianity, its praxis, and the actions of communists in Africa, with a focus on South Africa, which was identified by the retired commandant-general of the South African Defence Force, Stephen Melville, as 'the foremost battle line against the Communist attack on the free world'.[102]

This geopolitical role was relished by the National Party and encouraged by the Western powers. Apartheid South Africa could be relied upon. This was reaffirmed in 1964 when Justice Quartus de Wet sentenced eight of the Rivonia trialists to life imprisonment. 'It is to the advantage of the West as a whole that the Republic succeeded in good time in exposing a plot which aimed at unleashing a communist revolution here,' explained Hendrik Verwoerd, who had succeeded Strijdom as prime minister in 1958.[103] Across the white political spectrum there was a sense of relief.[104] Liberal and left-wing tyranny had been unmasked 'as no other revelation could possibly have done'.[105]

Draconian legislation and relentless oppression had certainly delivered results, but the struggle was far from over. Afrikaners in particular remained edgy and fearful.[106] In so far as Jewish involvement was concerned, a series of letters to the *EP Herald* showed that the presence of Jews among the trialists did not go unnoticed.[107] On the other hand, the *South African Observer* simply displayed the names of the whites, presumably a giveaway as to their Jewish identity.[108] In parliament, the National Party MP for Heilbron, Gabriël Froneman – who at one stage suggested that Jewish parliamentarians go back to Israel – was quite explicit: five Jews had incited the 'Bantu', he told the House. He did, however, point out that those radicals did not represent all Jews.[109] *Antikom* showed no such balance. A few months after the Rivonia judgment, it published an article entitled 'Aangename kennis, mnr. Haim Goldmann' (Pleased to meet you, Mr Haim Goldmann) that claimed Lenin was a Jew. According to the article, Lenin (nicknamed 'the bloodthirsty one') was born of Jewish parentage in a small town near Odessa and his real name was Haim Goldmann and his home language was Yiddish. Citing several so-called authoritative and confidential sources that dated back decades, the article implied communism and Bolshevism were of Jewish origin – a widely shared trope, both abroad and in South Africa.[110]

Jews were understandably angered, with their wrath directed at Koot Vorster (now *actuarius* of the General Synod of the NGK) because of his known ties to the journal.[111] However, in an interview with the *South African Jewish Times*, Vorster denied *Antikom*'s relationship with the National Council Against Communism, which had been established at the Pretoria Volkskongres, and, quite remarkably, denied that the articles were antisemitic; but, oblivious to any irony, he then called on Jews to 'come out openly against communism'.[112] This, he maintained, was why *Antikom* had published the questionable articles. When asked by *Die Transvaler* to comment on Vorster's views, an obviously fearful Board effectively distanced itself from the Jewish radicals, arguing that the community had no official political stance qua community. The fact that some high-profile Jews had been involved in communist endeavours was not a reason to cast aspersions on all Jews, stated the Board:

> No less than any other section of the population, the Jewish community seeks to advance the welfare and peaceful development of South Africa in the interests of all its inhabitants. Representative Jewish spokesmen, both lay and clerical, have on numerous occasions affirmed that they stand for law and order and for political progress through constitutional means, and that they unreservedly condemn and reject subversion and violence in the political field.
>
> The underlying assumption of Ds. Vorster's call seems to be the mistaken idea that the Jewish community somehow constitutes a political unit or a political entity. It is surely well understood by now that Jews act politically as individual citizens. There is no political regimentation and there cannot be. Any attempt by a Jewish body to interfere with the legitimate political freedom of the individual Jewish citizen would be immediately repudiated.[113]

While the views of *Antikom* did not represent all Afrikaners (or the NGK), and while some important NGK figures distanced themselves from the diatribe, many ordinary South Africans shared its sentiments.[114] *Antikom* had related 'indisputable facts', claimed one Kurt Edwards (father of a later apartheid spy) in a letter to *Die Oosterlig*. 'Karl Marx was a Jew and New York Jews did finance the Russian Revolution. Soviet Communism and political Zionism basically materialised simultaneously from Czarist Russia,' maintained Edwards. In his view the NGK owed no apology to the *South African Jewish Times*. The truth was that South Africa was confronted by several 'diabolical enemies, i.e. Black Nationalism, Communism or Political Zionism'.[115] In a letter to *Die Burger*, one S Conradie expressed similar views: 'While recognising a place for Jews in a Christian South Africa, it has, however, come to the attention of all South Africans that whites with Jewish surnames time and again appear in court or flee the country, because they have played a leading role in undermining activities against the lawful government of the land.'[116]

Newspapers were now peppered with correspondence on the alleged nexus between Jews, communism and the Russian Revolution.[117] Some interventions were guarded and nuanced, but many were blatantly antisemitic. 'Reader', for example, quoted from a range of international sources that highlighted the prominent role played by Jews in the Russian Revolution.[118] Tellingly, the NGK's own mouthpiece, *Die Kerkbode*, also expressed concern about the number of Jews listed as communists and empathised with those voicing concern:

> Lately it has now happened that the attention of many people has been drawn to what they regard as a high percentage of Jewish names among listed communists. These people can surely not be blamed for noticing this. And that Jewish leaders are apprehensive about anti-Jewish feeling which could be fed by this phenomenon is understandable. Should someone observe how tragic it is that persons with Afrikaans names are being accused of sabotage and undermining activities, then every true Afrikaner would feel himself answerable thereby.[119]

The 'red peril' and the noticeable presence of Jews among so-called subversives were manifestly of concern. Letter writers to the press persisted in pointing to the high number of Jewish names among those who had been incarcerated under the 90-day clause of the 'Detentions Act' embedded within the General Law Amendment Act No. 37 of 1963.[120] This raised questions about Jewish loyalty to the country, wrote Dirk Richard, the editor of *Dagbreek en Sondagnuus*. Richard, a pugnacious scribe, was provoked to address the issue by the editor of the *South African Jewish Times*, Leon Feldberg, who had called on the government to resist the 'extremist right' – a reference to battles raging within the National Party over crude racial discrimination and the need for reform. 'Waar staan die Jood in die Blanke bestaanstryd?' (Where does the Jew stand in the white struggle for survival?) asked an angry Richard in his weekly column 'Na my mening' (In my opinion). As far as he could see, the Jew was looked upon with suspicion, a fact 'kindled by the numerous Jewish names which have been found among underminers, leftists, NUSAS leaders and the most poisonous journalists – Goldreich, Wolpe, Rubin, Leftwich and others'. Richard also noted that Goldreich and Wolpe were seen not as saboteurs 'but Jews who wish to undermine South Africa'. The average Nationalist, he asserted, believed 'the Jews are not well disposed to his party and its policy of separate development – that they are even hostile to it … so that he cannot rely on the Jew at a time when his country has to be defended at the last ditch'.[121]

An avalanche of correspondence followed in the wake of Richard's column, much of it in agreement with the author.[122] RC Smith questioned Jewish patriotism and claimed a large proportion of Jews were communist-inclined,[123] while L van der Vywer claimed Jews had no respect for the Afrikaner and refused to endorse national policy. The Jew was more interested in 'the purchasing power of the Bantu than his welfare', asserted Van der Vywer.[124] PJ de Flamingh congratulated *Dagbreek en Sondagnuus* for its brave objectivity when examining the position of the Jew. 'They are merciless in their attacks on the Government and the Afrikaner,' he wrote, 'and any report is good as long as the Afrikaner and his Government are besmirched by it.'[125]

The twin threats of liberalism and communism were once again highlighted at another international conference, this time hosted by the National Council Against Communism. One of the international speakers was Major Edgar Bundy, the American evangelist and Cold War militant, who denounced the World Council of Churches as a 'Communist front',[126] while others targeted liberalism for its tolerance of communism and its quest for equality.[127] It was a 'fifth column', warned Koot Vorster in a hard-hitting address.[128] Major-General Hendrik van den Bergh too spoke of communists infiltrating newspapers, but he also spoke of communist infiltration of student organisations and the Church. In response to a question regarding the prominence of Jews in the anti-apartheid movement, he answered by saying communism was the highest form of capitalism.[129] It was left to one of the guests, the distinguished Professor Stefan Possony of the Hoover Institute at Stanford University, to 'discredit the prevailing antisemitic undertones and to warn that antisemitism in fact harmed the fight against communism'.[130]

Many Cold War warriors and their supporters clearly saw the Jew as destructive and hypocritical. This was especially the case of the radical right, as illustrated in Brown's *South African Observer*:

> The audacity of the Harry Oppenheimers, Helen Suzmans, Joel Mervises – as well as their co-racials who have played and are playing leading parts in liberal and progressive and all-far-Left organisations in South Africa – never ceases to amaze me ... In the guise of fighting for human rights and against 'racial discrimination', they seek to break down the racial and national integrity of our Western nation, whereas the racial and national exclusiveness they themselves practise so assiduously far surpasses anything practised by Western man anywhere.[131]

Hendrik van den Bergh put this charge in even stronger terms, albeit privately. Infuriated that so many Jews opposed apartheid, he told the spy and journalist Gordon Winter that Jews were in fact responsible for its invention: 'The Jews invented the idea of keeping their tribe apart,' he told Winter. 'They don't like people who marry out of their faith; or outsiders marrying into it either. That's their brand of apartheid, so why do they criticize ours? Why do they get involved in Communist sabotage and agitation activities?'[132] This so-called hypocrisy was a common criticism. Endogamy was good for the Jews – but for others, integration was necessary.[133] Liberalism and communism – two sides of the same coin – were also allegedly and cynically used by Jews for their own interests. Liberals wanted one man one vote, said a senior Nationalist, Connie Mulder, while communists wanted international equality in a single world state.[134]

Not surprisingly, Piet Meyer, SABC Board chairman, had warned that he would do everything possible to check these two ideologies.[135] This did not bode well, given the fact that the SABC was the only legal broadcaster.[136]

Adding to the Mix: The Israel Question

Alongside concern about Jewish subversion was an increasing disquiet about Israel's vocal opposition to apartheid, which had initially become apparent in July 1961 when the Israeli prime minister, David Ben-Gurion, issued a joint statement with Maurice Yaméogo, president of Upper Volta (now Burkina Faso), condemning 'any manifestation of racial discrimination' and alluding to apartheid as 'detrimental to the interests of the African majority'.[137]

Although relatively moderate in tone, Israel's attempts to curry favour with the African bloc shortly after the creation of the Jewish state in 1948 embarrassed South African Jews, who would soon be reminded that the government regarded Israel's actions as hostile.[138] Indeed, immediately after Ben-Gurion's statement, *Die Transvaler* considered it incumbent on the Jewish community to enlighten 'Jerusalem'.[139] In a strong statement a few months later, the Nationalist MP 'Blaar' Coetzee somewhat paternalistically called on 'every Jewish citizen of the Republic to make Israel understand in no uncertain manner that they condemn and reject its attitude. That is the least that South Africa can expect from her Jewish children.'[140] His comments came after Israel had joined the Netherlands in condemning foreign minister Eric Louw's defence of apartheid at the United Nations.[141] More ominously, *Die Oosterlig* warned that Israel's actions could 'disturb and disrupt' relations between Afrikaners and Jews.[142] How ironic it was, said Verwoerd, that while Israel refused to merge into the surrounding Arab states, it was asking South African whites to do just that.[143]

Israel's anti-apartheid stance was particularly hurtful for Afrikaners, many of whom had great sympathy for the 'People of the Book' and identified with the Jews of Israel, who they believed faced similar challenges to them.[144] As a punitive act in late 1961, the government refused financial transfer facilities for South African Jews seeking to help the fledgling Jewish state.[145] A few months later, when a Jewish delegation met with the minister of finance, Eben Dönges, it was bluntly told that Israel had 'slapped South Africa in the face and ganged up with her enemies'.[146] A short while later tensions escalated when Israel voted in the General Assembly of the United Nations in support of sanctions against South Africa and its expulsion from the body.[147] Relations deteriorated even further when Israel withdrew its minister plenipotentiary to South Africa, Simcha Pratt, in September 1963 and replaced him with a chargé d'affaires. 'Israel has chosen to attack South Africa in the hope that she will win the favours of the non-white states,' an angry Verwoerd told an audience in Heidelberg. 'I can do nothing else but deprecate this action.'[148]

Pressure was mounting. A short while before his speech, a letter writer to *Die Burger* had expressed revulsion 'against my country being sacrificed for [Israel's] self-interested strivings or that money earned in this country, by no matter whom, should be used to buy the knife for cutting my country's throat'.[149] By contrast, an empathetic editorial in *Die Vaderland* dealt with the 'severe trials' facing local Jews, noting that it was beyond their control that Israel had turned on South Africa. On the other hand, some Jews had 'chosen to be internationalists rather than Jews loyal to South Africa' and they had 'brought suspicion on the whole community'.[150]

Die Vaderland was not alone in empathising with the Jewish community's predicament.[151] Many correspondents, however, attacked what they identified as Jewish double standards and even raised the charge of dual loyalty.[152] A call by Jewish educationalists to develop a 'national-traditional' curriculum in the Jewish day schools was further grist to the mill. 'National traditional education is the counterpart of South African Christian National Education and places equal emphasis on the religious and the national content of Judaism,' noted the *Die Transvaler*.[153] This curriculum, explained Professor Barend Nel, dean of the Faculty of Education at Pretoria University, would cultivate political and cultural dual loyalty.[154]

The modus vivendi or 'emancipation bargain' between the Jews and the Nationalists was now clearly strained by Israel's actions and policies. This combined effortlessly with concerns about Jewish political subversion in South Africa. Menacingly, Koot Vorster warned that Israel's assistance to pro-communist African leaders – as in the Congo – could harm Jews.[155] Indicative of the mood, the words 'Hang Ben-Gurion' and a swastika were painted on a desecrated Jewish grave in Pretoria, while another gravestone was defaced with the slogan 'Down with all Jews', and yet another with a hammer and sickle.[156]

The connection between Israel's policies, domestic Jewish subversion and dual loyalty was neatly captured in a letter from 'Anti-Humbug' to the *Rand Daily Mail*. The writer – who proudly acknowledged his antisemitism – asserted that Jews themselves had provoked anger and needed to be brought into line. Ninety per cent of the whites behind all the subversive activity in South Africa were Jews who had prospered at the expense of the local population, he claimed. 'They live here off the fat of the land and show their gratitude by biting the hand that feeds them and by trying to wreck this country.' More than that, their money was sent to Israel, a country that attacked South Africa at the United Nations. 'No Jew can ever seriously be considered a South African. Israel is their own country and they made so much fuss over its creation that the hoary old piece of hypocrisy about "Jewish" being a religion and not a nationality can be completely discounted.'[157] Indeed, the fact that South African Jews sang 'the anthem of their country of origin' at occasions like bar mitzvahs and weddings upset 'Boerklong'. 'If this is also a demand of Zionism, then I must deduce that the Jewish faith forbids its follower to become a full citizen of any country other than Israel.'[158]

Revered journalist and *Beeld* columnist Rykie van Reenen echoed (at least in part) these sentiments when she called on Saron, executive director of the Board, to explain (in his anticipated new history of South African Jewry) why so many Jews were suspected of subversion and disloyalty.[159] Dr MW Retief was more expansive, identifying Jews at the centre of global liberalism. Writing in the influential *Kerkbode*, he attempted to explain the reason for the world's acceptance of the idea of equality between the races, and thus its opposition to apartheid, by identifying the three villains: communism, international Jewry and Americanism. This notion of the equality of races had emerged from a sick Europe and was taken further by the 'great money power' to whom a large part of the world press belonged.[160]

The notion of Jewish subversion was indeed commonplace. Being Jewish and being a communist were equated by the country's security police, recalled Raymond Suttner, a twice-detained senior anti-apartheid Jewish activist. 'They were obsessed with my being Jewish, absolutely obsessed,' he said. 'My Jewishness was relevant to the detainers. For the people who detained me my being Jewish was an essential element of criminality.'[161]

Fissures in Afrikanerdom

Muller's attack on Jewish students in 1968, discussed at the start of this chapter, had patently emerged after years of Nationalist concern about what it considered to be Jewish political subversion. At the time he condemned NUSAS, both communism and liberalism were well-established terms of abuse in the apartheid lexicon, and the state had begun to act purposefully against such perceived enemies. Over two thousand persons had been convicted of political offences, and many prominent black leaders were in exile, banned or imprisoned.[162] One year after Muller's speech, he introduced the framework of the new Public Service Amendment Bill, which he said was to be responsible for security co-ordination and would draw personnel from other security and intelligence organisations. It outlined the structure of a proposed Bureau for State Security, whose control would rest solely with the prime minister, independent of any parliamentary or other oversight.[163]

Yet for all its force or *kragdadigheid*, the National Party was considered too soft or progressive by its far-right wing led by the minister of posts and telecommunications, and of health, Albert Hertzog, son of the former Boer War general and prime minister JBM Hertzog. Prime Minister Vorster, who succeeded Verwoerd after the latter was assassinated in 1966, had indeed begun to soften the cruder aspects of 'petty apartheid' while shaping, albeit at a tortoise-like pace, a more plural social structure.[164] His government embarked on an 'outward' foreign policy, seeking accommodation with hostile neighbours, while relations with Israel also began to improve, much to the chagrin of the *South African Observer*, now the champion of the National Party's right wing.[165] The Six Day War in 1967 – a David and Goliath victory for Israel – had indeed evoked much sympathy for the Jewish state across South Africa's white population. Military and government officials now 'clamoured to visit Israel and learn from the victorious generals', writes Sasha Polakow-Suransky.[166] Indicative of the new mood, Helen Suzman – for so long a thorn in the flesh of the National Party – was greeted with 'Mooi skoot, Helen' (Good shot, Helen) by Nationalists in the corridors of parliament following Israel's spectacular military victory.[167] Significantly, special permission was granted by the South African government to transfer funds to Israel raised by the South African Jewish community.[168]

Muller's 1968 comments must therefore be seen in the context of a debilitating debate within the National Party between '*verligtes*' (the enlightened ones) and '*verkramptes*' (literally 'cramped ones' or unenlightened reactionaries), with the former attempting to appease the latter.[169] Despite its electoral growth through the 1960s at the expense of the opposition United Party (which was itself weakened by the creation of the more liberal Progressive Party in 1959), the National Party was threatened with a breakaway by its restive ultra-conservative wing. Afrikaner unity or *volkseenheid* was under strain. In August 1968 Vorster reshuffled his cabinet and removed Hertzog. Eight months later an angry Hertzog lambasted 'liberal' English speakers, whom he accused of having no empathy for Afrikaners.[170] The final straw for Hertzog was Vorster's softening stance on race policy towards sport. When he refused to endorse the changes, Hertzog was expelled together with Jacob Albertus ('Jaap') Marais, the MP for Innesdal, and Louis Stofberg, the MP for Worcester.

In October 1969 Hertzog founded the Herstigte Nasionale Party (Reconstituted National Party, or HNP), leaving the National Party with a fresh challenge.[171] The HNP would now be the standard-bearer of Afrikaner exclusivism. It would occasionally mobilise anti-Jewish stereotypes, but, at the time it was founded, issues of race were paramount and there was little appetite for Jew-hatred.[172] Despite the noise around Jewish subversion, the scale of antisemitism in South African society was negligible. Occasional anti-Jewish letters to the press, or even hostile pamphlets (emanating in the main from fantasists), minor explosions at the Great Synagogue and the West Park cemetery in Johannesburg, and the odd cemetery desecration at no time threatened to translate into programmatic political action.[173] Too many Afrikaners (and indeed whites in general) had benefited from economic growth through the 1960s. They had, in the words of the author and journalist Bernard Sachs, 'made a solid invasion of industry and commerce'.[174]

Unsurprisingly, a 'Jewish question' had hardly featured in the general elections of 1961 and 1966. A new Afrikaner entrepreneurial class no longer looked upon the urban Jew with envy. Canards about 'Hoggenheimer' and capitalism as well as Afrikaner dreams of socialism evaporated. Successful Jews were now valued for their entrepreneurial contributions. Even Israel's condemnation of apartheid had failed to generate meaningful outrage. In fact, before the Six Day War of 1967 there was a grudging sympathy for the Jewish state. None other than Koot Vorster spoke in glowing terms of Israel on his return from a visit there in 1965.[175] Nevertheless, a few months after the Six Day War, tensions between South Africa and Israel were briefly reignited when Israel's representative at the United Nations, Joel Barromi, appealed to the world to concern itself with the struggle against apartheid, an action referred to by the minister of transport, Ben Schoeman, as a 'slap in the face'.[176]

Meanwhile, behind the scenes South Africa and Israel had developed closer ties.[177] Angered by their country's repeated condemnations of South Africa, right-wing Israeli politicians established an Israel–South African Friendship League in 1968 to promote commercial contacts.[178] In February 1969 Yitzhak Unna was sent to South Africa as Israel's consul-general with the goal of improving ties between the two countries. It was the start of a mutually beneficial relationship that effectively put paid to previous anti-Jewish Nationalist hostility. Two months later, Ben-Gurion visited South Africa and was photographed with Prime Minister Vorster. The Nationalist press was ecstatic. 'When we, from our side, look realistically at the world situation, we know that Israel's continued existence in the Middle East is also an essential element in our own security,' opined *Die Vaderland*. 'If our Jewish citizens were to rally to the call of our distinguished visitor – to help build up Israel – their contribution would in essence be a contribution to South African security.'[179] A new chapter in Afrikaner–Jewish relations had begun.

At the far right of the South African political spectrum, however, the new partnership provoked heated opposition.[180] Led by Brown's *South African Observer*, English- and Afrikaans-speaking fanatics – on the fringe of South African political life – persisted in denouncing Israel and characterising it as the centre of a vast global conspiracy, with the Zionist project depicted as a threat to world order.[181] Brown had peddled such ideas in his monthly from the moment it was established in 1955. A fantasist par excellence, he had never come to terms with the modus vivendi between the National Party and the Jewish community. His discourse (and, as we will see, that of other fantasists) illustrated vividly the tenacity of malevolent ideas. Grand conspiracies were obsessively borrowed from abroad, and some, refashioned in a South African idiom, found an appreciative audience. The power of the irrational should never be underestimated.

In the next chapter we will examine how, in the aftermath of the Second World War, that toxic brew of fantasy evolved, one that paralleled mainstream accusations of Jewish subversion and disloyalty but with more sinister underpinnings.

TWO

Neo-Nazis, Fantasists and Conspiracists: 1940s to 1960s

We are all sufferers from history, but the paranoid is a double sufferer, since he is afflicted not only by the real world, with the rest of us, but by his fantasies as well.
Richard Hofstadter, *The Paranoid Style in American Politics and Other Essays*, 1964

'Experience teaches', said Gletkin, 'that the masses must be given for all difficult and complicated processes a simple, easily grasped explanation. According to what I know of history, I see that mankind could never do without scapegoats.'
Arthur Koestler, *Darkness at Noon*, 1940

[Racism] satisfies a need common in complex societies – the need to give body to vague hostility, to find excuses for what goes wrong, to fear aliens or curse them, while enjoying self-approval from within the shelter of one's own group ... It satisfies the starved sense of kinship and it promises a vast supernatural community.
Jacques Barzun, *Race: A Study in Superstition*, 1965

Nationalists of all lands Unite – You have nothing to lose but your Jews.
Ray Rudman, letter, 1953

What became of the Fantasists and Fascists?

What became of those vociferous conspiracists and fantasists who in the 1930s and early 1940s had peddled *The Protocols of the Elders of Zion* and made outrageous claims about Jews? At the time of Hitler's defeat, a great number were still operative, but most were quickly absorbed into the National Party and some even found political positions within the apartheid state. The pro-fascist South African National Party (Greyshirt) leader Louis Weichardt, for example, had formed the Blanke Werkersparty (White Workers' Party) shortly before the 1948 general election as a precursor to joining the victorious Dr DF Malan. Declaring himself prepared for any sacrifice that might have to be made for a white South Africa, he was ultimately rewarded with a seat in the Senate under Prime Minister Strijdom in 1955.[1] Another antisemitic firebrand and fantasist, Johannes von Strauss von Moltke, entered parliament as a South West Africa National Party MP for Karas in 1950, while many others simply terminated their anti-Jewish activism, leaving only a handful to persist with their obsessions undeterred by the awful legacy of Nazi barbarity. But they now operated at a less frenetic pace and with less hullabaloo than in the 1930s. Rather than public meetings, their preferred modus operandi was the distribution of pamphlets and booklets, often supplied from abroad (and sometimes adapted to local conditions) by a global nexus of like-minded fantasists. All shared a mode of thought – best described as crackpot or paranoid – that was laced with beliefs in secret plots and international cabals. Such 'thinking' has a long pedigree and is certainly not unique to the twentieth century.[2] At its root, argues Richard Hofstadter, is a 'paranoid style' – a cast of mind characterised by 'heated exaggeration, suspiciousness and conspiratorial fantasy' in which 'a nation, a culture, a way of life' are believed to be under threat.[3]

The Protocols of the Elders of Zion – a notorious Tsarist forgery – vividly illustrates this world of mythological fantasy. Emerging early in the twentieth century in Russia and spreading across Europe after the Bolshevik Revolution, the *Protocols* portrayed Jews as plotting to destroy Christianity and attain global supremacy.[4] By the 1930s South Africans had encountered these fabrications courtesy of the Greyshirts. Adapted to local conditions, the *Protocols* provided simple answers to complicated social, economic and political questions and served as a political device at a time of instability and hotly contested politics. Even a Supreme Court judgment in the 1934 'Greyshirt Trial' declaring the *Protocols* a fabrication failed to curtail its dissemination.[5] The document clearly appealed both to the *déclassé* or 'poor white' Afrikaners whose sense of worth had been gutted by rapid urbanisation and rural transformation, and also to more affluent individuals inclined to paranoia. It was an explosive arsenal whose claims would not be easily jettisoned.[6]

It certainly had special resonance in a country long dominated by powerful mining interests, often with international connections. Indeed, the 'spirit of Mammon' had been highlighted from the late nineteenth century following the discovery of diamonds in the 1860s and gold two decades later when a flood of fortune-seekers established themselves in Kimberley and Johannesburg. Among them were Jews, some from Germany and England, but most from the 'western' Russian empire (or Pale of Settlement), many of whom attracted negative attention. The mining magnates, or 'Randlords', were also particularly visible, and people who were the casualties of social and economic transformation were quick to blame their reduced circumstances on those they considered rapacious and alien. The Jameson Raid of 1895–6 – effectively a failed *coup d'état* – illustrated this vividly, as did the Anglo-Boer War (1899–1902), which consolidated the idea of a conflict fought at the behest of international financiers, often identified as Jewish.[7] In the immediate post-war years, DC Boonzaier's cartoon caricature of the grossly Semitic plutocrat 'Hoggenheimer' exemplified this perception, much as Otto von Bismarck's real-life financial guru Gerson Bleichröder was, in the words of the historian Fritz Stern, 'held up as the principal exhibit of mysterious Jewish power' in Imperial Germany.[8]

'Hoggenheimer' was a composite cartoon character, but he was clearly Jewish and embodied decades of hostile depictions that ranged from the *smous* (rural peddler) to the urban huckster.[9] By the 1930s, he was the personification of capitalism, the cunning and predatory *éminence grise* directing South African affairs.[10] Exuberant Afrikaner nationalists, evidently swamped by rampant capitalism, focused on this sinister figure who exploited them, undermined the *völkisch* project, and ultimately dragged South Africa into the Second World War. But, as noted previously, hostility and coarse anti-Jewish stereotyping generally waned with the reversal of Hitler's fortunes in the early 1940s. Attitudes shifted as the reality of Nazi racial madness was revealed. Photographs of mass graves and images of emaciated survivors of concentration and death camps consolidated this shift, as did the Nuremberg Trials of 1945–6. Yet, for those with a conspiratorial cast of mind, little remorse or empathy was forthcoming. They claimed that the destruction of Europe's Jews was an invention and that all evidence was concocted, serving as further proof of a sinister Jewish cabal.[11]

Malan had already laid the groundwork for such conspiracism. Soon after South Africa entered the war in 1939, he had spoken at a party congress held in Bloemfontein of 'organised Jewry backing England'. 'Janowitz Smutsowitz' was the way in which he referred to Prime Minister Jan Smuts on that occasion.[12] No one could have missed the implication of his words. By the end of the war, however, Malan and most mainstream Nationalists had turned away from such crass rhetoric. With the destruction of Europe's Jews, Jewish immigration – the engine of anger in the 1930s – was no longer a threat. On the fringes of the radical white right, however, old-style hatred fired by paranoia and riddled with fantasies, including the circulation of *The Protocols of the Elders of Zion* in Afrikaans, persisted.[13] Numbers may have been small and organisational activity minimal, but some hard-core individuals remained determined believers, finding common cause with a post-war international web of fascists and neo-Nazis, and doing their best to keep alive the flame of antisemitic thought.

Determined Believers: Ray Rudman and Johan Schoeman

Raymond Kirsch (RK) Rudman was one such believer. Tall and lean, and sporting a clipped Hitler-like moustache in his later years, Rudman had a long history of Jew-baiting and demagoguery. Born in Humansdorp in the eastern Cape in 1898 and claiming 1820 Settler origins, he left school after Standard 7 and subsequently served as a member of the SA Horse IX Regiment and the SA Motor Cycle Corps in the First World War before going to the United States to be

Raymond Rudman. Courtesy: Special Collections, National Library of South Africa, Cape Town

trained in horticulture. On his return he opened Rudman's Edendale Nurseries.[14] As a member of the Sons of England – a colonial club for immigrants and their descendants – Rudman apparently identified with imperial interests, but his later move to the National Party and the NGK suggests otherwise. That move would have served as a bridge into the Greyshirt movement, which Rudman headed in Natal from 1933 to 1934. It was during these years that his fiery anti-Jewish oratory (the 'raving of a lunatic', as Smuts put it in 1934) attracted attention.[15] Evidently seduced by European fascism, Rudman maintained that the Greyshirts remained South Africa's only hope of salvation.[16] Yet, together with Weichardt, he moved easily into an association with the GNP in early 1939 and a year later was happy to see the Greyshirts formally merge with Malan's party.[17] Thereafter, he aligned himself with Pirow's Nuwe Orde and subsequently with the paramilitary Ossewabrandwag, in which he was appointed an adjutant-general in Natal.[18] In 1942 Rudman was interned by the government at Koffiefontein, a small farming town in the Orange Free State. After four months he was released and placed under house arrest.[19]

A year before his arrest, Rudman had founded the NS Boerenasie (N[ational] S[ocialist] Boer Nation), effectively a resuscitation of the antisemitic and National-Socialist, anti-parliamentarian Volksparty, or People's Party, founded by Manie Maritz, a prominent rebel in the 1914 Boer insurrection and a rabid Jew-hater, who had died in a motor car accident in 1940. Rudman became commandant-general of this 'semi-military organisation', as the press styled it.[20] In the post-war years he boasted that the NS Boerenasie had 40,000 members. This is highly unlikely. What cannot be denied, however, is the movement's vile injunctions. 'No Jew or any non-European dares to be put forward or become a member,' read its manifesto, and candidates for parliament would only be supported if they endorsed the movement's views on communism, Judaism and Zionism. The aim of the movement, explained Rudman, was the seizure of power and a solution to the colour problem through 'Third Reich' methods.[21] 'We have borrowed much from Nationalism as proclaimed by Adolf Hitler in the Third Reich and have adapted it to South African conditions,' said Rudman. 'Above all it is our aim to free our Fatherland – which we love fanatically – from forces which undermine our state and people. These include international capitalism, Roman Catholicism, the Jews, and other secret movements which aim at forming a state within a state.'[22] 'Blood is everything,' Rudman explained in a letter to the secretary of the World

Aryan Union (WAU), which he represented in South Africa. Jews, he claimed, weakened the National Party under Malan.[23] Little wonder that members of the NS Boerenasie saluted each other with an '88', which meant 'Heil Hitler' – 'H' being the eighth letter of the alphabet.

The NS Boerenasie's mouthpiece, *Die Dapper Boodskapper* (The Brave Messenger), was dominated by anti-Jewish and anti-Zionist propaganda, but substantial attention was also devoted to the differences between blacks and whites, a common shift in focus among those who had formerly prioritised the 'Jewish question' in the 1930s.[24] Communications from the organisation were filled with admiration for Hitler and warnings about the Jewish peril and Zionist threat.[25] Propaganda focused on the insidious threat posed by *The Protocols of the Elders of Zion*, the Talmud, Freemasons, communists and Zionists, as well as the 'liberal' menace. Classic conspiracies were commonplace and included warnings against polio immunisation and bizarre claims about kosher slaughtering, as well as attacks on the 'Jewish-created' Genocide Convention of the United Nations.[26] Accusations were peddled in propaganda sheets as well as in *Die Nuusbrief* (The Newsletter) – an illustrated broadsheet issued by the NS Boerenasie – and a monthly newsletter, *Feite – Facts*.[27] Rudman also circulated *Natinform*, a news bulletin of the global far-right fascist Nationalist Information Bureau (an answer to the communist Cominform), which Rudman represented in South Africa.

In effect, the NS Boerenasie was a vehicle for Rudman to disseminate his antisemitic fantasies and prejudices through what were largely ineffectual mailshots and flyers posted on shop windows and buildings in urban centres.[28] Engaged in a private war with demonic forces, his was a relatively lonely and low-level voice, but he remained well connected with a range of neo-Nazis and fascist organisations abroad, absorbing and distributing the worst of European Jew-hatred through publications and pamphlets.[29] This concerned Jewish leaders. Indeed, shortly after the National Party came to power in 1948, the Board began communicating with the Anti-Defamation League (ADL) in the United States as well as the Board of Deputies of British Jews about Rudman's distribution of anti-Jewish material and his ties with antisemites abroad. Focus was on Rudman's Aryan Bookstore in Pietermaritzburg, described by the Board as probably the largest single distributor of antisemitic material in South Africa.[30] In fact, the Aryan Bookstore was only a postal address that served as the centre of pamphlet and book distribution.

Although Rudman's domestic audience was small and his impact limited, the Board kept an alert eye on his activities, and for good reason: Rudman was in contact with a web of international neo-Nazis.[31] Among them was Wolfgang Sarg, a neo-Nazi German publicist;[32] Norman Thompson, a well-known British antisemite;[33] and Bruno Peter Kleist, who had worked under the arch-Nazi racial theorist Alfred Rosenberg in the Reich Ministry for the Occupied Territories during the war. Kleist subsequently became foreign editor of *Deutsche Wochen-Zeitung*, the antisemitic organ of the right-wing Reich Party in Germany, where he devoted himself mainly to conservative politics in the Federal Republic of Germany with a focus on *Ostpolitik*, the normalisation of relations between the Federal Republic of Germany and Eastern Europe, especially the German Democratic Republic. He was also an executive member of the (German) Friends of Cairo organisation.[34] Rudman also communicated with Johann von Leers, a professor at the University of Jena. As an *Alter Kämpfer* ('old fighter' or early member of the Nazi Party) and an honorary *Sturmbannführer* in the Waffen SS in Nazi Germany, von Leers was known for his anti-Jewish polemics and publications. Rudman could also count among his friends Arnold Leese, the British fascist and author of *The Jewish War of Survival* (a book published in South Africa by Rudman); Hilary Cotter, the British far-right nationalist; and Cevat Rifat Atilhan, the leader of the Turkish Islamic Democratic Party, who published Izmir's antisemitic newspaper *Anadolu*.[35] In addition, Rudman established ties with far-right extremists like Martin Hughes, national secretary of the National Socialist Party of New Zealand;[36] the Ku Klux Klan; George Lincoln Rockwell, commander of the American Nazi Party; Bradley J Smith, the editor and publisher of the far-right *American Victory*;[37] and Richard Verrall (aka Richard Harwood), editor of the British National Front journal *Spearhead* and a vociferous Holocaust denier.[38]

Clearly concerned about Rudman's distribution of antisemitic books, the Jewish Board of Deputies asked Gustav Caminsky, a Pietermaritzburg lawyer, to investigate the source of Rudman's funding and whether the Aryan Bookstore was indeed simply a post box number.[39] By then the Board had been provided with a list of people, both local and foreign, who were associated with Rudman, as well as a description of the nature of the distributed material. Most of it consisted of fabricated stories about Jews, including accusations that they massacred Gentiles throughout the ages, wooed Afrikaners by pretending that they were Israelites, and even backed the Salvation Army, declaring its founder William Booth to be a Jew. Zionism was also in the firing line, with Jewish 'terrorist' activities in Palestine prior to the establishment of Israel in 1948 presented as evidence that Jews planned to conquer the Middle East and, indeed, the world. Invariably Judaism was equated with communism. One circular (allegedly from the well-known Swedish antisemite Einar Åberg) went as far as recommending that Jews be transplanted to Madagascar.[40]

According to the ADL, Rudman's efforts were part of an extremely active international network of antisemites that were of concern to Jewish organisations abroad.[41] In March 1949, the editor of *Common Sense* (an organ for the Society of Jews and Christians published by the South African Jewish Board of Deputies) received a letter requesting information about Rudman from the American investigative journalist Stetson Kennedy, who had heard that Rudman was organising a World League of Fairplay and Decency whose members included the most notorious fascists and antisemites in Europe and America.[42] The editor's reply outlined Rudman's political activities and noted that his movement reprinted a great deal of Nazi racial propaganda that fanned the flames of antisemitism.[43]

It was obvious that Rudman was obsessed with Jews. Letter after letter to his numerous contacts, as well as his voluminous clippings focused on Jews both in South Africa and abroad, attest to that. He even maintained that 'Malan and his colleagues have FALLEN to the "30 pieces of silver" to [*sic*] the yids and they now hobnob freely with Jews and they voted together!' In grandiose imaginings that he had 'several ministers on his side', Rudman also indicated that he was gradually establishing cells throughout the country and that once this was accomplished, he would demand an election.[44]

Rudman patently lived in a fantasy world peopled by sinister and cunning Jews. Plots and conspiracies laced his communications.[45] The depth and fabricated crudity of his hatred are reflected in a note he penned about Morris Kentridge, following the death of the eminent Jewish parliamentarian in 1964. Readers were reminded that his real name was Kantorowich and that he was one of 'the filthiest Jews that ever appeared in our land', responsible for the legislation that had enabled 'the Asiatic-Mongole-Khazaar-Ashkanazim jews' to enter South Africa.[46] One year earlier, Rudman had informed the British antisemite Norman Thompson that he had founded an English organisation called the South African Anglo-Nordic Union, which would be sister to the Afrikaans NS Boerenasie.[47] We have few records of the South African Anglo-Nordic Union, which kept a low profile; but its unadulterated racist sentiments are well captured in a confidential call to a meeting: 'You are invited to an ACTION COMMITTEE SITTING of very great importance. The Timeglass runs empty and the "Black Gorillas" and White Asiatics (Jews) are hoping to eradicate Christian White Civilization and Whiteman's existence in Africa.'[48]

By the late 1950s Rudman had largely faded from public view, only to enjoy a brief flurry of media interest with his creation of SONOP/SUNUP (the South African National Union of Patriots – the 'political instrument' of the NS Boerenasie and the South African Anglo-Nordic Union), which planned to contest elections in the early 1960s.[49] Prime Minister Verwoerd's alleged soft-pedalling on race policies and his supposed ties to Jews were at the core of this movement's concerns, whose national-socialist agenda called for the 'nationalisation' of all mineral wealth, the abolition of the 'treacherous' Marxist foreign income tax system, and the abolition of education for 'kaffirs', as well as for the repatriation of South African 'Asiatics' to their homelands and the expulsion of all Jews to Israel.[50]

While Rudman was acting out his obsessions in his home town of Edendale in Natal, another fantasist of concern to the Board (unconnected although known to Rudman) was Johan Schoeman. Tilting at global Jewish conspiracies from his home named 'Yasnaya Polyana' (presumably after the estate of Leo Tolstoy) in Broederstroom, near Hartbeespoort Dam in the Transvaal (now North West Province), Schoeman did his best to alert the world to what he perceived was a global Jewish threat. He expended great effort to elaborate and diffuse a Manichaean worldview in which powerful and subversive Jews in alliance with communism increasingly took centre stage. In touch with publications of the (antisemitic) Britons Publishing Society, which had been founded in 1919 by Henry Hamilton Beamish (a man who had given evidence in support of those charged with peddling *The Protocols of the Elders of Zion* in the Greyshirt Trial of 1934),[51] Schoeman gave vent to his own fantasies in numerous publications, while at the same time peppering newspapers with letters, distributing pamphlets and brochures, and sending telegrams and cablegrams to government ministers and international leaders warning them, inter alia, of the evils of the United Nations and Zionism and, after the war, disputing the number of Jews killed during the Holocaust. Described by the journalist PC du Plessis as an inveterate letter writer, Schoeman was known to every South African editor and cabinet minister. Even Churchill, de Gaulle and Truman had been the recipients of his cablegrams.[52]

Little is known about the early life of Johan Schoeman other than a youthful enthusiasm for socialism that was shattered by the way in which he perceived Afrikaners were being treated by labour leaders. We can assume that the young Schoeman was deeply traumatised not only by British soldiers setting fire to the family house during the Anglo-Boer War, but also by his father, General Hendrik Schoeman, being charged with treason towards the end of the conflict and sentenced to death. A combatant who had surrendered (a so-called *hensopper* or hands-upper), Schoeman père died soon after his release from gaol when a lyddite shell – which he was using as an ashtray – exploded when he dropped a match into it after lighting a pipe.[53]

It is unclear what lay behind Schoeman's obsession with Jews. What is clear, however, is his efforts to promote fantasies about Jews and communism, albeit with limited resonance. His writings are informed by an imaginative belief in vast, evil and impersonal forces, coupled with a whiff of social Darwinism. Here he shared much with Rudman. But Schoeman was a more serious thinker (albeit not a man of original ideas) than the horticulturist from Edendale. By all accounts an eccentric, he was considered something of a seer among the locals of Hartbeespoort. As the scion of the renowned Boer fighter and a huge landowner (Hartbeespoort was formerly known as Schoemansville), his pedigree alone accorded him a measure of gravitas.

*Johan Schoeman. Courtesy: Special Collections,
National Library of South Africa, Cape Town*

A sense of Schoeman's eccentricity emerges in an article by Sidney Barnett Potter, editor of the *Union Review*, who recalled a chance meeting he had with Schoeman in 1940 when he was camping in the Hartbeespoort area and had come to Schoeman's house to buy supplies. Potter vividly described Schoeman as 'a rather rough, shaggy and unkempt person' and 'a queer combination of garrulousness and courtesy, squalor and dignity'.[54] Schoeman took exception to this description – especially to the word 'squalor' – and successfully sued

Potter for defamation. Significantly, Schoeman was able to marshal supportive testimony from Professors Daniël Johannes Keet and Jacobus Christiaan Bosman of Pretoria University, while his son told the court that visitors to his father's farm included Jan Smuts and other personages of note. Among them was RC Hargreaves of the 'Office of the Governor General in South Africa' who, following the visit, thanked Schoeman for entertaining him at his home and 'for your kindness in sending his Excellency and Her Royal Highness some of the first fruits of your farm, and especially to thank you for the loaf of bread, which Princess Alice thought really excellent'.[55]

A dyed-in-the-wool Nationalist who shared much with the Afrikaner mainstream, including a belief in white supremacy as well as an abiding hatred for perfidious Albion, Schoeman directed his attacks frequently at the South African (and later United) Party of Smuts. He had opposed South Africa's entry into the First World War, challenged Smuts in the Pretoria West constituency for the National Party in March 1920, considered South Africa's entry into the Second World War a great mistake, and was furious that his country had allied itself with Bolshevist Russia.[56] Schoeman was, to be sure, obsessed with communism – which, as noted earlier, he associated with Jews and Judaism – and believed Hitler to be the last bulwark against Moscow. More than that, he rejected the demonisation of the Führer and, like Rudman, he considered the National Party to be too cosy with the Jews. 'The collusion of you and the church leaders with the self-acknowledged historical bearers and distributors of the Marxist leprosy over the whole world', he told the government in December 1953, 'makes your half-baked anti-communist efforts a farce... Alas, that an Afrikaner Government meekly tightens the slave-chains of the century of injustice, of the anti-Christ and of the UNO deception and monster.'[57] It is not clear what precisely precipitated this attack. Perhaps it was the visit of Prime Minister Malan to Israel, which we do know was vigorously opposed by Schoeman.

In early 1960 Schoeman distributed a collection of several of his previously published articles in a 160-page booklet, *Vistas 59: Die krisis in Suid-Afrika en ander stories* (Vistas 59: The Crisis in South Africa and Other Stories). The book's cover indicated that income from sales would go to the Anti-Satan Fund, intended to foil the Jews' capitalistic and communist plot to rule the world. The title page listed a series of articles beginning with 'Die krisis in Suid-Afrika, 1952', which raised the Jewish liberal and communist spectre. He also included a reprint of a February 1939 speech delivered in parliament by Eric Louw when introducing the second reading of the Aliens (Amendment) and Immigration Bill, intended to curtail the influx of German-Jewish refugees. In addition, the booklet featured a bogus speech supposedly made by the 'Rabbi of Budapest' depicting non-Jews as slaves and describing Hermann Goering as a 'son of the highest western culture'. Hitler in turn is characterised as a man sent by God 'to rebuild Germany and thereby Europe', and the Allied armies depicted as 'monsters of decadent Europe and America and the lepers of Bolshevism'. Discussing the murder of the Jews, Schoeman says 'gassing was a gruesome job, but you will also have to admit that Hitler had no alternative UNDER THE CIRCUMSTANCES'.[58] Predictably, the booklet included a summary of *The Protocols of the Elders of Zion*, by now a favourite document for conspiracists. A section was also devoted 'to exposing the Jewish capitalistic Cause and Jewish Revolutionary Communism' – described by Schoeman as a 'solitary alliance between two apparently conflicting theories against the "gentile common enemy"'. Taking his cue from Eric Louw, Schoeman characterised all Jews as unassimilable. His solution was to remove them from their homes and dump them in their own country – not Israel, though, because that country had been 'stolen' from the Arabs. Finally, the booklet included falsifications and distortions of the Jewish religion and Jewish religious teachings.[59]

This was vintage Schoeman: eclectic, imaginative, fanciful and crude. The collection essentially propagated in defamatory terms the outsider status and subversive qualities of Jews, citing references garnered from a range of spurious anti-Jewish sources. But besides slandering Judaism and depicting Jews as the hand in the communist glove, Schoeman also asserted that the Anglo-Boer War had been engineered by Jewish capitalists who were still maligning and blackmailing the Afrikaners. In addition, Jews were exploiting the 'Native problem', and were also responsible for Pearl Harbor, Amritsar, the Black and Tans, the Anglo-Boer War concentration camps, the Purim massacre of Persians, Jesus' death, and the bombing of Nagasaki and Hiroshima.[60] Such twaddle was also apparent in *The Hand behind the Scenes*, a pamphlet Schoeman published in 1963, which accused the Afrikaans and English press of preventing him from being published 'for fear of a Jewish boycott'.[61]

For all that, Schoeman declared that he was only against Jews who were communists and that he indeed had Jewish friends.[62] This appears to have been true in at least one case. Well-known businessman IW Schlesinger, who had a holiday home at Hartbeespoort Dam, was a house guest of Schoeman, according to the neo-Nazi Wolfgang Sarg.[63]

Stoking the Conspiratorial Fires

To most observers Rudman and Schoeman would have appeared as charlatans and crackpots, but they did manage to keep alive a world of anti-Jewish conspiracy that was nourished by the inflow (a 'flood', according to the *Sunday Times*) of anti-Jewish material from abroad.[64] Among this material were the well-known Jew-hating bi-monthly *Common Sense* (published by the Christian Educational Association in the US and edited by the well-known antisemite Conde McGinley), the British National Party's *Combat*, *Thunderbolt* (US), and the *Intelligence Digest* (London). The antisemitic California journal *New Patriot* was even sent to some South African university libraries. In addition, propaganda material from George Lincoln Rockwell's Nazi Party in the United States found its way into the country, as did other anti-Jewish books from abroad.[65]

Besides this imported material, locally produced 'antisemitica' was also available. Oswald Pirow, for example, published (in roneoed form) the *Adv. Pirow Newsletter / Adv. Pirow se Nuusbrief* from 1948 till 1958. Although concerned primarily with domestic politics, communism and – in alliance with the British fascist Oswald Mosley – the racial partition of Africa, the newsletter was not averse to including conspiracies and anti-Jewish commentary.[66] In one issue it quoted with approbation an article from the American *Common Sense* that accused Jews of wishing to dominate the world through their control and manipulation of Moscow and the United Nations. 'Every extension of the powers of UNO must therefore necessarily amount to a greater extension of the power of the Jews over other Peoples,' warned the newsletter.[67] Two other local publications also targeted Jews and Zionism: *Helikon*, a bi-monthly organ of the South African Literary and Cultural Society in Randburg, and *Boomerang*, an organ of the Patriots Society for Race Friendship, based in Pretoria, which aimed to 'fight the international world dictatorship through the study of the international conspiracy'.[68] Like other anti-Jewish tracts, both were informed by pure fantasy. *Boomerang* (edited by Noel Crowd, a pseudonym for Leon Menge, a teacher at Pretoria Boys' High School) was especially widely distributed, and although the publishers denied being antisemitic, the articles it published were invariably penned by well-known Jew-haters.[69] In identifying Zionists as authors of the world's evils, *Boomerang* echoed the hostility towards Zionism expressed in many of Johan Schoeman's publications. One of its pamphlets, *Pattern of Assassination*, drew parallels between the assassinations of Kennedy and Verwoerd and sought to implicate Jews while simultaneously propagating the myth of Zionist involvement in a world conspiracy.[70] 'Many Zionists are self-confessed atheists and communists – all of them fear what South Africa's policy of separate freedoms will do to impede their goal of world government,' explained the authors.[71]

It was SED Brown's *South African Observer*, however, that best exemplified the fantasies surrounding Zionism and the Jewish state and Jewish power. Indeed, soon after Brown had founded the Sons of South Africa (discussed earlier), he issued a pamphlet that claimed Jews were not true South Africans because of their support for Zionism. In addition, he averred 'that there are too many Jews in South Africa and they are making themselves and their power and nation too conspicuous. A saturation point has been reached …'[72] Unsurprisingly, Brown's monthly included tirades against so-called Jewish liberalism, and Jewish loyalty to South Africa was always questioned. Conspiratorial articles from far-right journals abroad were regular features.[73] These invariably characterised the United Nations as a creation of three 'unholy triplets' – Soviet communism, international finance and political Zionism – whose central ambition was a world state 'dominated by, and for, them'.[74] Contributions from AK Chesterton characteristically attacked the relationship between the United States, Britain and Israel, and what he termed the propaganda techniques of 'the Jewish international money power'. Articles by the far-right journalist Eric Butler, founder of the Australian League of Rights, also appeared in the pages of the *South African Observer*, while letters frequently contained anti-Jewish tropes and inventions about Israel's ties with Russia. South African mining magnate Harry Oppenheimer was a constant target and, despite his conversion from Judaism to Christianity, was regularly tied to communism and Zionism.[75] Even the National Party, an enemy of the *South African Observer* from the late 1960s, was accused of benefiting from leftists, liberals and the 'money power'.[76]

Ultimately, in the minds of these fantasists, communism and Zionism were twin conspiracies, each beholden to the international 'money power'.[77] This was reflected in the *South African Observer*'s angry response to the South African security chief, Hendrik van den Bergh, who visited Israel in 1973 and praised its accomplishments. Apart from fulminating against Israel as a nerve centre of world Zionism and world communism, the monthly attacked Van den Bergh's 'newfound enthusiasm for Israel and for things Jewish' while ignoring 'Israel's long anti-white and anti-South African role in Africa – not to mention the increasingly active role being played by Jews in Black Power and far-left politics in South Africa'.[78]

The *South African Observer* similarly criticised Prime Minister John Vorster after he visited Israel to sign military and trade agreements in 1976:

> One wonders whether in his wildest dreams in the early 1940s – when he was interned in Koffiefontein, and he inveighed bitterly against Communism, Democracy, the British, and Jewish Bolshevism, and prayed for a German victory – Balthazar Johannes Vorster ever imagined that thirty-five years later, he would desert the conservative principles of his forebears to accept the Zionist-Communist equality doctrine ... become a crusader for Zionism; turn his country into an ally of Israel; and find himself on a pilgrimage to Israel and, as his first official act during his visit, solemnly laying a memorial wreath on the shrine in Jerusalem of the 'Six Million Jews murdered by the Nazis'.

Ivor Benson. Courtesy: Special Collections, National Library of South Africa, Cape Town

Thereafter, in a manner reminiscent of Schoeman, editor Brown repeated accusations of world Jewry and Israel's total war against the Gentile world that threatened the future of the white man in South Africa.[79]

Journalist Ivor Benson's *Behind the News: A Southern African Bulletin* – a monthly he founded and edited in 1969 – echoed Brown's fantasies.[80] Born to Swedish parents in 1907 in Bethlehem in the

Orange Free State, Benson grew up in South Africa and Rhodesia. After completing his secondary schooling at Durban High School, he joined the *Natal Mercury* in Durban as a cadet reporter and subsequently the (London) *Daily Telegraph* and *Daily Express*. During the early stages of the Second World War, Benson was a freelance journalist in Poland, Finland and Sweden, leaving Norway shortly before the German occupation in 1940. Thereafter he served as an officer under British command in North Africa and Italy. Subsequently Benson became chief assistant editor of the (Johannesburg) *Rand Daily Mail*, and then worked on the *Sunday Tribune* before serving as information adviser (and chief censor) to Ian Smith, prime minister of Rhodesia, and as a news commentator for the SABC.[81] Under the pseudonym 'Candide', Benson also wrote conservative commentary for the *Nataller*, where his political predilections were clearly on display,[82] as they had been since the early 1960s when he served as a contributing editor for *Western Destiny*, a journal edited by the racial anthropologist, biological racist and eugenicist, and antisemite Roger Pearson. By the 1980s, Benson had developed an international reputation, lecturing and speaking at numerous far-right conferences, and serving on the editorial board of *Spotlight*, the newspaper of Liberty Lobby, the largest and most well-financed of American antisemitic organisations.[83]

Benson was a classic Cold War warrior, well read in conservative geopolitics, relentless in his anti-communist crusade, and a believer in Jewish conspiracies.[84] For him, the news was managed and orchestrated by Jews with the help of bottomless funds that enabled manipulation and pernicious brainwashing. Like so many Nationalists, he conflated liberals with communists, and prided himself on removing some of them from the *Rand Daily Mail* when he was chief assistant editor.[85] At heart Benson was a segregationist with a hatred of finance capitalism and multiracialism, and with an essentialist understanding of group identities which he placed in a social Darwinist frame. The Jew, he wrote, 'is racially strong in an environment which makes others racially weak'.[86]

Cold War fear-mongering dominated Benson's *Behind the News*, as did attacks on Zionism and the National Party, which he accused of ideological deviation from apartheid.[87] In Benson's view, Israeli nationalism was a sham and Israel, a home for communists, used as a 'pivot or pressure point for power which is worldwide in its sources and its reach'.[88] The 'money power' (Jewish financial manipulation) in politics was of particular concern to Benson, who believed that Jews enjoyed a competitive advantage over others through an intense 'race consciousness and the shared loyalty of nationalism which is all the more intense for being geographically dispersed'.[89]

A Disturbing Fringe

Although largely restricted to the fringes of public life, the dissemination of anti-Jewish and anti-Zionist material (much of it under the guise of combating communism) deeply concerned the Jewish Board of Deputies. A special report was drawn up in 1967 by Gus Saron pointing out the close connections of antisemitic groups in South Africa with their counterparts abroad, especially in the United States and Great Britain.[90] A similar message had been spelled out a short while earlier by the president of the Board, Teddy Schneider, who was concerned about the arrival in South Africa of Nazi and other antisemitic material emanating in particular from 'radical right groups in the Southern States of the USA which have been busy spreading reactionary and anti-Jewish poison to many parts of the world'.[91]

This was certainly the case. But besides the penetration of antisemitic material, prominent antisemites also visited South Africa. One such visitor was British fascist AK Chesterton, who in 1964 founded the Candour League of South Africa in Cape Town, a branch of the anti-communist Candour League in England, which emerged out of the League of Empire Loyalists, also founded by Chesterton in 1954.[92] In an inaugural address, he spoke of a 'world government plot', directed not by 'Russians or Chinese or Cubans' but by 'financial Jewry in New York'. The 'Jewish propaganda machine', he asserted, 'having created immunity for the Jews from criticism, is now in the process of creating a similar immunity for the coloured races, who seem to have become their special protégés'.[93] Members of the Candour League were sent lists of books that included *The Protocols of the Elders of Zion*, *International Jew* and *World Conquerors*.[94]

A year before the founding of the Candour League, a group of

German neo-Nazis had toured South Africa on a visit organised by the Hanover *Deutsche Wochen-Zeitung*, the antisemitic organ of the right-wing Reich Party. Among them were Peter Kleist (one of Rudman's friends) and Adolf von Thadden (the leader of Germany's extremist National Democratic Party, the NDP), who, on a later visit, connected with the Candour League in Cape Town and established ties with two Germans now living in South Africa: Oskar Sheffler (leader of the Friends of the NDP) and Rolf Wenzlaff, a fitter and turner who claimed to have spent six years in a communist concentration camp.[95]

These international ties were scrutinised by the *Rand Daily Mail*'s Michael Cobden in an investigative article that spelled out the deep connections between the German right and South African radical rightists. Cobden reminded readers of the visit organised by the *Deutsche Wochen-Zeitung* and claimed that these Germans considered South Africa fertile ground. 'They have left their mark in little patches here and there, in the people they have infected and the organisations they have instituted and inspired,' he wrote. Cobden also discussed the writings of Brown, *Boomerang*, and the activities of other far-right groups. 'How well organised this sort of activity is, is difficult to tell,' he explained. 'The probability is that there is no large-scale organisation, yet there is enough activity in South Africa, with its racialistic atmosphere, to make Jews feel uncomfortable. They have long memories and they certainly have not forgotten what happened in the thirties and forties of this century.'[96]

Cobden's assessment was echoed by the English-born conservative journalist Aida Parker, who claimed that neo-Nazis in South Africa were following *Der Freiwillige*, an official publication of the former SS, the conservative John Birch Society's *American Opinion*, and the publications of Ron Gostick (founder of the far-right antisemitic Canadian League of Rights).[97] Conspiratorial thought was percolating. As early as 1960, the Australian conspiracist Eric Butler had given a series of talks for the SABC in which he claimed that the first major act of the United Nations (described as a 'collaboration between the Money Power and Communism') was to support Zionist aggression in the Middle East.[98] Many years later Butler was a guest speaker at an HNP fundraiser.[99] Even more disturbing, in 1965 the blackguardly

Louis Weichardt was happy to host Otto 'Scarface' Skorzeny (Hitler's one-time bodyguard who had been involved in the rescue of Mussolini and the removal from power of the Hungarian regent, Miklós Horthy) in the South African parliament.[100]

In essence, neo-Nazis and fascists visiting South Africa were anti-Jewish Cold War warriors who empathised with the National Party's apartheid policies and shared its fear and loathing of communism. Information was exchanged about Jews, who were accused of controlling and manipulating world events through international financiers. For these fantasists, Wall Street rather than Moscow was the home of communism. Jews were blamed for undermining the 'Aryan' people and deliberately weakening Gentile religion. As was so often the case, Zionism loomed large in the conspiratorial arsenal.[101]

Some of this madness may have translated into sporadic action, but at no time did it dominate mainstream discourse. There was no appetite in South Africa to revive the pre-war 'Jewish question'. Under the National Party, Afrikaners were 'on the move' (as the historian Hermann Giliomee puts it) and crude antisemitism had little appeal.[102] By way of illustration, Rudman was prevented from speaking in Brits by the local town council.[103] Nevertheless, as mentioned in the previous chapter, there had been explosions at the Great Synagogue in Johannesburg and the city's Jewish West Park Cemetery in the early 1960s.[104] Swastikas were displayed from time to time and anti-Jewish pamphlets (both local and foreign) distributed. At Pretoria University, notices saying 'Communism is Jewish – Hitler was right' were pinned on noticeboards.[105] In 1967 Hitler's birthday was celebrated at the Crown Beer Hall, known as the Deutscher Keller or German Beerhall in Johannesburg, at which German songs were sung, 'Sieg Heil' was chanted, and a photograph of Hitler allegedly displayed. Not surprisingly the incident provoked clashes between outraged Jewish youths and German immigrants.[106]

This 'Hillbrow Affair' (named after the cosmopolitan suburb in which the event took place) attracted substantial attention. Indeed, in his Sabbath sermon, South Africa's chief rabbi Bernard Casper warned of the dangers of Nazi-oriented symbols and antisemitic literature being disseminated as well as visits by 'individuals with a pronounced

Nazi antisemitic background'. It was the duty of the government, he said, to denounce all neo-Nazi activities.[107] The government did, in fact, take the matter seriously and Prime Minister Vorster declared that his administration dissociated itself from events such as the 'Hillbrow Affair'.[108] He also made it quite clear that antisemitism was unacceptable and had been so since the days of Malan.[109]

In so far as the radical white right was concerned, his words fell on deaf ears. Hitler's birthday continued to be celebrated by neo-Nazi elements,[110] while another 'Sieg Heil' incident occurred in 1971 near the Deutscher Keller where two swastika flags were brandished.[111] Four years later, 'Sieg Heil' and 'Raus Juden, raus Juden' were chanted at the Deutscher Keller.[112] A swastika was also unfurled at the funeral of Karl Heusler, a Pretoria bookseller and distributor of Nazi and other right-wing publications,[113] and there were calls for the release of Rudolf Hess, the imprisoned one-time deputy leader of the Nazi Party.[114] In an official Orange Free State University rag procession, a small car carried a Nazi flag,[115] while in Johannesburg, Albert Greene, an American member of the John Birch Society who had been living in South Africa for three years, printed flyers suggesting Jews were controlling the free world through power wielded by the likes of the Rockefellers and Rothschilds.[116] From time to time Jewish institutions were daubed with ugly anti-Jewish graffiti and vicious antisemitic pamphlets were distributed.[117] Under the name of the 'Institute of Jewish Research' in Natal, pamphlets claimed that Jews 'wanted to bastardise the white race and to achieve world domination' through a genocide of the 'Caucasoid' peoples. As we have seen, this was a commonplace trope on the radical white right: endogamy was quite in order for liberal, communist and Zionist Jews, but non-Jews were to forgo their identity.[118] This double standard was spelled out by Brown:

> Vorster did not seem to care that the world-wide campaign against racial discrimination is the result of deliberate calculation on the part of White liberals, Communists and Zionists whose aim is to arouse anger instead of reason, to inflame the Black man against the White man, and ultimately to eradicate the races and nations of the world, in their drive towards their New World Order. In their drive for universal racial equality they have found a doctrine which not only makes the

small nucleus of Jews in the world perfectly safe to practise their own rigid racial and national exclusiveness, and at the same time to pursue their own national and international objectives, but a doctrine which also effectively conceals from the non-Jewish masses of the world one of the fundamental objects of their whole drive against discrimination, which is precisely this safety and immunity to indulge their own age-old ethno-centricism to the full.[119]

Quite clearly, the lessening of tensions between Jews and non-Jews after the Second World War meant little to the likes of Ray Rudman, Johan Schoeman, SED Brown and Ivor Benson. Anti-Jewish fantasies aided and abetted by a small circle of neo-Nazis and fascists from abroad, continued to circulate and inform their world and that of other like-minded conspiracists and fantasists. They indeed shared much with major Nazi ideologues like Alfred Rosenberg, Adolf Hitler and Dietrich Eckart.[120]

Fantasies and Holocaust Denial

The most commonplace fantasy on the radical white right involved the 'myth of the six million', as *Die Afrikaner* put it in 1976.[121] Such thinking was already evident soon after the Second World War when many far-right extremists refused to acknowledge the horrors perpetrated by the Nazis.[122] The Nuremberg Trials were deemed a travesty of justice by the likes of Johan Schoeman, who produced his anti-Nuremberg publication *Small Essays on Big Subjects* to enable him to raise money for the dependants of the Nazi trialists.[123] Prior to that, Schoeman had written *Hear the Other Side: The Afrikaner Side and the German Side* in 1946; *In Gods naam! ontwaak: As Duitsland sterf (of verplig word Stalin te steun) sterf die Christendom!* (In God's Name! Awake: If Germany Dies (or Is Obliged to Support Stalin) Christendom Dies!) in 1948; and in 1949, *Goering's Last Letter! Field-Marshal Hermann Goering Speaks from His Grave to His Accuser, Prosecutor, Judge, Hangman – Winston Churchill and the World Christian Conscience.*[124] By the late 1950s Schoeman was claiming that treble the number of Jews who died in the war had been killed by 'our ally Bolshevism at that time'. He also told *The Star* that gassing was a preferable option to being bombed, as had been the case for the Japanese in Hiroshima.[125]

Relativisation of the Holocaust soon morphed into gross fantasy and classic denial. This was apparent in the wake of the capture of Adolf Eichmann (the main organiser of the 'Final Solution') in Argentina in 1960, when Schoeman raised funds for Eichmann's defence, personally offering the not insignificant amount of R200. 'I don't think Eichmann did the right thing, but he was under orders, and it is the only practical thing he could have done,' Schoeman told a reporter. 'Anyway, I don't think that six million Jews were murdered. I doubt even whether the figure comes to 500,000.'[126] In a twenty-page booklet entitled *Eichmann Is Not Guilty*, Schoeman went further. Displaying a deep and wide-ranging knowledge of conspiratorial literature, he defended Hitler, denied the gas chambers, belittled Nuremberg, relativised murder by raising the atom bomb attacks on Nagasaki and Hiroshima, and betrayed a profound hatred of Jews. He pleaded with readers to get rid of their 'pro-Jew prejudices' and wake up. 'We, South Africa, and the West, are actually facing the Jewish Marxian hell. The sun of the West is setting in the East, but most of our leaders are fast asleep in the laps of the Delilahs of Jew-design – like Vashti's husband.'[127]

Schoeman's views had undoubted support. The treatment of Boers during the Anglo-Boer War (especially the concentration camp deaths) was frequently raised in exchanges, as well as the suffering of Germans and others during the closing stages of the Second World War. Double standards, it was argued, had been applied at Nuremberg. 'Matriculant' said much the same in a letter to *Dagbreek en Sondagnuus* which reminded readers of the cruel bombing of 'Japanese cities' and Dresden, 'while Goldman (alias Lenin) had apparently murdered millions of White Russians without being charged with war crimes by the world'.[128]

By the mid-1960s, the 'myth of the six million' was increasingly articulated by the radical white right. 'Afrikaner' questioned the figures in a letter to *Die Transvaler*,[129] while one correspondent, GA Cole, displayed gross ignorance when he expressed doubt in a letter to the *Daily Dispatch* that Hitler could have killed six million Jews when there had been only 600,000 Jews in Germany.[130] More significantly, *Die Vaderland* summarised an article by Richard Cotton which had appeared in (the American) *Common Sense* describing the murder of six million Jews as a 'great lie'. In any event, asserted Cotton, it was the Jews who had declared war on Germany.[131]

Revisionist ideas about the Second World War in general, and the destruction of European Jewry in particular, had clearly penetrated South Africa – fuelled by a radical white right and neo-Nazi presence in South Africa that not only hated Jews, but sought to rationalise its wartime pro-Nazi stance. On the other hand, mainstream Afrikaners for the most part felt distinct discomfort with the peddling of such errant nonsense. In fact, the editor of *Die Vaderland*, Adriaan Mynhardt van Schoor, apologised to the Board when the latter brought to his attention the publication of Cotton's article in his newspaper. The policy of the newspaper, he explained, was not to publish anything anti-Jewish.[132] Yet small pockets of conspiracists continued to spread falsehoods. In 1971 a Holocaust denial pamphlet ('Falsehood about the Six Million Jews Said to Be Gassed by Hitler Exposed') was distributed at the Jewish Westpark Cemetery on Holocaust Remembrance Day and, a few weeks later, placed in letter boxes in Johannesburg by Rudman's South African Anglo-Nordic Union.[133] Evidence of these ideas gaining currency can be increasingly discerned. *Op en Wakker*, a magazine allied to the HNP, published a letter that questioned the figure of six million Jews,[134] while a correspondent to the *Daily Dispatch*, H Viedge, argued that the Anne Frank story was invented.[135] *Brandwag*, an Afrikaans magazine published by *Ster* (also connected to the HNP), went so far as to deny the Holocaust altogether, while extolling Hitler as a man of high morals.[136] Remarkably, a sixteen-year-old girl told an audience on *Stryddag* (Battle Day, a festive-like occasion used by Nationalists to mobilise political support) that the Hitler Youth had set a good example.[137] Perhaps more disturbingly, a conservative Pretoria daily, *Hoofstad*, carried an article that was favourable towards Hitler.[138] *Ster* also published a lengthy piece on Hitler which ended with a question as to whether the Nazi leader was good or bad.[139] Some months earlier the magazine had seen fit to publish a long letter from one JK Strydom who contended that Hitler had made Germany the most 'effective and powerful bulwark against communism, which was nothing other than a front organisation for Jews. Hitler knew that his National Socialist political and economic system would release the world from the clutches of Jewish imperialism, but the Jews also realised this. Therefore, the Second World War had to be forced upon Germany.'[140]

More significantly, the newly founded HNP-supporting weekly, *Die Afrikaner* (edited from 1970 to 1972 by the theologian Willem Jacobus Gerhardus Lubbe, a Greek and Latin scholar and editor of *Die Kerkbode* from 1967 to 1970), portrayed Jews as outsiders in a way that nourished paranoia and fantasy.[141] The international 'money power' and 'international communism' were conflated, and canards such as the Wall Street banker Jacob Schiff funding the Russian Revolution and American financier Bernard Baruch conniving with Roosevelt and Lenin were popularised.[142] Under the guiding hand of the historian Beaumont Schoeman, who succeeded Lubbe as editor, the HNP mouthpiece became even more determined to rehabilitate Hitler's Germany and challenge the veracity of the Holocaust. Indeed, using the work of the respected British historian AJP Taylor, Schoeman wrote a lengthy nine-part article examining the question of blame for the Second World War. However, by citing the Holocaust denier Richard Harwood as an authoritative source, Schoeman's real predilections were apparent. To be sure, he even employed the old canard that the Zionist leader Chaim Weizmann was responsible for the declaration of war on Germany – a crude argument used in the 1980s by the German right in the *Historikerstreit*, or historians' dispute.[143]

Similar crudity was displayed in the *South African Observer*'s warm review of *The Hoax of the Twentieth Century* (a classic of Holocaust denial literature) by the Canadian author Arthur R Butz. Editor Brown applauded the publication, asserting that it 'demolishes the greatest propaganda legend of our times – the legend that the Germans attempted to exterminate the Jews during World War Two' and claiming that it 'will remain the standard volume for many years to come'. The review included a chapter-by-chapter summary in which Jews, Zionists, the World Jewish Congress and the Nuremberg Trials were vilified, while subjects such as the concentration and death camps were tendentiously discussed. Readers were invited to order the book through the *South African Observer*, which also advertised and distributed a pamphlet, *Did Six Million Die? The Truth at Last*, by Richard Harwood.[144] After the Board of Deputies successfully applied to the director of publications in June 1976 for a ruling under the terms of section (10)(1)(a) of the Publications Act No. 42 of 1944, Harwood's booklet was classified as 'undesirable' and banned.

In August 1976, Brown (as editor of the *South African Observer*) and two private individuals (Pol Hyacinth Jozef Doussy, a Belgium-born medical practitioner, director of companies, and, later, member of the Afrikaner Nasionaal Sosialisties Party, or Afrikaner National Socialist Party; and Helmut Hänsel, a chemical engineer and secretary of the Bund gegen die Verleumdung des Deutschtums, or League against the Defamation of Germanness) lodged appeals against the Publications Board's ruling, but when the case came before the Publications Appeal Board on 7 September 1977, the appellants withdrew their appeal and the publication therefore remained banned.[145] The Board of Deputies then published *Six Million Did Die: The Truth Shall Prevail* – a rejoinder that garnered favourable responses, revealing that most South Africans, including mainstream Nationalists, acknowledged the truth about this period.[146] Indeed, most school textbooks, despite praising Hitler's domestic successes, also 'provided unguarded descriptions of Nazi racism and its consequences', as Shirli Gilbert puts it.[147]

In radical white right circles, however, the veracity of the Holocaust remained an issue, as evidenced in the heated debate that preceded the screening of the 'Genocide' episode in the television series *The World at War*. Letters of objection flooded the press from the moment the SABC announced the broadcast.[148] One GJ Rico made this clear in a letter to *The Star*:

> It is very unfortunate that the responsible authorities have seen fit to include 'The death camps' part of the 'World at War' series in our television programme. As a matter of historical fact, it has been proved that the figure of 6 million Jewish war victims is grossly exaggerated, furthermore, any such casualties that did exist were not the victims of any premeditated extermination. Certainly, there were many Jewish casualties during the war, but regard must be had for the millions of all nationalities and races who died and suffered in that tragic event as well. It is 30 years since the war ended, and the untruths about that war are all being forced on a sympathetic world. In the interests of historical honesty and justice, these falsehoods should be exposed, not repeated.[149]

Acceding to substantial pressure, the SABC reversed its decision to screen the 'Genocide' episode on the grounds that it might give offence to some; but, in the face of widespread anger and criticism, it went ahead with the screening, which was widely acclaimed in mainstream English and Afrikaans newspapers. Antisemites especially should have watched the transmission, argued *Beeld*,[150] while Brian Barrow, a prominent columnist on the *Cape Times*, wondered who would have been offended. 'The Jews? The Germans? Our children? Or was there a fear that black men would see that white men could commit barbarities unheard of even in Darkest Africa? Every reason that comes to mind seems utterly childish compared to the far more important message of the death camp episode, namely that man's inhumanity to man is a universal condition…'[151]

Barrow's appropriation of this specifically Jewish tragedy and its universal message was echoed by other commentators. 'No narrative of World War 2', noted the *Cape Argus*, 'could be complete without the story of the extermination camps. It does not simply show what Hitler's Germany did, it shows what people can do to other people. It shows the inhumanity that can emerge in even the most advanced societies. It is a dreadful warning to us all.'[152] Much the same approach was taken by Dr Louw Alberts, founder and member of the conservative religious group Action Moral Standards, who stressed the universal message of the Holocaust.[153] But approval was not universal. H Hauptman, the chairman of the German Club in Durban, referred to the episode as 'Jewish propaganda',[154] while Ivor Benson (writing as director of the far-right National Forum) called it a 'falsification of history'.[155] The Natal Afrikaans-language newspaper *Tempo* wondered why this 'dark episode' should be remembered and then raised questions about the authenticity of films and books dealing with the subject.[156] *Die Afrikaner* was less guarded. 'The alleged slaughter of six million Jews is based on falsification and fraud and lies,' it claimed.'[157] On the other hand, *Die Vaderland* and *Volksblad* did their best to be even-handed about the 'controversy', with the former publishing a rebuttal from Denis Diamond, the executive director of the Board of Deputies, and the latter suggesting that the persecution of the Jews in Germany was a fact, but that 'the precise extent of and nature of that persecution remains subject to debate'.[158]

Predictably, the most vicious attack on the screening of 'Genocide' came from the *South African Observer*, which described the decision to go ahead as 'the capitulation of the Vorster Government to the forces of world Zionism'. The whole series, argued the monthly, was 'nothing more than history of the last war selected, compiled and purveyed, *not* by qualified historians, but by two Zionist Jews, Jeremy Isaacs and Charles Bloomberg', with the 'other side of the story' having been completely obliterated. It was 'nothing else than another instalment in the gross continuing libel against Germany and the German people as a whole at the hands of Zionists'. Not surprisingly, the monthly cited 'denial' literature and quoted an early revisionist American historian, Harry Elmer Barnes, and the Frenchman Paul Rassinier, whose denial of the Holocaust would win him notoriety in the late 1970s.[159]

Brown concluded his diatribe in typical fashion with an attack on Jews, Judaism and Zionism:

> For our part, if 'The World at War' series – including the Genocide episode 20 – has one lesson for the people of South Africa, it is the pressing need for the whole question of Zionism, Judaism and the Talmud, 'anti-Semitism', the myth of the Six Million, and the whole matter of ethnocentricism to be opened up to free discussion and enquiry – in just the same way that Western man's customs, his traditions, his racism, his nationalism and his Christian faith have since the end of the last war been subjected to the fierce and unremitting glare of public scrutiny by the Zionists themselves.[160]

It is not without significance that Albert Hertzog, the leader of the HNP, refused to come out unequivocally against Holocaust denial.[161] Perhaps he sensed the mood and would have been acquainted with the spread of denialism and the penetration of Harwood's revisionism. As 'Audi Alteram Partem' put it in a letter to the *Sunday Tribune*, the evidence assembled by Harwood in his *Did Six Million Really Die?* was 'strong enough to dispose of the TV film frame by frame'.[162]

The radical white right clearly situated its hatred of Jews within a conspiratorial framework that encompassed notions of Jewish omnipotence, with Israel at the heart of international capitalist and communist machinations, a belief bolstered by the United Nations equating Zionism with racism in its General Assembly resolution in November 1975. But we need to note that the radical white right remained relatively small. It was, however, increasingly energised by fears of political reform. It also needs to be noted that it was not only those on the political margins who shared anti-Jewish fantasies. For example, a SABC religious programme 'Crossroads' – under a deeply committed Christian, William (Bill) Chalmers, who was responsible for English religious programmes on both radio and television – spoke of 'Western high finance' and 'a financial elite' that included 'top banking families' being behind international communism and bent on the destruction of 'Western-style governments, property rights, family life and religion'. No specific mention of Jews was made but, as critics pointed out, Chalmers's ideas echoed *The Protocols of the Elders of Zion*.[163] On an earlier occasion Chalmers had referred to the Illuminati (a secret society that allegedly controlled the world and that was supposedly organised by Jews) and had recommended that listeners read *Pawns in the Game* by William Guy Carr, an English-born Canadian conspiracy theorist. Based on the *Protocols*, the book takes seriously the Illuminati and focuses on the dangers of international communism and capitalism.[164] Questioned about the programme that had alluded to the *Protocols*, SABC spokesman Hein Joubert said Chalmers had 'not mentioned the Jewish community – so if the glove fits wear it'.[165]

Three years later Chalmers was again the subject of controversy. His booklet *The Conspiracy of Truth*, which purported to be a 'Christian response to Communism', accused Jews of having infiltrated high ecclesiastical positions in the 'Middle Ages', while the 'Rothschild Empire' and 'Wall Street Oligarchy' – obvious allusions to Jews – were depicted as part of a worldwide communist-inspired plot or 'Grand Design'. According to Chalmers, it was 'International Finance' created by Jews 'but willingly adopted by Westerners' that was behind the conspiracy.[166] Unsurprisingly, the leader of the NGK's committee Antikom, Koot Vorster, wrote a glowing preface to the booklet, illustrating a bond between conservative Afrikaners and at least some English speakers arising out of a visceral Christian anti-communism.[167]

A media furore followed the publication of *The Conspiracy of Truth*.[168] Chalmers was condemned by Jewish leaders and his work was raised in a parliamentary debate by Rupert Lorimer, the PFP MP for Orange Grove, who accused Chalmers of peddling *The Protocols of the Elders of Zion*. 'I may say that this document is a discredited document; it has been proved to have no substance at all and is, furthermore, banned,' he told the House. 'It is a highly antisemitic document and quoting from it certainly amounts to a deliberate affront to another religious group.'[169] The SABC came to the defence of Chalmers, saying the ideas expressed in *The Conspiracy of Truth* were his private views and had not been aired by the broadcaster.[170]

Sinister Movements

In 1975, Manfred Roeder, a leader of West Germany's militant right-wing Deutsche Bürgerinitiative (German Citizen Initiative), who was classified as a terrorist by the German Office for the Protection of the Constitution, visited South Africa and expressed pleasure at his warm reception.[171] In addition to praising Hitler for disciplining the German people, Roeder publicly denied that six million Jews had been murdered by the Nazis.[172] He clearly felt he was among friends. According to the *Sunday Times*, there were indeed secret Nazi cells in South Africa that met in private homes bedecked with swastikas, where proceedings began with a Nazi anthem.[173] The liberal *Rand Daily Mail*'s full-page article 'Voices from the Far Right' also attested to the spread of extremism.[174]

Anti-Jewish attitudes were gaining traction.[175] It was even reported that the Ku Klux Klan – in close contact with its parent body in the United States – was operating in South Africa.[176] The journalist Keith Abendroth warned that materials denying the Holocaust were formally included in propaganda aimed at recruiting members for the Afrikaner Weerstandsbeweging (Afrikaner Resistance Movement, or AWB), a far-right movement founded in 1973 to protest against the Westminster system of government and any relaxation of apartheid polices under Prime Minister Vorster.[177] Three years later, the RSA-Front was founded by Dr PHJ Doussy.[178] Typically its focus was on 'another race' which, it claimed, dominated the super-big financial powers, communism and the Vatican.[179] The Anglo-Afrikaner Bond with its youth arm, the Odal Clan, was another group that attracted attention. According to the *Sunday Times*, the Odal Clan was a white youth supremacist group based in Krugersdorp (although originating in Cape Town) that was allegedly financed by the Anglo-Afrikaner Bond and inspired by Hitler. Its founder, Rudolf Schmidt, was a former member of the Hitler Youth who subsequently made his way to Paraguay with his wife to establish a settlement of like-minded people on land allocated to them by the government.[180] More significantly, in 1977 the South African National Front (SANF, also known as the National Front of South Africa) was established. It was a sister organisation of the racist British National Front (although this was denied by the British organisation) and linked to an international group of neo-fascist organisations, including the Ku Klux Klan.[181] In addition to its international ties, the movement had links with both the HNP and the AWB. The SANF published and distributed several anti-black, anti-Jewish and anti-Zionist pamphlets, and some were even sent to state schools.[182] It also had its own military wing, the Wit Kommando (White Commando), which began a campaign of terrorism against blacks and liberal institutions.[183] Meanwhile, Rudman's NS Boerenasie continued to distribute Nazi-like pamphlets, especially in the Eastern Cape, and gained special attention when its publication *Son-op* had the first three issues banned.[184] Even Rudman's death in 1978 failed to dampen its operations and NS Boerenasie's new leader, Ludiwicus Erasmus, reported that the 42,000-strong movement remained anti-black and anti-Jewish.[185] Some months after the change of guard, Erasmus claimed that hand grenades had been thrown at his house. He speculated that they might have originated from the Broederbond, Zionists, Rotarians or Freemasons, 'to name only a few'.[186]

Anti-Jewish incidents were now increasingly reported: a 'Nazi Victory Feast' dinner at a residence at the University of Pretoria;[187] a display of swastikas at the Orange Free State University;[188] antisemitic jokes in Pretoria University's rag magazine;[189] threats against a Jewish SRC candidate at the University of the Witwatersrand;[190] and a wave of anti-Jewish graffiti that included Nazi slogans.[191] Pamphlets claiming that the Holocaust was a hoax were widely disseminated in Cape Town,[192] and swastikas were painted across Pretoria.[193] In Aliwal North, an Eastern Cape town, vandals wrecked a synagogue,[194] while the home of a Jew in Johannesburg was defaced and swastikas painted on an apartment block in the city.[195] A wave of antisemitism was sweeping the country, warned Judge Kowie Marais, the PFP MP for Johannesburg North, who ironically had been a founder member of the OB four decades earlier.[196]

This burgeoning hostility towards Jews reflected tensions within the white body politic. Cracks and fissures in Afrikaner nationalism evident since the 1960s had widened, as disenchanted extremists felt that the country they knew was being taken away from them as the National Party tentatively explored power-sharing with blacks.[197] Enjoying greater room for debate under Prime Minister Vorster, intellectuals and clergymen were questioning a failing and morally indefensible apartheid policy. When Vorster's successor, Pieter Willem Botha, signalled even greater change in the late 1970s and spoke of the need to 'adapt or die', the radical right was incensed. It now clearly represented a threat to public order. The country's security experts recognised the challenge, as did the Board of Deputies.[198] The latter indeed looked on anxiously at the proliferation of radical white right antisemitic movements and, with good reason, included the HNP among these threats.[199] Importantly, the highly respected intellectual Willem ('Wimpie') de Klerk, one-time editor of *Die Transvaler* and *Rapport*, shared these concerns, warning of a 'whole string' of far-right movements, which included the AWB, the Odal Clan and the NS Boerenasie:

> The vast majority of these people are nationally rooted, inspired and proud Afrikaners. It is easy to swear at them, but we must rather make them have some insight. To ignore them is equally easy because they are not a political factor, but to keep on talking to them is better. The idealism which inspires these movements is of a very suspicious character. The spectre that haunts them must be very clearly seen. It is not nationalism that consumes them but racism at its most dangerous.
>
> By claiming all rights for one's own people, by declaring one's own people as sacred and to look upon others as dirt ... It is not democratic action, but a resuscitation of German Nazism transplanted on the Afrikaner people, that is why I say it is as un-Afrikaner as it can come.[200]

In so far as Jews were concerned, we need to ask how widespread were these conspiracist fabrications and outlandish fantasies. For the *Rand Daily Mail*, the fact that a weekly such as *Die Afrikaner* – affiliated to a mainstream political party, the HNP – had denied the Holocaust at the time of the 'Genocide' debate was a cause for alarm:

> Should any attention be paid to *Die Afrikaner*, the organ of the Herstigte Nasionale Party, when it dismisses as fabrication what was presented in the Genocide episode of the World at War series? Or should it be shrugged off as simply making clear to those who might not have fully understood it, the meaning of the political phrase the 'lunatic fringe?' It is tempting to do so. Yet *Die Afrikaner* and the party it speaks for represents a definite body of opinion in South Africa. True, a small body of opinion; but one which constantly presents itself to the public, which contests parliamentary elections, and which has as its leader a former Cabinet Minister and in its ranks a number of former Members of Parliament.[201]

THREE

The Resurgence of Exclusivism and Neo-Nazism: 1970s and 1980s

For nearly two thousand years the inherited fibres of every Jew's being has been saturated with his race's two-fold mission of supplanting Christian civilisation and establishing Israel as the dominant ruling power of the world.
South African Observer, March 1978

There is no doubt in my mind that the Jews and the Muslims and other non-Christians cannot be part of the true belief and we must try to bring them to the path of light.
Ada Claasen, *Sunday Times*, 16 May 1982

...they openly identified themselves with world Zionism's "total onslaught" on South Africa ... in complete phase with the "total onslaughts" of world Communism and the forces of international finance.
South African Observer, February 1986

There are more pro-Hitler people in South Africa than I have found anywhere else, the reason is unknown to me.
David Irving, *Pretoria News*, 25 September 1986.

Brandishing the Exclusivist Flag

The Herstigte Nasionale Party (HNP) may have been on the fringe of white politics, but it was undoubtedly part of the political mainstream. The party was able to air its views through *Die Afrikaner* and enjoyed the support of Brown's *South African Observer* and Benson's *Behind the News*. As we have seen, these outlets – and the ongoing efforts of fantasists – ensured the survival of derisory accusations against Jews. However, the reach of these extremists was marginal and the message hardly resonated. In fact, there was no fertile ground for nurturing a 'Jewish problem', as had been the case in the 1930s. South African whites were enjoying economic prosperity, while Afrikaner cultural concerns were insufficient to morph into serious political discomfort. Added to that, Jews had benefited from a more inclusive (white) South Africanism (apparent in a new discourse that greeted the creation of a Republic in 1961), which had brought English and Afrikaans speakers closer together. Historical animosities dating back to the nineteenth century between Boer and Brit were, in the main, relegated to the dustbin of history. 'By the late 1960s', writes Aletta Norval, 'the language of *volkism* was virtually absent from NP discourse. It was now replaced by a discourse on *multi-nationalism*, considered to be more suited to the "realities" of the South African situation.'[1]

Nationalist ideologues had indeed begun to grapple with South Africa's so-called ethnic nations (the emergent Bantustans), as well as the urban black African, Coloured and Indian questions. New political and social frameworks were being sought in which Jews joined English- and Afrikaans-speaking whites as part of a dominant and privileged population. Growing ties between Pretoria and Jerusalem cemented this, and the widespread respect for Israel's feisty militarism enhanced the image of the Jew. In radical-right (predominantly Afrikaner) circles, however, fantasies about Jews bubbled beneath the surface, ready to be exploited by politicians and demagogues. It was even reported that in 1968 the Broederbond had launched an investigation into the 'Jewish problem' and the 'influence' of Jews on the South African economy, as well as ways to restrict Jewish immigration.[2] For some, Jew-baiting was patently a political ploy; for others, it amplified and connected with past conspiratorial fantasies that were being increasingly nourished by growing challenges to the old order.

These challenges, which marked the erosion of the relatively calm late-1960s, became evident by the early 1970s, with major textile strikes in Durban in 1973, violent stoppages in the mining industry, and the growing rhetoric of the Black Consciousness Movement, a grassroots anti-apartheid Christian-oriented movement that emerged in the 1960s. Further challenges accompanied the collapse of Portuguese colonialism after the overthrow of the Portuguese regime in Lisbon in 1974 (which had serious implications for neighbouring Mozambique and South Africa's *cordon sanitaire*), and the significant national and international reverberations of the Soweto uprising of 1976, in which thousands of protesting black African schoolchildren confronted the state and hundreds were killed.

Political anxiety and stress exacerbated white fears as international hostility towards apartheid grew. The mood among whites became increasingly gloomy. The HNP did its best to build on this sense of unease by promising a return to *kragdadigheid* (forcefulness), a pristine neo-Calvinism and white supremacy. Its worldview – a relic of Malan's GNP of the 1930s – was driven by a bellicose and racial ethno-nationalism, coupled with a chauvinism that was at odds with pluralism and liberalism. Undesirable changes and perceived disintegration of the normative order were blamed in conspiratorial terms on liberalism, the loss of an unambiguous faith, and 'a small international moneyed elite' that 'manipulates world affairs and strives to create a centralised one-world government'.[3]

Representing the so-called *verkramptes* (unenlightened Afrikaners), the HNP fought tooth and nail against the reformers (*verligtes*) and were supported by Afrikaner trade unions and elements within the Broederbond and the media as well as the NGK.[4] However, few parliamentarians had followed Hertzog when he broke from the National Party in 1969 to form the HNP. Equally significant was the fact that Andries Treurnicht, editor from 1967 to 1971 of *Hoofstad*, failed to throw his weight behind Hertzog. A man of considerable intellect and political acuity, the one-time NGK theologian, editor of *Die Kerkbode* from 1960 to 1967, National Party MP for Waterberg from 1971, and chairman of the Broederbond from 1972 to 1974 had yet to reach his tipping point. His failure to join the HNP effectively put paid to the hopes of the new party. In any event, it had little appeal to an emerging Afrikaner bourgeoisie that had enjoyed years of unprecedented economic growth and that, in the words of the historian Albert Grundlingh, 'helped to shape a new Afrikaner social world'.[5] Stability had begun to return in the wake of the 1960 Sharpeville massacre and foreign investment had increased. Afrikaner financiers, businessmen and industrialists were narrowing the gap with their English counterparts. *Völkisch* solidarity eroded and a new Afrikaner bourgeoisie looked askance at the HNP. 'The new class has cut itself adrift from the main Afrikaner stream,' wrote an AWB supporter, Chris Beyers, 'and their inborn conservative instincts have tended to become liberal so that they feel themselves more at home in a liberal atmosphere than among their own people.'[6]

In an early general election that had been called by Prime Minister Vorster in 1970 to destroy the HNP, the breakaway party garnered a paltry 53,735 votes against the National Party's 822,034, representing only 3.59 per cent of the total poll.[7] Its politics were stale. Few Afrikaners shared the party's distrust of English speakers, including Jews, who were by now mostly urbanised and a relatively successful section of the population. For the radical white right, however, Jews remained outsiders, an image built upon decades of hostile stereotyping that was informed, at least in part, by religious differences. Hertzog explicitly stated that members of the HNP would have to accept Calvinist principles, including the 'triune' – which meant no 'Catholics, atheists, freethinkers and Jews'. It was also formally agreed that no Jew should be a member of a provincial council, parliament or cabinet.[8]

Given such exclusivism, it is hardly surprising that in HNP circles the 'Jewish question' was raised from time to time. At one election meeting in 1970, MW ('Boet') Pretorius, HNP candidate for Pretoria Central, adamantly asserted that his party did not want Jews as members.[9] Similar sentiments were articulated by Willem Lubbe, who had replaced Treurnicht as editor of *Die Kerkbode* in 1967. For this conservative intellectual, armed with a doctorate in Latin from Leiden in the Netherlands, the religious freedom permitted in the National Party went against 'the triune God'. In his view, it was not enough for the National Party to say that it was a Christian party. It needed to spell out what this meant. 'How can a Party call itself Christian and seek the development of our national life on Christian national lines when it numbers among its members also those who reject the New Testament and do not recognise Christ?'[10]

Christians of a conservative bent clearly tended to frame the Jew in religious terms, and theological journals frequently grappled with the divide between synagogue and church.[11] Koot Vorster even criticised attempts to get the Catholic Church to drop deicide charges against Jews and suggested that any initiative to absolve Jews of that crime would anger Christians, while Ds. Nik Lee claimed that non-Christians such as Jews and Hindus had the Devil as their father.[12]

Unsurprisingly, evangelising missions persisted in efforts to convert Jews.[13] Such religiously conservative thinking – inspired by an *adversus Judaeos* tradition – was fairly widespread and included mainstream Nationalists such as Ds. D Pepler of the National Party, who asserted that the first question a political candidate should answer was whether he was a redeemed child of God through Jesus. Of course, this meant that Jews should be barred from holding public office.[14] Such views were not new. Similar sentiments had been expressed, albeit infrequently, by the Nationalists in the 1950s and 1960s, and school textbooks were often Christocentric.[15] It was certainly not uncommon to hear voices within the Church objecting to non-Christians being returned to parliament. The Southern Transvaal Regional Synod of the NGK, for instance, had resolved in 1958 that all parliamentarians were to be 'of unimpeachable Christian character and behaviour'.[16] When approached by *Die Volksblad* for comment, Dr LB Rex, a member of the Synodal Commission, side-stepped the issue and insisted there would be no attempt to stop Jews from entering parliament and that it was character rather than faith that was at issue. However, Ds. HJ Kriel, *scriba* of the Southern Transvaal Regional Synod, contradicted Rex and affirmed that 'it would be positively undesirable that members of our congregations should support or return persons whom they know are not Christians'.[17] The Synod had, in fact, made its position clear in an official statement: 'The Synod makes an earnest appeal to members of the Church to see to it through their personal influence as people of faith that only persons to whom as avowed Christians they can with confidence give their support should be sent to governing and administrative bodies.'[18]

Despite these voices, the National Party had, in the main, come to terms with admitting Jews as members as long as they did not undermine its Christian character.[19] Only occasionally did one hear accusations of Jewish religious deviance such as that expressed by the chairman of the Free State Teaching Association, Petrus ('Piet') Clase, who maintained that it was 'unthinkable that someone who is not a professing Christian should be permitted to teach. It was impossible for a world citizen to be responsible for the education of the descendants of the Afrikaner people ... There was no place for a teacher whose attitude towards life is not Christian National.'[20]

It is difficult to assess the extent and significance of such thinking. However, it is reasonable to accept that, at the least, theological impulses did inform perceptions of the Jew. As noted earlier, many white South Africans and especially Afrikaners were religiously conservative.[21] Christian National Education, or CNE, was an endless subject of debate and church attendances remained relatively high. Sunday observance or 'blue laws' operated without serious objection as did religious broadcasts by the SABC. It was not altogether surprising that Ds. Jacobus Badenhorst of the NGK objected to Joseph ('Yokkie') Shill, a Jewish businessman, throwing his hat into the ring for a provincial seat in the Transvaal, because of his Jewish descent. Indeed, National Party canvassers were asked if the lives of their children could be put in the hands of a Jew. Although Badenhorst denied saying these things, they were widely reported and there were no repercussions for his statement.[22] In similar fashion, the NGK in Odendaalsrus, a rural mining town in the Orange Free State, objected to the election of Edel Cohen as mayor. Christians should be ruled by a Christian, said Ds. David Hermanus Botes.[23] Two years later the same Botes attacked Judaism as a religion but not Jews as a people. 'Among no one else did he encounter such venomous slander against Christ as among Jews, and nowhere else had he seen more dedicated Christians, who believed so passionately in Christ, as converted Jews,' Botes told an NGK Synod in the Orange Free State. 'If one examines their writings, one would be astonished about everything that is said about Christ. I have never come across people who have attacked Christ in such defamatory words.'[24] It is perhaps not surprising that a meeting of the Komitee vir Volksoorligting (a committee to inform the people), organised by a group opposed to Prime Minister Vorster's reformist initiatives and attended by some NGK clergymen, was, according to the monthly *To the Point*, notable for a number of antisemitic statements.[25]

Overall, however, religious or theologically based hostility towards Jews had little purchase. Antisemitism in a programmatic sense was effectively absent, but there were still accusations of Jews dominating commerce and conducting underhand business practices,[26] buying too much land, or exploiting and wresting control of South Africa from the Afrikaners.[27] Importantly, such charges, as well as the circulation of anti-Jewish pamphlets and leaflets or the occasional daubing of Jewish institutions, were invariably condemned by the National Party.[28] Yet conversely, Harry Schwarz, the pugnacious Transvaal leader of the United Party, was the endless target of anti-Jewish barbs in the Transvaal Provincial Council.[29] Literature, both English and Afrikaans, also revealed the tenacity of stereotypes that had developed over decades, with the 'evil money power' and 'subversive' Jew never far from the surface.[30] Jews were invariably associated with money and business, while a new symbol (in many ways reflecting the upward mobility of Jews) was the emergence of the 'kugel' in popular discourse in the late 1960s. A South African version of the Jewish American princess (JAP), she confidently walked the shopping malls of Johannesburg's affluent northern suburbs and was regularly parodied on stage by the likes of Pieter-Dirk Uys, South Africa's master satirist, and was also the subject of countless 'kugel jokes' enjoyed by Gentile and Jew.[31]

This shared humour was, it seems, a barometer of the comfortable place the Jew was beginning to enjoy in South Africa. It was certainly not a harbinger of hostility. Most social clubs at this time admitted Jews, and few businesses or industries precluded their employment. Ugly incidents were indeed few and far between, and a 'Jewish question' per se never seriously entered the political arena. In 1972, the chair of the Public Relations Committee of the Jewish Board of Deputies, Arthur Suzman, could, with justification – and despite the rantings of fantasists and the actions of some people discussed earlier – report that antisemitism in South Africa had declined massively despite the persistence of a subtle 'othering' of the Jew.[32]

Persisting Fantasies

Notwithstanding Suzman's optimistic report, there remained anti-Jewish fantasists who persisted in peddling outrageous conspiracies. As pointed out in the previous chapter, Holocaust denial had become a staple of the radical right by the early 1970s and *Die Afrikaner* was comfortable with such journalese. It will be recalled that its editor, Beaumont Schoeman, who succeeded Willem Lubbe, had done his best to rehabilitate Nazi Germany by regularly publishing articles throwing doubt on the veracity of the Holocaust.[33] One such article was by the notorious German revisionist and Holocaust denier Wilhelm Stäglich, a one-time Nazi officer and author of *Der Auschwitz-Mythos* (The Auschwitz Myth).[34] It is also noteworthy that the Jewish Board of Deputies' publication *Six Million Did Die* – a refutation of *The Hoax of the Twentieth Century* by Arthur Butz – was the subject of scathing criticism in the columns of *Die Afrikaner*, which characterised the Board's critique as misleading and tendentious.[35] *The Hoax of the Twentieth Century* was in fact referred to with approbation by *Die Afrikaner*:

> Butz writes that it is not the extermination of the Jews which will attract the attention of future generations, for the simple reason that nothing like that happened. It will also not be the German programme for the expulsion of Jews from Germany because this was in no way a unique phenomenon. What will be unique will be the establishment of the legend of the 'great slaughter' in the West and also the exploitation of this legend to a point bordering on insanity … The fact that there is no German document which makes mention of the extermination of the Jew is well known. The documents simply make mention of the 'final solution', the ultimate banishment of all Jews from Europe and a wartime procedure of resettling them in the Eastern parts which were occupied by Germany.[36]

Die Afrikaner also extended its sympathy to the German-born Canadian

Holocaust denier Ernst Zündel, who had been on trial several times in Canada for 'spreading false news'.[37] Shortly after the centenary of Hitler's birth, it even attempted to rehabilitate the Führer, arguing that he needed to be seen and understood in a broader perspective and appreciated for his considerable contribution to the German people.[38] More disturbing were the conspiracies periodically raised by this HNP mouthpiece. Old canards that Jews had fomented the Anglo-Boer War were rehashed,[39] and *The Dispossessed Majority* by Wilmot Robertson, an American right-wing conspiracist who denied anything positive about Jewish economic contributions, was favourably reviewed.[40] The Jewish origin of communist leaders was also identified as the reason for secret understandings between Jerusalem and Moscow, and for Russia's support for Israel's expansionist policies.[41] *Die Afrikaner* even claimed that by focusing on the fiftieth anniversary of Hitler's rise to power, the South African press hoped to deflect attention from the 1982 Israeli invasion of its northern neighbour Lebanon.[42] In similar fashion, the radical-right labour unionist, member of Antikom, and one-time secretary of the National Congress for Combating Communism, Gert Beetge, lodged an objection with the SABC over its reportage of the fortieth anniversary of the Auschwitz liberation, which he dismissed as malicious, unfounded and discredited propaganda. The 'myth of Auschwitz', he maintained, was kept alive 'to serve the political aims of certain international organisations'.[43]

By the 1980s it seems as if *Die Afrikaner* had become the home of respectable Holocaust denial, which meshed with the trope of devious and malevolent Jewish power. In a letter published by the weekly, the former Greyshirt leader and one-time HNP MP for Germiston District, Theunis Stoffberg, captured this sentiment:

> As one who has a knowledge of the Jewish question, I realise that the Jews dominate us, something that is never mentioned in party politics. The Jewish question is naturally untouchable and is rejected in party politics like the plague, which is the reason for the lack of understanding of the realisation that the Jews totally dominate our people. No party politician will ever admit that... Unless we throw the whole Westminster system overboard, we will become slaves of the Jews.[44]

This sense of Jewish domination and, ultimately, power – persistently employed by *Die Afrikaner*, the *South African Observer* and *Behind the News* – nourished fantasies about Jews and their global ambitions, at the root of which were the alleged ties between Moscow and Jerusalem, as well as communist links with Zionism. SED Brown was a particularly prominent exponent of this view:

> As we have pointed out in the past, no one can begin to understand the world power structure, and what is happening in the world today, unless he realizes that the two Asiatic movements which arose in the first world war, and which reaped the victory of the second, were Communism and political Zionism. These two revolutionary movements, which sprang from a common root in the ghettos of Russia, are only as separate as the two main branches of the one tree ... In America and other countries of the West, the rise of Zionism has gone side by side with the rise of Communism. The Zionists work from the top, the Communists from below. The power exerted by Zionism in the world today is power at the highest political level; in world affairs it is a 'world power'. The conquest of Palestine was not merely a return to an 'ancient homeland', but an attempt to set up world power there. Empires in the past wielded great power over large areas but they were visible bodies. But not so with Zionism, which is advanced in all countries of the world through tremendous financial and other power brought to bear on leading politicians, editors, Christian leaders and public men generally. The influence of Zionist organisations reaches into the inner policy-making groups of nearly every government in the world, particularly the Christian West. This influence causes those groups to adopt pro-Zionist and pro-Communist policies which are often in conflict with the real interests and the very survival of the peoples and nations they govern...[45]

Focusing on the Jewish menace was a way of undermining the National Party, perceived as supporting the Zionist enemy. Indeed, shortly after PW Botha became prime minister in 1978 and signalled a move away from crude apartheid, the *South African Observer* blamed 'the communists, the men of international finance or the political Zionists' for the new prime minister's 'headlong retreat from discrimination'.[46] Jews were accused of undermining order and stability – a familiar chant that was linked to the well-worn stereotypes of the liberal and communist Jew. Not coincidentally, the *South African Observer* perceived Henry Kissinger, the American secretary of state, as an *éminence grise*.

> Just who is this Henry Kissinger, with his horn-rimmed glasses, heavy German accent, kinky hair, double chin and expanding waist line – the man who has never left the corridors of power in the State Department and is still a guiding light on African and Southern African policy? ... Who we may well ask is this Jewish immigrant to the US in 1938 who once established a vice-like grip on the American foreign policy machine and who executed policies which flew directly in the face of one-time entrenched conservative State Department thinking? ... But of course, Kissinger is no stereotyped communist. He is no stereotyped anything, except a stereotyped political Zionist. The truth about Henry Kissinger is that he proved himself to be one of the most pragmatically successful and, if one recognises the Communists as the maliciously satanic enemies of man and God, then the most dangerous and treacherous political careerist on the contemporary scene.[47]

Jewish Perfidy and the Myth of the Holocaust

It is difficult to know the extent of ideas surrounding the 'myth' of the Holocaust and notions of Jewish perfidy, but frequent letters to the press denying the murder of European Jewry provide an indication of their proliferation.[48] What we can be certain about is that questioning the Holocaust was not the sole preserve of the uneducated and unemployed. In 1980, Theodor Eberhardt Werner Schumann, a leading Afrikaner scientist and deputy chair of the South African Atomic Energy Board, called for a judicial investigation into the veracity of the Holocaust.[49] Five years later, Schumann – who was now chief counsel of a far-right cultural organisation, Die Afrikaner Volkswag (The Afrikaner People's Guard, or AV) – forwarded a well-supported motion for the AV to consider a request for a three-man commission to probe the veracity of the murder of six million Jews. It was the astonishing control the Zionists had over bookshops, claimed Schumann, that was responsible for Afrikaners remaining in the dark about the 'fable of the six million'. He personally knew of ninety books that had disproved the allegation and were not made available in local bookshops.[50]

It needs to be stressed that Schumann had a well-established reputation as a scientist and intellectual. Trained as a meteorologist at Stellenbosch, Göttingen and Yale, he headed the South African weather service and even received attention from geneticists and those concerned with geopolitics.[51] More than two decades earlier in *The Abdication of the White Man*, Schumann had revealed a Spenglerian obsession with the decline of the white race and the global threat of communism.[52] Jews hardly featured, but, when they were referred to, the emphasis was on their putative strength that derived from their monotheism and belief in Chosenness.[53] Significantly, his description of events minimised Hitler and the growth of fascism. Instead, he stressed the threat of Marxist communism. At that time, however, there was no hint of animus towards Jews per se or intimations of fantasy.[54] Yet two decades later Schumann was denying the Holocaust. Perhaps the tone of *The Abdication of the White Man* and Schumann's inclination towards conspiratorial thinking provide a hint of his turn in the 1980s. But this is mere speculation.

About Ivor Benson there is no need to speculate. His *Behind the News* harped monotonously on Jews and their machinations, and his numerous pamphlets and books remained a consistent outlet for anti-Jewish fantasies.[55] His was a dark world ruled by the 'money power', which in turn was connected to both 'political Zionism' and communism. For Benson the Holocaust never happened. He even claimed that the Genocide Convention, ratified three years after the Second World War, had been a set-up to protect Jewish national interests by the Jewish Polish jurist Raphael Lemkin.[56] Patently conversant with Holocaust denial literature, Benson made his own contribution and, as we have seen, was well known and tightly connected to a global web of like-minded colleagues. As an independent political writer and analyst, he travelled and lectured widely and commented on world affairs. In 1970 he joined Albert Hertzog's HNP while widening his networks within far-right circles. Two years later Benson addressed the far-right World Affairs Council in Seattle,[57] and in 1986 and 1990 spoke at conferences hosted by the Institute for Historical Review, an organisation promoting the denial of the Holocaust. He in fact published two articles in the

Journal of Historical Review, the primary organ for revisionists. In 'The Siege of South Africa', published in 1986, he placed the Jew at centre stage by tendentiously excavating secondary sources that focused on the machinations of 'Hoggenheimer' and the Rothschilds. He quoted with approbation the American conspiracist Carroll Quigley, as well as JA Hobson, whose book *The War in South Africa* had postulated the notion of the Anglo-Boer War having been fought in the interests of a 'small group of international financiers, chiefly German in origin and Jewish in race'.[58] Benson also reminded readers of the Treason and Rivonia trials of the 1950s and early 1960s in which Jews (as discussed earlier) had been particularly prominent.[59]

Four years later, in 'Russia 1917–1918: A Key to the Riddle of an Age of Conflict', Benson described the destructive role of the Jew in history as well as Zionist manipulation of global affairs and the central role of Jews in the Russian Revolution of 1917. 'In Russia in September 1917 power finally passed into the hands of Lenin and his fellow Jewish conspirators,' explained Benson, 'and in the same week Prime Minister Lloyd George and President Woodrow Wilson, yielding to pressure exerted by Jewish leaders, committed Britain and the United States to the recognition of a future state of Israel and its people as a nation.' In addition, Benson highlighted Jewish subversion in South Africa, asserting that the ANC and SACP masqueraded as 'Black Liberation' movements when in fact they 'are only other names for a chauvinist Jewish nationalist imperialism'. For Benson, the 'Jewish role in history has been undeviatingly *destructive*, the very opposite of *creative*'.[60]

Benson's more circumspect language of the early 1960s had clearly given way to unguarded and vicious anti-Jewish bigotry from the 1970s. The 'money power' or Hoggenheimer was real for him, with Jewish evil an overarching explanation for human affairs. In addition to his lectures, journalese and publications, Benson wrote several books including *The Opinion Makers*, *The Worldwide Conspiracy*, *The Battle for South Africa*, and *The Zionist Factor: The Jewish Impact on Twentieth Century History*.[61] Each revealed his conspiratorial inclinations and his hostility towards the subversive Jew, with the pernicious power of 'high finance' a common thread. In *The Zionist Factor*, Benson connected his fantasy-driven demonisation of Jews to major global events, supposedly uncovering hitherto suppressed evidence of the sinister role of Jews in the Bolshevik Revolution as well as the ties between communism, capitalism and the State of Israel.[62] 'Zionist imperialism', he asserted, had patently replaced an 'Anglo-Saxon imperialism'.[63]

Besides his own publications, Benson added to the corpus of Douglas Reed (a notorious British Holocaust denier and antisemite) when he published a manuscript recovered after Reed's death in Durban in 1976.[64] Importantly, Benson wrote a laudatory preface to the book, published as *The Controversy of Zion* by his own Dolphin Press in 1978. In a work riddled with prejudicial historical allusions, Reed dissects Zionism with crude, simplistic and vulgar observations tied to biblical references. At all times, Jews direct world affairs and revolution. *The Protocols of the Elders of Zion* – a world conspiracy first disclosed, according to Reed, by the founder of the Illuminati, Adam Weishaupt – is treated as authentic, and Israeli machinations are scrutinised and framed within the context of omniscient world Jewry.[65]

While Benson's publications and his pathological fantasies published in *Die Afrikaner* and *Behind the News* might have had some resonance, for the most part white South Africans of a conservative bent had little affinity with such nonsensical claims. They certainly paid little attention to Jaap Marais, the firebrand white supremacist who replaced Albert Hertzog as leader of the HNP in 1977. Cursing Afrikaner monopolies such as the insurance giant Sanlam or claiming that the National Party had sold out to 'Hoggenheimer' made little impact. The same was true for his use of terms like '*vuil Jood*' (dirty Jew),[66] or his assertion that 'political power lies in the hands of a Jewish-dominated worldwide conspiracy'.[67]

Marais's fiery oratory was simply too extreme: his appeals to *völkisch* myths and symbols had depreciating returns for most Afrikaners. 'They were more concerned with freeing themselves from indebtedness than escaping the clutches of "cosmopolitan" culture,' explains the historian Dan O'Meara. 'Ditto the Afrikaner civil servants and workers, who were far more interested in their pay cheques than "their" culture.'[68]

Eugene Terre'Blanche (right) in conversation. Courtesy: Special Collections, National Library of South Africa, Cape Town

Enter the Conservative Party

Notwithstanding these new priorities, there was a growing and not insignificant group of Afrikaners who were unhappy with the reformist direction of the National Party. In the 1981 general election, the HNP succeeded in gaining the support of 13.1 per cent of the white electorate, but that did not translate into even one seat in parliament.[69] Nevertheless, the performance of the HNP appears to have encouraged Andries Treurnicht (minister of public works, statistics and tourism in Botha's government) to break from the National Party. He had long been wary of plans to share power with 'non-Whites' and feared that the President's Council – a body comprising whites, Indians and Coloureds that was created in 1980 to advise the state president on constitutional reform – would undermine *magsverdeling*, or the division of powers. 'If you share power, you lose it. If you share power, you are no longer in control,' warned Treurnicht.[70] His fears were increasingly reinforced as 'grand apartheid' threatened to crumble and as Botha, who was often under pressure from big business, pressed ahead with plans to create a tricameral parliament that would include Coloured and Indian elected representatives.

Matters came to a head in February 1982 when the National Party parliamentary caucus overwhelmingly supported a motion of confidence in Botha. Those like Treurnicht who opposed the motion were given eight days to reconsider their objections or leave the party. Treurnicht, as the leader of the powerful Transvaal National Party, took the matter to his provincial caucus where he anticipated full support; but, after the dramatic and surprise entry of PW Botha, he was defeated and replaced as Transvaal leader by FW de Klerk. Far-right groups outside the hall made their support for Treurnicht obvious and some even went to Johannesburg's Jan Smuts (now Oliver Tambo International) airport to give him a rousing farewell on his departure for Cape Town.

With tensions running high in the House and a Treurnicht-inspired walkout from the National Party anticipated, Harry Schwarz (now PFP MP for Yeoville) implored the renegade Treurnicht not to embrace the attitude of the many reactionary radical white right splinter groups that had emerged in the 1970s. 'Nobody gainsays him his right of starting a new political movement,' Schwarz told the House. 'But let it be said that there are some of us who perhaps represent minority views and are members of minority groups in South Africa who are a little concerned about some of those who are hailing his actions. Some of the badges and banners, whether at the airport or in Pretoria, of those who seem to be those of the ultra-right, give us a degree of concern as to the people who want to be led by him.'[71]

Shortly after Schwarz's warning, Treurnicht, Ferdinand ('Ferdi') Hartzenberg, minister of education, and fourteen other MPs were expelled from the National Party and were later joined by two other resignations.[72] For his followers, Treurnicht had now become a symbol of Afrikaner resistance and a saviour of the *volk*.[73] He moved quickly to form the Conservative Party (CP), which was inaugurated in Pretoria on 20 March 1982. The boisterous crowd of 8,000 included members of white supremacist movements such as the Afrikaner Weerstandsbeweging (AWB), the Kappiekommando (Bonnet Commando, an ultra-conservative women's organisation), Aksie Eie Toekoms (Action for Our Own Future, a political breakaway from the Broederbond, founded by the irrepressible Willem Lubbe) and Connie

Mulder's National Conservative Party (NCP), which had broken away from the National Party in 1979 in the wake of the Information Scandal, by which the state sought to influence the American government. Schwarz's fears were well founded.[74]

With great speed, the CP established its own newspaper, *Patriot*, and enjoyed favourable coverage in *Oggendblad* and *Hoofstad* – the latter, as noted earlier, edited by Treurnicht from 1967 till 1970. It will be recalled that *Hoofstad* had cast doubts on the veracity of the Holocaust and had regularly raised the issue of domestic and international Jewish power. It had even attempted to rehabilitate Hitler,[75] and had called for the release from prison of Rudolf Hess.[76] And yet, the CP had no desire to whip up a 'Jewish question'. Its primary goal was racial partition and the perpetuation of white supremacy in South Africa. Treurnicht's essential commitment was to the idea of a (white) Christian republic. Under such a government, wrote Hartzenberg, his right-hand man, there would be religious freedom, but only Christianity would be promoted. Education would be Christian National, and there would be no provision in schools for other religions.[77]

How did all this relate to Treurnicht's attitude to South African Jews? In a 1988 interview the CP leader made it clear that although his was a 'Christian National' party, Jewish membership was permitted. 'Should Jews be interested in our party, the main question would be, could they subscribe to our policy? If they could do that, then it's up to them. Even the National Party, its political policy still on paper as Christian National, has accepted Jewish membership over the years.'[78] Jews, then, were regarded as part and parcel of the white community.[79] Even 'dual loyalty' was not an issue for Treurnicht.[80] When asked about his stand on Holocaust revisionism, he indicated that 'I may have certain reservations about the Holocaust, but I do not think it could contribute to good race relations to make that a bone of contention'. Asked what he meant by 'certain reservations', he replied: 'There are people who think six million may be a rather high figure, but I am not making an issue of that. We know, as Afrikaners, what we went through during our second war against the British in 1899, and it's a sensitive issue.'[81]

It is apparent that Treurnicht did not see antisemitism as a 'real factor' in South African politics. 'I think in any country where there is a considerable Jewish population, I think people are aware of the presence of a Jewish community ... I do not think that anti-Semitism is something real or organised in South Africa.'[82]

The AWB

Foremost among those small, reactionary and menacing radical white right movements that had mushroomed in South Africa from the early 1970s was the AWB. It was founded by Eugène Terre'Blanche, a 32-year-old policeman turned farmer who had unsuccessfully stood as a candidate for the HNP in the Heidelberg constituency in 1970. He and six collaborators met secretly in the garage of Terre'Blanche's house in Heidelberg on 7 July 1973. At that time, the Bureau for State Security was monitoring the activities of the radical right, and it was prudent for Terre'Blanche and his colleagues to be cautious.[83] Public awareness of the AWB would only come later.

At the meeting, the seven men explored the possibilities of non-parliamentary Afrikaner action to block National Party reforms and curtail the influence of aliens and enemies of the Afrikaner. Jews were among those enemies – if not *the* enemy, at least for some. Indeed, when Terre'Blanche had stood as a candidate for the HNP in Heidelberg three years before founding the AWB, he spoke of the Afrikaner having to defend South Africa while 'the Englishman and Jew is at home with their millions of rands' acquired by exploiting the *volk*.[84] But the fundamental aim of the AWB was to maintain white supremacy and racial separation, which were seen to be under threat as Prime Minister Vorster deviated from apartheid's fundamental premises. Primarily, the AWB targeted the support of disillusioned and fearful Afrikaners whose numbers had grown as popular pressures, both international and domestic, gathered momentum.

Within a year of the movement's founding, the press was commenting on the AWB's subversive political agenda. *Beeld*, a *verligte* daily, was the first to raise the threat, reporting that members of the AWB 'were racist, antisemitic people who were expelled from the Broederbond, Ruiterwag and Rapportryers, former members of Dr Albert Hertzog's Afrikaner Order, militant Hertzogites and other Verkramptes'.[85] In other words, supporters of the movement were political dropouts on the margins of mainstream Afrikaner politics. In fact, AWB henchmen could be likened to the Freikorps or early Nazis in Weimar Germany rather than the disgruntled Afrikaners who had joined the HNP.

Informed by an exclusivist *Weltanschauung*, the AWB employed a fundamentalist Christian and *völkisch* vocabulary. Its Programme of Principles clearly stated that the movement wished to do away with the 'British-Jewish parliamentary system' and unite all 'White Christians' into one great Afrikanerdom, but only white Christians who were fluent in Afrikaans and possessed undivided loyalty to the *volk* and the Republic could be admitted.[86] This was the language of the 1930s echoing, and in parts almost replicating, the language of the radical right 'shirtist' movements of earlier decades. According to a contemporary analyst of the movement, it was fair to characterise the AWB as 'a combination of the outward characteristics of National Socialism, while on a purely philosophical level it is a combination of extreme Afrikaner nationalism and Christian anti-Semitism'.[87]

Like its forebears, the AWB depicted the South African government as 'a victim of the British-Jewish money power', which, it claimed, 'softens the resistance of the white'.[88] Here was the classic bogey: the Jew as a subversive threat to the status quo. In line with SED Brown and Ivor Benson, the AWB looked askance at Israel, describing that country as the locus of global Jewish hegemony and Prime Minister Vorster as 'a pawn of Zionism'.[89] Greyshirt leader Louis Weichardt (by then retired from the Senate) would certainly have felt comfortable with such language, as would Ray Rudman. International Jewish conspiracies had always been a staple of the radical right.

Significant elements within the Afrikaner population applauded the efforts and goals of the AWB and, rather worryingly, *Die Transvaler* expressed concern that senior officers in the police and defence force were being recruited to the movement within two years of its founding. It now had 'enough support to move in the open', claimed the National Party daily.[90] Alarm bells were also sounded in the *Sunday Times*: 'Leading lawyers, former members of the security forces and at least one leading Transvaal Nationalist are involved with a paramilitary movement which is planning an anti-Black and anti-British-Jewish dictatorship in South Africa,' wrote the journalist JHP Serfontein.[91] This growing support for the AWB was reiterated by the *Rand Daily Mail*'s Keith Abendroth:

> The militant extreme right-wing organisation, the Afrikaner Weerstand Beweging [sic] has started actively recruiting members from South Africa's armed forces and police – backing recruitment with anti-Semitic propaganda. Recruiting letters have gone out from the organisation to senior officers of the Air Force, Navy, Army and Police. With each letter is a mass of literature, most of it anti-Semitic, accusing South African Jewry of being 'leftist' and behind anti-Government moves... The letters say the organisation wants to mobilise the forces of Afrikanerdom against communistic influences – largely backed by South African Jews it says – at work in South Africa. They quote largely from a publication by the Historical Review Press of Richmond, Surrey, written by Professor Richard Harwood, of the University of London. The import of the work is that international Jewry is making political capital out of the 'massacre of 6-million Jews' by the Nazi regime during the Second World War. In fact, says Prof Harwood, there were only 3-million Jews altogether in Germany when war broke out and he quotes documents to state that not more than 1.5 million Jews died of all causes during the war.[92]

The matter was clearly of concern. Indeed, the *Rand Daily Mail* devoted an editorial to the subject:

> We are dealing here with a group of people who make mischief with the hoary old anti-Semitic smears that South African Jews are leading an anti-Government movement. And the calibre of the movement can be gauged by the fact that its source of inspiration is a British professor who claims it is untrue that 6-million Jews died in Nazi hands during the Second World War. The figure, he says, in callously dismissive terms, was probably 'no more' than 1.5-million – including 900,000 in concentration camps. The Prime Minister has said we must build friendship between the races in South Africa. The Afrikaner Weerstandbeweging [sic] is doing just the opposite – and the consequences can only be dangerously harmful.[93]

Yet despite its apparent success at recruitment, it took three years before the AWB held its first public meeting. This took place in the small Transvaal town of Brits, where speakers spelled out the movement's message to an audience of about 300. The hall was noticeably decorated in a manner reminiscent of the Nazi party rallies of the 1930s. Two large Vierkleur flags and an enormous banner with the insignia of the AWB were used to enhance the fascist-like aesthetic that served as a backdrop to the speakers on the stage. From the windows hung ten red banners with a white circle enclosing what appeared to be a three-legged swastika. Military marches were played over the public address system, amplifying the fascist ambience and enhancing the militant messages of the speakers, who made it clear that the aim of the AWB was to abolish democracy (including political parties), and to create a third Republic of South Africa governed autocratically according to the true 'will of the people'. This would replace rule by the 'obsolete British-Jewish parliamentary system'.[94]

Here was neo-fascism in action despite AWB denials.[95] The *mise en scène* mattered. Even the language employed by the charismatic and demagogic Terre'Blanche (which the BBC's Graham Leach described as 'a symphony') was *völkisch* and, as the infamous Holocaust denier David Irving said on a visit to South Africa many years later, was reminiscent of the Führer.[96] Like his putative Nazi mentor, Terre'Blanche had his own elite paramilitary youth brigade, the Stormvalke (Storm Falcons), which resembled Hitler's Brownshirts, and, like Hitler, Terre'Blanche's greatest asset was his oratory. His booming voice and studied theatrical style, with its appeal to Afrikaner history and myth, never failed to arouse an audience.[97] The movement's swastika-type emblem clearly implied that Jews would not be comfortable in a 'Christian country' under Terre'Blanche's leadership.[98] Certainly, the AWB's Programme of Principles of 1979 left no room for ambiguity:

Eugene Terre'Blanche. *Courtesy: Special Collections, National Library of South Africa, Cape Town*

> To all fellow Afrikaners! The AWB introduces itself to you, not as an organisation with new and unreasonable claims, but as the movement which is the medium for the continued struggle for Christian self-preservation.
>
> Nineteen centuries ago the Christian decided to offer resistance when the Jews crucified Christ. He (the Christian) became a soldier and fighter, for he had to fight and to offer resistance against the devious methods of the anti-Christ. The Afrikaner volk, true to generations past, has not disturbed that continuity. He rose up and offered resistance when the Christian National view was threatened by an Anglo-Saxon world.
>
> True to the methods of the anti-Christ, which resides in International Judaism, [this anti-Christ] has carefully stretched its tentacles around the resources of the fatherland. With the help of a denationalized government the Afrikaner has been disinherited of his greatest asset – the natural wealth of his land.[99]

Unlike the efforts of Rudman, Schoeman, Brown and Benson, the AWB's were focused not on print propaganda but on political action. This was vividly apparent in March 1979 when a group of AWB thugs marched into a hall where the well-known Afrikaner historian Floris Albertus ('Floors') van Jaarsveld was delivering a lecture and proceeded to tar and feather the learned and terrified professor because he had earlier upset the AWB when he raised questions around the interpretation of the Day of the Covenant (an Afrikaner commemoration of the Battle of Blood River of 1838). This fascist-like behaviour was widely covered in the press, which highlighted the threat posed by the militant movement.[100] The AWB could not have hoped for better publicity. It had finally achieved national prominence.

The incident set off a panic, with commentators talking of a dangerous turn among Afrikaners and comparing the rhetoric and message of the AWB to that of Weichardt's antisemitic Greyshirts in the 1930s. 'The Afrikanerweerstandsbeweging (Afrikaner Resistance Movement) in whose name Professor FA van Jaarsveld was tarred and feathered is a clandestine militant National Organisation with a neo-Fascist outlook,' wrote Patrick Laurence in the *Eastern Province Herald*. 'It symbolises the embodiment of militant Afrikaner nationalism and neo-fascism through its emblem – the Vierkleur of the old South African Republic and a three-legged Swastika formed by figure sevens.'[101] Writing in the *Sunday Tribune*, Peter Fabricius claimed the movement reeked of antisemitism and naked racism. 'The movement does not categorically deny its resemblance to the Nazis, preferring to leave that decision to observers, but it is obvious the resemblance is not coincidental.'[102]

Fears of a radical white right resurgence were exacerbated when the HNP increased its support five-fold in the Randfontein by-election in July 1979.[103] As mentioned earlier, the HNP also increased its vote in the 1981 general election, capturing nearly 200,000 votes or 13.1 per cent of votes cast. Subsequent by-elections revealed that the National Party was haemorrhaging Afrikaner votes while the AWB was simultaneously gaining more attention. For most Afrikaners, however, the bombastic style of Terre'Blanche was unappealing and, for the disillusioned on the far right, the formal politics of Treurnicht's CP were considered a more realistic option.

Terre'Blanche, meanwhile, relished the media attention. His fiery speeches were replete with attacks on the National Party and promises of safeguarding the future for whites. The anti-Jewish vitriol was unabashed. Shortly after the Van Jaarsveld incident, Terre'Blanche claimed that the Information Scandal was nothing compared to 'money bled out of the South African economy by the forces of international monetary Zionism'.[104] The 'octopus arm of Anglo American, international Jewry, the anti-Christ, the international money-powers … have bought our country and now rule it,' declaimed Terre'Blanche at a political rally in Pretoria.[105] On another occasion, Freemasons (long associated with so-called subversive Jews) were described as a threat and a 'tool in the hands of international Jewry'.[106]

Clearly encouraged by the political mood, and anticipating growing political support, the AWB declared in April 1980 that it would become a political party, fighting for a *volkstaat* (ethnic Afrikaner state) under the Blanke Volkstaat Party (White People's State Party, or BVP). In effect the BVP would be the political wing of the AWB, whose aim was self-determination in an Afrikaner fatherland.[107] Predictably exclusivist, the *volkstaat* would be socialist in orientation, and the mines – hitherto in in the hands of *volksvreemdes* or aliens, a clear reference to Jews – would be nationalised.[108]

Towards a Volksfront

As tensions mounted and the Botha administration moved further along the path of reform, hate-mongers and fantasists, desperate to block the forces of change, threatened the South African state. Terre'Blanche slammed the creation of the President's Council, expressing horror at its multiracial composition, even though black Africans were excluded from it. But the inclusion of Muslims, Chinese and 'leftists' was unacceptable.[109] In fact, reform of any kind was unacceptable – and Jews were to blame. The villains targeted by Terre'Blanche were the mining magnate Harry Oppenheimer and the 'International-Zionist-Leftist-communist money powers' who had stolen the country's wealth from the Afrikaners.[110] At a meeting in Krugersdorp, he told a large audience that 'the Jews, the British, the Indians and the Chinese will never get the *volk*'s country'. 'Kill the bastards' was the roaring response of the crowd.[111]

Focusing on outside forces – especially the Jewish, communist and Zionist threat – was patently a way of exploiting the fears of both Afrikaners and English speakers that the Christian order and racial status quo were under threat.[112] Labour laws had been liberalised, black African squatter settlements had expanded around the larger cities, personal income per head for whites had declined, and unrest was endemic.[113] Indicative of growing anger, a large rally of the right was held in Johannesburg in November 1981.[114] A few months earlier, Connie Mulder had launched an umbrella right-wing organisation, Aksie Red Blank Suid-Afrika (Front for Saving White South Africa, or ARBSA). Among those who joined this initiative were the National Conservative Party, AWB, Kappiekommando, Aksie Eie Toekoms, and the South Africa First Campaign, set up by Brendon Wilmer, a renegade British fascist and friend of Ivor Benson who had come to South Africa in 1971.[115] Here were the early beginnings of what the sociologist Janis Grobbelaar refers as a *volksfront* or people's front – 'a network of organisational complexes and formations' with the CP at the helm.[116]

Tensions heightened as the National Party embarked on its tricameral initiative whereby parliamentary representation would be shared with Indians and Coloureds. That the black African majority was excluded (ensuring a white veto over policy) made little difference for the CP. A common legislature was seen as a vehicle to erode the Christian state: it was entirely unacceptable.[117] Even the promise made by the National Party that one of the goals of the new constitution was 'to uphold Christian and civilised standards with recognition and protection of freedom of faith and worship' failed to assuage the opposition forces.[118]

Support for the CP grew, while Terre'Blanche continued to scapegoat 'subversive' Jews, whom he accused of pulling the political strings. In a speech at Kroonstad he warned that foreign capital was enriching itself through '*boeresweet*' (Boer sweat) and that the 'Boer' would no longer 'be a slave to the small political smurfs ("*die klein politieke smurfies*" or "money launderers") who are nothing but the backscratchers of the Oppenheimer regime and international Jewry'.[119] In similar fashion he complained that the *volk* was being exploited by the mine owners, who were replacing white mineworkers with blacks. 'I say send the fat Jew who owns the mine down and make him do the work.'[120] This sort of rhetoric was the stock in trade of Terre'Blanche.

Given such vilification, it is difficult to reconcile the claim made by Terre'Blanche to the journalist Kitt Katzin that Jews had nothing to fear from the AWB and that there would be no discrimination. 'You don't understand that neither I nor the AWB are anti-Semitic,' he told Katzin. 'Rather we are pro-Christian – and Christian ideology, which is the fundamental pillar of Afrikaner nationalism, and of an AWB government, remains non-negotiable. Nobody who is not a Christian will ever sit in our parliament.' The Jews 'can remain in South Africa, but they will never be given the right to vote or to participate in an exclusive Christian White Afrikaner government. They are not Christian and South Africa is not their fatherland. Jews could enjoy political rights in Israel, their fatherland,' insisted Terre'Blanche.[121]

A few months later, a row broke out after Terre'Blanche – in a rousing rally in the Johannesburg City Hall – complained about the rapid de-racialisation of the densely populated and historically cosmopolitan suburb of Hillbrow. Once in power, he warned, the AWB 'will chase all the Kaffirs out of the Jewish buildings'.[122] Apparently, he believed that a great many of the apartment buildings in the suburb were owned by Jews. But the press understood the AWB leader to be saying that, once in power, Jews and blacks would be chased out of Johannesburg.[123] A media furore erupted, with the Jewish Board of Deputies issuing a statement in which it expressed its horror and shock. But Terre'Blanche never tried to correct the misunderstanding.[124]

Given Terre'Blanche's vituperative and ugly utterances about Jews, it is not surprising that an investigation by the Hervormde Kerk found that the AWB 'had a strong anti-Jewish attitude which was based on the acceptance of a Zionist conspiracy towards world domination and a manipulation of the money power of the world'. 'A general hatred of Jews is often apparent,' noted its report.[125] Yet Terre'Blanche persisted with the line that he was not an antisemite. 'I am an Afrikaner Nationalist. I am not a fascist or national socialist,' he told Patrick Laurence.[126] Blacks would be guest workers in his *volkstaat*, and non-Afrikaners would have the vote so long as they became naturalised citizens of the *volkstaat*. But they would have to be Christians. Jews were excluded. 'I am a Christian,' explained Terre'Blanche, 'and Christian convictions are the reason for the *volk*.' The AWB, as he put it, 'was a cultural political movement. We are what you call a "volks" movement.'[127] He rejected the Westminster parliamentary system, which he characterised as a 'British Jewish' concept foisted on the Afrikaners after the Anglo-Boer War.[128]

This outlook, coupled with a hostility to liberalism and Marxism, remained a constant. For Terre'Blanche, Jewish loyalty was primarily towards Israel and was rooted in their religion. 'They are not Christians,' he told Tzippi Hoffman and Alan Fischer in an interview conducted in 1988: 'they themselves don't want to marry out of the Jewish religion. They stick by the laws of Moses. It's religion for them to be loyal to their people and their beliefs. I don't hate them. There is just a great difference between the Jew and the Christian.'[129]

New Radical Groups

While the AWB was by far the most prominent movement on the radical right through the 1980s, it was not the only extremist group. As we have seen, several fringe groups had been established in the wake of the Second World War, among them Rudman's resuscitated NS Boerestaat and its English counterpart, the South African Anglo-Nordic Union. Similar groups proliferated through the 1970s and 1980s as domestic and international pressures mounted to dismantle apartheid. Among those that pockmarked the political landscape through the 1980s – effectively constituting a *volksfront* engaged in *kultuurpolitiek* or cultural politics – were:

- Die Vereniging van Oranjewerkers (The Society of Orange Workers), founded in June 1980.[130]
- Toekomsgesprek (Forum for the Future), established in 1983 as an alternative to the Broederbond.
- Die Afrikaner Volkswag (The Afrikaner People's Guard), an exclusivist Afrikaner right-wing organisation established in 1984.
- The Afrikaner Nasionaal Sosialisties Party (Afrikaner National Socialist Party, or ANS), founded by Koos Vermeulen in 1987 after he had broken away from the AWB.[131]
- The Blanke Bevrydingsbeweging (White Liberation Movement), or BBB, founded in 1985 by Johan Schabort, a professor of biochemistry at the Rand Afrikaans University, and Jan S Smith,

who held a master's degree in nuclear physics.[132]
- The Boerestaat Party (Boer State Party), founded in 1988 by Robert van Tonder.[133]
- Die Kerk van die Skepper (Church of the Creator, or KVS) – a South African offshoot of Bernhardt (Ben) Klassen's American Church of the Creator – founded in about 1980 by Jan S Smith, formerly of the BBB.[134]
- The Stallard Foundation, an English right-wing organisation established in 1985.[135]

While memberships of these groups were small and fluid, and while their ideas were not always aligned, all were distinguished by brazen racism, invariably informed by a pernicious social Darwinism. 'We believe in the genetic superiority of the white race, and we believe it is the duty of the white race to stop the natural increase and decadence of the black races from destroying this planet,' the BBB's Schabort told Helen Zille, a journalist at the *Rand Daily Mail*.[136] Their agendas – often informed by a conspiratorial outlook – were driven by the gradual erosion of apartheid, widespread 'township' unrest, significant labour instability, including major mineworkers' strikes, and the increasing prospect of power-sharing or majority rule, epitomised in a meeting between liberal and reformist Afrikaners and the ANC in Dakar, Senegal, in 1987.[137] For the BBB, the Jew, inhabiting a grey zone between white and black, was considered alien and disloyal and became a convenient scapegoat. According to *The Star*, its founder, Johan Schabort, went so far as to claim that if it came to power, South Africa's 130,000 Jews would be banished:

> The Blankebevrydingsbeweging (BBB), South Africa's newest and most right-wing order, classifies 'groups from the Middle East', such as Jews, as non-white, along with blacks, coloureds and Asians. All such people are regarded as undesirable and decadent under the terms of its blueprint for a new, white-dominated South Africa. The 'Middle Eastern' groups, says the BBB, though classified today as white, were originally declared non-white and will accordingly be reclassified under a BBB government and 'repatriated' along with blacks. Urban blacks would be banished to the homelands – and Jews could opt to join

The Resurgence of Exclusivism and Neo-Nazism: 1970s and 1980s

them or settle in a foreign country of their choice ... The BBB, also known as the White Liberation Movement, and which boldly claims to be more radical than the Afrikanerweerstandsbeweging (AWB), links South African Jews to the SA Communist Party, the ANC, and to acts of terrorism, and says their presence is not conducive to peace and security in this country... The BBB's emergence as a Nazi-like pressure group has drawn severe criticism from National Party MPs and other political leaders, who say it should be banned. But Professor Schabort, who believes that Adolf Hitler's cause was just, and that the Holocaust never happened, says the BBB has come to stay.[138]

Like the BBB, Robert van Tonder's Boerestaat Party hankered after a pure white state for 'Boers'.[139] His wish was to resurrect the old Boer Republics. Fiercely anti-English, Van Tonder in fact left the National Party in 1961 after Verwoerd had appointed English speakers to his cabinet. His views were outlined in his book *Boerestaat*, which argued that South Africa's declaration of a Republic in 1961 had been a betrayal of the nineteenth-century South African Republic and the Orange Free State and was a threat to Boer identity. Two years before publishing *Boerestaat* in 1987, Van Tonder had written a five-page article lauding Hitler in *Die Stem van die Boerevolk*, described as an independent right-wing newspaper.[140] 'An Open Letter to the Rellys, Cohens, Blooms and Oppenheimers' by Johann Pienaar provides a taste of its journalese and is a reminder that in radical right circles Jews were still considered disloyal and hypocritical:

> Sirs, when you without any fuss drove the Palestinians out of Israel and took the country in 1948 and established a National State there, what you did was right. Today you say it is still right. Why then do you whine when the Boers also demand their own National State and are also going to get it? ... When it will become too hot for a Jew in South Africa, then he will flee to his National State, Israel. Well then it is becoming too hot for our decent Boers and that is why we will all move over to the National State. Just as you don't want to mix with Arafat, the Boers don't want to mix with Mandela and Tutu ... I think you ought to understand us better because we recently received a document from Israel in which we Boers were requested to continue ruling the country because you are safer in a Boer government.[141]

Die Kerk van die Skepper was even more obsessed with Jews. This is not surprising since its leader, Jan S Smith, had drawn his inspiration from the notoriously antisemitic Russian-born Bernhardt ('Ben') Klassen, who had founded the Church of the Creator in the United States in 1973.[142] Believing in the subversive qualities of Jews and especially the danger of communism – and combining these fears with the prospect of black rule in South Africa – Smith expressed hatred for 'Jews, Kaffirs and the mud races' and went so far as to advocate their extermination.[143]

Far-right movements were clearly burgeoning in the 1980s and displayed a discernible interconnectedness.[144] Several of these organisations gathered at the Rebecca Street cemetery in Pretoria in 1987 to mark the death of Rudolf Hess. Organised and hosted by the ANS, the gathering included the AWB as well as the BBB. 'The Good Comrade' (a popular post-First World War German song) was sung,[145] and Dr WR Helm, a retired German scientist, gave a Nazi salute. Some guests even wore Nazi armbands.[146]

In the tempest that followed, Terre'Blanche announced that he had wanted to pay homage to a great German leader.[147] 'Although Jewish capital controls the economy of the country, right-inclined people in the country will not allow their thought process to be controlled,' he told *Die Vaderland*. The press, he asserted, was controlled by 'arrogant Zionists'.[148] Schabort too defended the presence of the BBB at the memorial. 'There would be a dangerous situation for South Africa if Jews are allowed to bring to a head the victimization of Nazis,' he told *Business Day*. He then went on to link Jews to the Anglo-Boer War and the SACP, and commented on the over-representation of Jews among the white accused in the Rivonia Trial. 'Jews have no sympathy for whites and are on the side of those who murder whites,' he said.[149]

Such rhetoric – as well as the singling out of the 'liberal' and 'communist' Jew – had little traction at this time. Jews were well integrated into white society and whites were preoccupied primarily with the race question. Moreover, growing ties between South Africa and Israel ensured the erosion of antisemitism. In fact, the 'Jewish question' was not even raised during the 1987 general election campaign in which the Conservative Party, supported in the main by lower-income Afrikaners, emerged as the official opposition, replacing the liberal PFP in that role. Treurnicht had benefited from a rash of strikes raging across the country, largely organised by the Congress of South African Trade Unions (COSATU), a labour federation that had been established in 1985. In addition, the CP's success emanated from the rise of the United Democratic Front (UDF), a non-racial and broad-based umbrella opposition movement that had been founded in 1983, as well as from growing economic sanctions and international pressure against the apartheid regime. The Conservative Party was now able to win 22 seats in parliament or 26.62 per cent of the total white vote. In the general election two years later, it increased its representation to 39 seats or 31.52 per cent of the total vote.[150] Once again there was no mention of a 'Jewish question' at the hustings.

A Last Gasp

For Afrikaner fantasists, however, the Jew remained the *éminence grise* in the South African political drama.[151] This was vividly illustrated when, within days of President De Klerk's 2 February 1990 'Rooi Vrydag' (Red Friday) speech – which announced the forthcoming release from gaol of Nelson Mandela and effectively demolished the apartheid order by unbanning the ANC, the SACP and the PAC – the AWB and other radical rightists protested on the streets of Pretoria. At the start of formal proceedings on Church Square, an Israeli flag was burned on the speaker's podium and a banner carried a Star of David and the words 'Hitler was right, Jews are communists'. Several swastikas were also held aloft, and Terre'Blanche and Van Tonder tried to hand over 'thirty pieces of silver' to a senior police officer observing the protest.[152] Thirty pieces of silver, of course, related to the price for which Judas Iscariot allegedly betrayed Jesus, according to the Gospel of Matthew.

A wave of anti-Jewish incidents was reported in the immediate aftermath of the release of Mandela.[153] Synagogues and Jewish schools received hate mail, the Kimberley synagogue was vandalised, and anti-Jewish graffiti sprayed on several Jewish institutions. Cemetery desecrations also occurred, and pig's heads with ugly slogans were placed at some Jewish centres.[154] Evidently the dramatic normalisation of South African political and social life unleashed what De Klerk described as a psychosis driven by the CP.[155] *Volksblad* shared these concerns:

> The intimidation of the Jewish community by for example the placing of bloody pig's heads at synagogues, offensive slogans against walls and the desecration of Jewish graves stems from anti-Semitism which has been fed throughout the centuries by hatred and small-mindedness ... And on top of that, successful Jews of whom there are many in all fields of life, are portrayed by witch hunters as the symbol of the international money power which ostensibly wants to dominate and rule everything and everybody ... In South Africa it is especially from far-right circles that the intimidation and insults originate, as well as attempts to sow animosity between Afrikaners and Jews.[156]

Although white radical rightists primarily feared the prospect of 'majority rule' and the demise of Afrikaner (and white) power, apocalyptic fears were, at least for some, entwined with sinister anti-Jewish motifs and sentiment. The Jewish Board of Deputies in fact recognised this and met with the commissioner of police and the head of the security police to share its concerns.[157] The meeting, however, appears to have had little impact. Protests persisted in the ensuing months: swastikas and AWB insignias were periodically painted on synagogues and cemeteries were desecrated.[158] But anti-Jewish extremists remained on the fringe of broader South African politics and their influence, though disturbing for Jews, was minimal. Individuals preaching Jew-hatred were leaders of marginal and disaffected groups; they did not represent an ethno-nationalist movement attempting to mould a 'people' or *volk* in terms of language, religion, culture and divine mission by using the Jew as a classic 'other' – as had been the case with *völkisch* Afrikaner nationalism in the 1930s. Nevertheless, anti-Jewish incidents were regularly reported and the threat from extremists never quite abated. Indeed, three years after the release of Mandela, white supremacists disrupted political negotiations at the World Trade Centre in Kempton Park and held a banner aloft which read 'Hitler was right – communism is Jewish'. When Terre'Blanche appeared in court a few months later for defying a summons to testify before the Goldstone Commission (appointed by De Klerk to investigate state-instigated destabilisation), a banner read 'Who is Goldstone? King of the Jews'. The placard also displayed both a Star of David and a hammer and sickle.[159]

Although the prospect of Eugène Terre'Blanche's white Christian society in which Jews would have no place might have faded, antisemitism on the radical white right – which included English speakers – continued alongside dreams of racial partition.[160] In a symbolic reminder that hope springs eternal, a one-time grand wizard of the Ku Klux Klan, David Duke, made a private visit to South Africa shortly before the country's first democratic election in April 1994. 'His purpose here', noted an official ANC statement, 'seems to be to stoke up the war psychosis which has already been ignited by a broad coalition of Black and White Right-wing extremists.'[161] By then, however, South Africa was on the road to a new non-racial and democratic future, and atavistic Jew-hatred would provide diminishing political returns. On the other hand, as politics and society normalised, Jew-hatred beyond the radical white right began to surface.

FOUR

Into the 'New' South Africa: 1990 to the Present

Hitler should have burnt all Jews.
Dawood Khan, member of the Western Cape ANC regional executive, speaking during protest outside the Israeli Embassy, *Cape Times*, 8 April 1993

I have nothing against Jews or against the Jewish religion. Jews as in practitioners of the Jewish faith but Zionism is an ideology of the devil. Zionism is an evil ideology. It's, it's an evil, it's an ideology of Satan. I will never say anything in support or good about Zionism never ever.
Talk-show host Jon Qwelane, Channel Islam International (Lenasia), 9 July 2008

I want to state for the record that we are not anti-Jew because that will be tantamount to racism. So we are not anti-Jew and we are not anti-Christian but we need to tell the world that Zionism is an entity, is an entity that hides Judaism. They do all these atrocities in the good name of Judaism, and the Jewish people.
Sheikh Alexander, al-Quds Mosque, speaking on Radio 786, 14 November 2014

There is no such thing as a good Jew...
Jan Lamprecht, History Reviewed website, 19 November 2019

Enter the Majority

Hitherto our examination of antisemitism in apartheid South Africa has been confined to the white population. Readers will understandably wonder why this is so. Whites, after all, numbered only one in five of the total population in 1948, a proportion that had declined to less than one in six by 1990. The reason for this is simple: Jews had never been a specific political concern for the black majority, which included black Africans, Indians and Coloureds.[1] Their struggle was against white domination and oppression. Colour was the cardinal divide. Blacks (in the broad 'non-white' sense of the word) and whites interacted on a daily level in the workplace, in domestic situations and other non-formal settings, but ordinary social engagement was the exception. Centuries of geographical separation built on slavery, colonialism, segregation and, after 1948, 'grand apartheid' ensured a separation of people's worlds. That is not to say that blacks did not construct views of the Jew, but, besides a tantalising hint or two, history has left scant evidence.[2]

Our first glimpse (and it is only a glimpse) into black attitudes towards Jews is to be found in a 1970 survey of black African and Coloured matriculants in Soweto. Here Stuart Buxbaum found that both Coloureds and black Africans in a Soweto matriculation group generally held unfavourable views of Jews. This he attributed to a 'carry over of a general attitude of social distance of many groups towards Jews' as well as the generalised phenomenon of 'haves' and 'have-nots.' Buxbaum surmised that Jews were 'singled out by the non-Whites as being the visible symbol of White financial wealth, a direct result of the depressed economic position of the non-Whites'.[3] Why Jews specifically were 'singled out' is not explained.

A year later, in a carefully crafted survey of black African matriculants in Soweto, the sociologist Melville Edelstein found that the pupils he interviewed experienced a greater 'social distance' in relation to Jews than to English speakers in general, although less than towards Afrikaners. Those interviewed told Edelstein that a black African who was loath to part with his money was described as being as 'stingy as a Jew'. In Edelstein's view prejudice arose from New Testament teaching in school and church.[4] It may well be that there is an added cause:

the resentment of blacks (including Coloureds and Indians) towards Jewish traders in town and country.[5] Marcia Leveson's examination of Jewish stereotypes in the fiction of black writers certainly reinforces this view, with the Jew typically portrayed as ugly, exploitative and powerful.[6] Saths Cooper, a psychiatrist and one-time president of the anti-apartheid Azanian People's Organisation (AZAPO), confirmed this perception in an interview conducted in the late 1980s. 'The common reaction – and this is throughout the black community – is to classify any exploiter as a Jew, even if he happens to have a black skin, he appears to be in the Shylock mould,' said Cooper.[7] Further attitudinal indications emerged in a 1990 survey conducted by the South African Zionist Federation among urban black African 'elites'. The study showed that they harboured substantial antipathy towards Jews. Almost one in five of the respondents said that the Jewish community 'irritated' them because, in descending order of frequency, they were parasites, snobs, racists, anti-Christ, and unpatriotic. Almost the same proportion approved of right-wing antisemitic actions, and nearly one in three considered the Jewish community to be 'mostly a liability' to South Africa.[8]

These attitudes surfaced publicly once the veil of apartheid was lifted. For example, during industrial action by black workers against the giant retailer Pick n Pay in 1994, a comment on one placard relating to the Jewish founder and CEO read: 'Mr Ackerman, remember Adolf Hitler'.[9] Specifically, Jewish 'capitalists' were identified as 'exploiters of the workers' at the time.[10] In the same year, antisemitic placards were displayed at six other strike sites around the country, and at some of these anti-Jewish slogans were chanted. A pamphlet accusing Jews of controlling the country and calling for the killing of the 'capitalist Jew pigs' was distributed at a Volkswagen strike in Port Elizabeth, although Volkswagen management had no Jewish members. Some of the placards read: 'Away with Jewish settlers!'; 'Jews dismiss innocent workers!' and 'Jews are union bashers'. In similar fashion, during a protest against the sacking of twenty workers in 1994 at Highlands House, a Cape Town Jewish aged home, two hundred workers shouted 'Away with Jews' and 'Jews are oppressing us and we are going to fight back'.[11] A further illustration that the anti-Jewish stereotype had penetrated beyond the white population is apparent in the words of the leader of the Johannesburg Tenants Association, Moses Moshoeshoe, who, during a strike in 1994, claimed (without evidence) that most of the slumlords were Jewish.[12] Little wonder that Saths Cooper told Tzippi Hoffman and Alan Fischer that, in the minds of 'blacks', Jews were associated with capitalism – which in turn meant propping up apartheid. Oppenheimer, he asserted, was identified as a symbol of exploitation.[13]

Clearly black Africans perceived Jews as an identifiable group within the broader white population, sometimes labelling them as outsiders or aliens. 'Our director Mr Victor Farkas is a foreigner i.e. a Jew,' wrote IT Zwelibanzi, National Union of Metalworkers shop steward at AfMag, to the Independent Exemption Board of the Metal and Engineering Industries Bargaining Council. 'He can leave and skip the country any time since his history with the company finance is not for good. Our previous management can witness to this.'[14]

The 'New' South Africa

The foregoing manifestations of strong anti-Jewish sentiments are not meant to suggest that the 'new' or democratic South Africa was awash with antisemitism. Deeper issues defined post-apartheid public life as the nation began to undo centuries of race-based policies. Renewal, redress and normalisation focused the attention of all politicians. Importantly, the 1996 Constitution celebrates cultural and religious diversity. Jew-hatred – like all forms of prejudice – is frowned upon. In fact, South Africa experiences relatively few anti-Jewish incidents. Yet it needs to be said that in certain quarters entrenched anti-Jewish stereotypes have persisted – albeit without great traction – and the harassment of Jewish individuals, vandalism of Jewish property and bomb threats, as well as offensive comments on radio talk shows and on television, accompanied the transformation from the old to the new South Africa. Tasteless editorial comment and newspaper cartoons occasionally appeared in the mainstream press, as did some blatantly antisemitic letters. The display of swastikas at sports matches at which Jewish day schools were competing and antisemitic attacks on university students also persisted,[15] as did reports of hate mail, threats of intimidation, social media abuse, verbal abuse, mass email postings, pamphlets, graffiti and vandalism.[16] One notorious Jew-hater, 'Snowy Smith', was charged with postings of antisemitic emails to Jewish individuals and institutions, journalists and news editors over three years. In one case, printed matter and DVDs containing similar material were sent to the office of a Jewish former High Court judge.[17] Violent incidents, however, were few and far between, but the language accompanying incidents was extreme and characterised mostly by expletives.[18]

South Africa has also not been immune to the uninhibited reach of social media. Facebook and Twitter posts contain threats and even calls to murder Jews. 'Attacking Jewish schools is mandatory till Jews go back to Poland. These bugs r a cancer' captures the tone of some anti-Jewish social media postings together with other examples:[19] 'Kill the Jew'; 'May you burn in Hell'; 'You must get out of South Africa and don't come back, you Jewish bastards'. 'Keep calm and kill the Jews' was posted on the ANC Youth League website.[20] At the outbreak of the Covid-19 pandemic in 2020, a social media post by Sebastian Sebbi Petersen, the leader of the fringe African Progressive Movement and a former deputy director-general of the Department of Correctional Services, claimed the virus was concocted by American and Israeli pharmaceutical companies.[21] Some talk shows have also provided a safe space for blatant Jew-hatred. For example, in a 2013 interview on Radio 702 (a Johannesburg station), the Pan Africanist Youth Congress spokesman, Sello Tladi, claimed that 'General Adolf Hitler' had been much better than Nelson Mandela. 'He did something for the German side, purging the Jews ... It is because of this Nelson Mandela that in South Africa the Jews and the white settlers don't even respect our human rights, they exploit our wealth and exploit our labour in this country.'[22]

Jewish businessmen were also frequently characterised as devious, and the Holocaust seen as a form of special pleading.[23] In 2015, a case of intimidation was laid against Thabo Elias Phahlamohlaka, who had repeatedly sent email messages to various leaders of the Jewish community blaming Jews for the prevalence of poverty in South Africa and, on frequent occasions, issuing threats if Jews did not remedy the situation.²⁴ Jews were also included in a tirade against business leaders by Edward Zuma, son of President Jacob Zuma. They 'are running the show without interference of the government', he wrote.²⁵ Although such pronouncements were tied to party-political factional battles within the ANC, it is not without significance that specifically Jewish business leaders were identified among those exploiting the country and ensuring poverty for the masses.

Extreme anti-Jewish statements or violent threats tend to coincide with tensions or conflict between Israelis and Palestinians. At such times a common feature of the discourse has been the ubiquity of the 'Hitler was right' theme.²⁶ 'I could have killed all the Jews, but I left some of them to let you know why I was killing them,' noted one observer with reference to the Nazi leader.²⁷ Invariably Jews were reminded of, and challenged on, their ties to Israel. Bongani Masuku, international relations secretary for COSATU, on several occasions threatened harm to Jews who continued to support Israel.²⁸ A popular radio talk show host, Jon Qwelane, did much the same at the time of Israel's Operation Cast Lead, a 22-day conflict with Gaza that began in late December 2008. 'I do agree totally with the theory that what the Jews are doing to the Palestinians right now renders Jews everywhere wherever they may be to be legitimate targets,' Qwelane told his listeners.²⁹

More disturbing were sentiments expressed by the Student Representative Council (SRC) and Progressive Youth Alliance (PYA) at the Durban University of Technology (DUT). Soon after former aeroplane hijacker and Palestinian activist Leila Khaled had spoken on the DUT campus in support of the (South African) Boycott, Divestment and Sanctions (BDS) campaign against Israel in 2015, the SRC and PYA presented a memorandum of demand to the vice-chancellor calling, inter alia, for the deregistration of Jewish students. 'As the SRC, we had a meeting and analysed international politics. We took the decision that Jewish students, especially those who do not support the Palestinian struggle, should deregister,' explained the secretary of the SRC, Mqondisi Duma.³⁰ Notably the vice-chancellor of DUT, Ahmed Bawa, quickly condemned the demand, which he called 'totally preposterous, unjust, unfair, unreasonable and unconstitutional', and added that the DUT did 'not discriminate against any person based on their race, religion, colour, ethnicity, sexual orientation or political affiliation'. Bawa committed DUT to working with the Jewish Board of Deputies and other civil society organisations in a programme of engagement with the SRC and PYA to address issues of tolerance and social cohesion.[31]

Notwithstanding Bawa's principled position, it became increasingly apparent that the line between 'Jew' and 'Zionist' was being blurred. Certainly, posters held aloft during anti-Zionist marches and graffiti often showed no distinction between opposition to Israel's policies, even its existence, and flagrant Jew-hatred.[32] Much the same applied to university protests where antisemitism was often blatant and sometimes violent. Jew-bashing had become increasingly acceptable. In 2016 the SRC president, Mcebo Dlamini, told a Human Rights Commission hearing into university transformation that Jewish students at the university received preferential treatment because of Jewish financial clout within the institution. Dlamini – described by the historian Vashna Jagarnath as a 'Hitler-loving homophobic fantasist' – also made anti-Jewish comments on social media, as well as in print and radio interviews, accusing Jews of exercising harmful and secretive control of everything through their financial power.[33] Even the Wits legal office was described by Dlamini as 'Zionist controlled'. One of his Facebook comments lauded Hitler and included a Nazi salute. In another he referred to Jews as 'Christ killers' who 'got what they deserved in the Holocaust'.[34] In yet another outburst on the Johannesburg radio station Power FM, he referred to the Jewish community as 'devils'.[35]

Clearly, the religious impulses that Edelstein had raised in his 1971 Soweto matriculant study as a possible source of anti-Jewish hatred cannot be discounted. In a 2018 Good Friday message issued in the name of the Economic Freedom Fighters (EFF), a parliamentary opposition party, its national spokesperson, Mbuyiseni Quintin Ndlozi, invoked the charge that Jews were guilty for the death of Jesus and drew parallels between what was referred to as 'the brutal death on the cross of Jesus Christ' and the alleged actions of 'the racist, murderous Apartheid Israeli regime'.[36] This might seem strange coming from a leader of a Marxist-oriented political party, but it may well reflect elements of Christian schooling (especially Catholic), which was a feature of black education even under the apartheid government.³⁷

From time to time, prominent public figures as well as academics have articulated a fundamental aggression towards and even hatred of Jews. For example, after covering a Jewish event, the deputy editor of the (Johannesburg) *Star*, Mathatha Tsedu, suggested that Jews should stop regarding themselves as exceptional. Israel and 'Jewish people' in general, he wrote, 'see themselves almost as a special breed that God loves more than others.'³⁸ Along similar lines, Mandla Seleoane, a research specialist in the Democracy and Governance Research Programme of the Human Sciences Research Council, used Karl Marx's writings to argue that as long as Jews persisted in the view that they were unique and God's chosen, they could not hope for acceptance by the rest of humanity. Seleoane went on to level wild charges regarding the 'extermination' of Palestinians by the Israelis.³⁹

Some politicians have also spoken negatively of Jews, but for the most part these outbursts are rare. They do, however, illustrate the tenacity and depth of Jew-hatred, not to mention a breach in the post-Holocaust norm against public antisemitic discourse. For example, Badih Chaaban, an African Muslim Party councillor in Cape Town, made his feelings quite clear when he allegedly said, 'There is something about Jews that everyone wants to "f**k them', that it was time for the Jews to be 'f**ked again' and that the final solution would be when 'five or six million Jews are bombed in one day'.⁴⁰ Less overt, but more insidious, the deputy minister of international relations and provincial leader of the ANC in the Western Cape, Marius Fransman, during a 2013 interview with Voice of the Cape (a Cape Town-based Muslim community radio station), alleged that Jewish businessmen in Cape Town were unfairly benefiting at the expense of the Muslim community because of the policies of the Democratic Alliance (DA), the ruling party in the Western Cape province.⁴¹ On being taken to task for his comments by the Jewish Board of Deputies, Fransman responded by accusing the Board of being disloyal to South Africa and of undermining the national interest by furthering Israel's agenda.⁴² Only a short time later, at a Cape Town Press Club meeting, Fransman claimed – without any evidence and quite incorrectly – that 98 per cent of land and property owners in Cape Town were white and most of these were Jews.⁴³ Fransman's colleague Sharon Davids also made an outrageous and invented assertion when she told the Western Cape provincial parliament that the DA had fabricated the drought-induced 2018 water crisis in Cape Town in order to obtain desalination contract kickbacks from the 'Jewish mafia'. In addition, she attributed opposition to Mayor Patricia de Lille within the DA to the fact that De Lille was opposed to the award of a Sea Point property in Cape Town for purposes of building a Jewish day school.⁴⁴ 'Premier Helen Zille is too much in love with the Jewish mafia,' claimed Davids. Ultimate proof offered by Davids that the DA was favouring Jews was supposedly evident in the party's leader, Mmusi Maimane, 'hanging out' with Michael Bagraim, a DA MP who had served in a senior position on the South African Jewish Board of Deputies.⁴⁵ This notion of the Board as a toxic institution reared itself again in 2021 when David Unterhalter, one of the finest legal minds in South Africa, was interviewed and rejected for a Constitutional Court position by the Judicial Service Commission. Representatives of the Black Lawyers Association questioned Unterhalter about his association with the Board, which they deemed was unaligned 'with the democratic values of the SA Constitution because of its support for "apartheid Israel"'.⁴⁶

Fantasies Persist

Holocaust denial and anti-Jewish fantasies have also persisted in the new South Africa,⁴⁷ as has the sale (albeit illegal) of *The Protocols of the Elders of Zion*.⁴⁸ In 1996 a former member of the National Intelligence Agency, PJ Pretorius, published *Volksverraad*, a book that ascribed the end of apartheid to the secret machinations of the Illuminati. In a work riddled with outlandish conspiracies, Jews were characterised by Pretorius as an unpatriotic transnational group bent on promoting their own interests.⁴⁹ A similar conspiratorial worldview informed *En Mammon het gesê: Laat ons geld maak* (And Mammon Said: Let Us Make Money) by Peter Banks (a pseudonym). In addition to claiming that the Holocaust was a fabrication, Banks accused the Rothschild family of manipulating the world.⁵⁰ Shortly after this book was published, Manie Maritz's *My lewe en strewe* (My Life and Struggle) was reissued as part of a series of works commemorating the centenary of the Anglo-Boer War. First published in 1939, the book was replete with anti-Jewish fantasies, including excerpts from *The Protocols of the Elders of Zion*.[51] Also of interest was the new 2018 edition of *Rivonia Unmasked: The South African State's Case against Nelson Mandela* by Lauritz Strydom, first published in 1963. Tellingly, the new edition included an 'Additional Appendix' entitled 'Mandela's Jews: Jewish Involvement in the Rivonia Plot'.[52]

In some ways these interventions were part of a 'pushback' on the part of an outraged radical white right that had not come to terms with democratic South Africa and laid blame for the new order on sinister, perfidious, cunning and powerful Jews. Omnipotent Jewry was a deep-rooted idea in these circles. The HNP's Leon Strydom, for instance, during a protest at the Union Buildings in Pretoria in 1997, accused 'Jewish financial power' of being responsible for the outlawing of Holocaust denial in Germany.[53] Two years later, Jani Allan, a journalist and Cape Talk radio host, interviewed Keith Johnson, leader of an American militia group who, in addition to diatribes against Israel, 'race-mixing' and homosexuals, called the Holocaust a hoax and claimed that rabbinical teachings promoted paedophilia.[54] Costas Zaverdinos, a mathematician at the University of Natal, had by then established an international reputation as a Holocaust denier through his letters to the press and public lectures.[55] Appointed to the editorial advisory committee of the *Journal of Historical Review* in 1997,[56] Zaverdinos was proof that South Africa remained a comfortable home for fantasists such as David Icke, a well-known British conspiracist who regularly visited the country. Adoring middle-class white audiences listened attentively to his bizarre theories, one of which claimed that an alien race of humanoid reptiles secretly controls the world. Icke also defended the authenticity of *The Protocols of the Elders of Zion* and accused Jews of having conspired to start both the first and second world wars.[57]

A young Cape Town sheikh, Mogamat Colby, studying at the Al-Azhar Institute in Cairo, speaking on Voice of the Cape, also attested to the veracity of *The Protocols of the Elders of Zion* and added that Jews controlled the 'economic systems in the world… all our land, all the means of the radio stations, the newspapers, the televisions – they are controlling all these things – and this is how they have full control over the whole world'.[58] In similar fashion, Sheikh Ebrahim Gabriels, president of the Muslim Judicial Council (MJC), the representative voice of the community, referred to Jews manipulating and corrupting the Gentiles through strategies spelled out in *The Protocols of Zion*.[59] The pugnacious Jon Qwelane also punted the *Protocols* and raised questions about what he termed the 'Holocaust business'. The numbers simply did not add up, he told listeners to Channel Islam International (CII), a 24-hour digital radio station broadcasting from Johannesburg and Durban to over 55 countries, with a claimed listenership of more than a million worldwide. Insisting that the *Protocols* were genuine, Qwelane disingenuously distanced himself from Jew-hatred by saying it was only Zionists – rather than Jews – whom he linked to the *Protocols*: 'The Zionists were so embarrassed when the *Protocols* came to light, they denied, they tried this, they tried that,' he said. 'Then you had Zionist-controlled courts in Switzerland and somewhere else declaring the book a fake and outlawing it, but Henry Ford would have none of that nonsense.' Events, continued Qwelane, have demonstrated the authenticity of the *Protocols*.[60] CII also hosted Daryl Bradford Smith, a well-known American-born anti-Jewish conspiracist based in Paris, who made no such distinctions: Zionism, Israel and Jews, together with Zionist bankers, the Rothschilds and 'billionaire Jewish money' in England, were all combined in a toxic mix. Smith made all kinds of bizarre claims, including an accusation that US president Barack Obama was working for 'the Zionist Jewish criminals' and that the ANC was in the hands of Zionists.[61]

In 2014 Steven Mitford Goodson, a former non-executive director of the South African Reserve Bank, published *Inside the South African Reserve Bank: Its Origins and Secrets Exposed* in which he wrote of Jewish skulduggery and machinations.[62] Unsurprisingly, Goodson denied the Holocaust and served as a contributing editor of *Barnes Review* (named after Harry Elmer Barnes, an early Holocaust denier), a publication run by the notorious American conspiracist Willis Carto. In a radio interview with Deanna Spingola, a well-known conspiracist working for the Republic Broadcasting Network in the United States, Goodson called the Holocaust a 'huge lie' that was created to extract large sums of money from Germany.[63]

It was, however, the HNP mouthpiece, *Die Afrikaner*, with its regular revisionist articles and letters, that remained a constant source of both Holocaust denial in South Africa and fantasies about Jewish financial power and machinations.[64] Zunata Kay was a particularly prominent contributor. For her, the Holocaust was a myth created by Jews in order to impose their so-called New World Order (NWO).[65] In a two-part article she claimed that the September 11 attacks on the United States had been orchestrated by the Jews and the Illuminati to justify a declaration of war against Islam, and were part of a conspiracy to force the United States into a war to enable the establishment of a new world order.[66]

The veracity of the Holocaust was also challenged in mainstream Muslim media and on Radio 786, the mouthpiece of the Islamic Unity Convention (IUC), an Islamist organisation founded in 1994.[67] Speaking from Switzerland on Radio 786 in 1997, Ahmed Huber suggested that the Holocaust was exaggerated,[68] and, one year later, on the same radio station, the Scottish historian Yaqub Zaki spoke at length about an 'imaginary Holocaust' and other Jewish conspiracies.[69] Falsity and truth were also tested by Jamiel McWilliams, a reporter from *Muslim Views*, who was among a group of journalists invited to the inaugural press briefing for the opening of the Cape Town Holocaust Centre in 1999. Although admitting to being moved by visuals of the death camps, McWilliams nevertheless alerted readers to the so-called controversies surrounding them. While acknowledging that they were 'terrible places', he noted that 'A lively "numbers game" has long been in play, and the exact purposes of the camps debated'.[70] In a subsequent series of articles McWilliams clarified his real sentiments about the Holocaust, invoking treacherous conspiracies, Zionist imperialism, Jewish dishonesty and denial of mass murder. For those wishing to face the 'truth', he recommended several 'denial' classics such as *The Hoax of the Twentieth Century*, by Arthur Butz; *The Six Million Swindle*, by AJ Rapp; and *Did Six Million Really Die?*, by Richard Harwood.[71]

Outbursts and irrational fantasies such as those described above need to be put in a wider context to avoid the impression that the 'new' South Africa is facing a 'Jewish problem'. This is not the case. By and large Jews have felt comfortable, and the community has continued to thrive, despite a wave of emigration in the 1980s, born of broader political fears shared with whites in general. Yet it needs to be noted that a 2008 Pew Global Attitudes Project reported that South Africans (along with Spaniards, Mexicans and Brazilians) harboured some of the most negative views of Jews outside the Muslim world. Forty-six per cent of respondents regarded Jews in a 'very unfavourable' or 'somewhat unfavourable' light, and of those, two-thirds disliked Jews in the extreme. Only 26 per cent of responses fell into the 'favourable' category.[72] When it came to antisemitic incidents, however, South Africa figured relatively low down on the table.[73] It had experienced nothing like the bombing of Jewish institutions and other incidents of violence in advanced Western democracies including the United States.

Six years after the 2008 Pew Attitudes survey, an ADL survey confirmed the prevalence of widespread anti-Jewish attitudes in South Africa, noting that about a quarter of the population harboured antisemitic stereotypes, with 38 per cent of those surveyed answering 'probably true' to a majority of the questionnaire's anti-Jewish tropes.[74] Similar findings emerged in a survey of black African attitudes towards Jews undertaken in 2016 by the Isaac and Jessie Kaplan Centre for Jewish Studies and Research at the University of Cape Town.[75] Three years later another survey undertaken by the ADL found South Africa to be second only to Poland in the rankings of hostile attitudes towards Jews, with nearly one in two South Africans apparently viewing Jews in an unfavourable light.[76]

On reflecting on the findings of the Pew, ADL and Kaplan Centre surveys, it is important to note that the last-mentioned survey revealed that the respondents demonstrated a low level of awareness about Jews and that while 38 per cent rated Jews unfavourably, this was the same for Muslims (38 per cent) and Indians (45 per cent). It is also important to recall Todd Endelman's distinction – raised at the start of this study – between 'ideational' and 'programmatic' antisemitism. The latter moves beyond attitudes and transforms into political action. Importantly, in the 'new' South Africa, anti-Jewish ideas or attitudes have never threatened to turn into party-political action or policy. While some politicians have displayed vile Jew-hatred, and while formal responses from the ANC to those of its members who have crossed the line have usually been weak, at no time has a 'Jewish question' been employed as a political plank. In the wake of the long struggle against apartheid, constitutional (Chapter Nine) institutions have been specifically designed to safeguard human rights and uphold the dignity of all. The celebration of diversity encapsulated in the notion of the 'rainbow nation' serves as an antidote to ethnic hatred.[77] Thus antisemitism cannot be identified as a serious or defining political factor in South Africa.

When it comes to the 'Zionist question', however, the situation is different. Here any sensitivity shown about undisguised Jew-hatred is invariably abandoned. Over many decades, an anti-Zionist discourse has evolved, nurtured by the ANC both in exile and after its unbanning in 1990. The movement's 'Third Worldist' and anti-Western worldview (supported and nourished in exile by the Soviet Union, which was especially hostile to Israel), plus its ties to the Palestine Liberation Organisation (PLO) and the anti-Zionist SACP, ensured animosity towards the Jewish state. *Sechaba*, the ANC mouthpiece in exile, toed the Soviet line and comment on Israel was generally hostile; this was so, too, for the *African Communist* and the (South African) *Guardian*, both SACP mouthpieces.[78] For ANC and SACP intellectuals, the idea of an ethnic state has always been problematic and Israel, long characterised by its enemies as an apartheid state, has been and is still seen as an outpost of the West, a colonial settler state. In 1988, Dr Neo Mnumzana, the chief United Nations representative of the ANC, who was still in exile at the time, put it bluntly: 'The South African people have never approved of Zionism. They see parallels of apartheid in Zionism and therefore their struggle against apartheid automatically has overtones of anti-Zionism which is not the same thing as being anti-Jewish.'[79]

It is not surprising that shortly after his release from prison, Nelson Mandela warmly embraced Yasser Arafat, the PLO chairman, in Lusaka, Zambia. The following day Mandela was quoted as saying that if his meeting with Arafat and his statements equating the struggle of the Palestinians with that of black people were to alienate 'South Africa's influential Jewish community', that was 'too bad'.[80] Eight years later Arafat gave a rousing address to a joint sitting of the National Assembly and National Council of Provinces in which he accused Israel of bringing the Middle East to the brink of 'violence, anarchy, war and destruction'. In thanking the PLO leader, ANC parliamentarian Ahmed Gora Ebrahim was loudly applauded when he equated Zionism with racism – effectively ignoring the ANCs long-standing endorsement of a two-state solution to the Israel–Palestine conflict, as well as contradicting the United Nations General Assembly Resolution 46/86 of 1991, which revoked the equation of 'Zionism and racism'.[81]

Contemporary South Africa has, to be sure, become a comfortable space for anti-Zionists. Both the electronic and print media are widely supportive of the Palestinian cause. Zionism is characterised – especially but not exclusively in the Muslim media – as immoral in conception and horrific in execution. In today's atmosphere it would be tantamount to political suicide for an ANC politician or public figure to say anything positive about the Jewish state. One saw evidence of this in the instantaneous condemnation of South Africa's chief justice Mogoeng Mogoeng when, in 2020, he lamented his government's 'lopsided' attitude towards the Israel–Palestine problem.[82] Within hours the ANC had issued a hard-hitting statement that referred to the 'Apartheid State of Israel' and called on the speaker of parliament to censure the chief justice.[83] The foreign minister, Naledi Pandor, viewed his comments 'with great dismay',[84] while the ANC MP grandson of Nelson Mandela, Mandla Mandela, called on the chief justice to retract his apparent support for 'apartheid Israel'.[85] A year later (when he addressed a Pan-African Palestine Solidarity Network meeting in Dakar, Senegal), Mandela lashed out at Israel being granted observer status in the African Union. 'We must reflect deeply on what has transpired on our continent and how the Apartheid Israel regime and its Zionist lobbying machine has crept insipidly into the African psyche and wormed itself into our structures overtly and covertly.' This was 'chequebook diplomacy', said Mandela, seemingly oblivious to his use of age-old anti-Jewish tropes.[86]

While antagonism towards Israel cannot be axiomatically equated with antisemitism – and this needs to be stressed – one must note that the discourse of anti-Zionism often goes beyond the bounds of normal political rhetoric and frequently betrays vulgar Jew-hatred. Israel alone is signalled out for obloquy, while the controversial human rights abuses of many other states are ignored. Anti-Zionism has become, at least for some, a hygienic form of antisemitism and a fig leaf for what the historian Robert Wistrich termed 'the longest hatred'.[87] In the words of Bernard Harrison, Zionism or Israel has replaced 'the role traditionally assigned in antisemitic theory to the world Jewish conspiracy'.[88] To illustrate this, we need to explore the evolution of an increasingly warped and rabid anti-Zionist discourse – often riddled with imaginative fantasies – in a changing domestic and international context. While the ANC (and its tripartite allies, the SACP and COSATU) and other 'progressive' voices have been party to this, it is the Muslim minority that, for obvious reasons, has been most exercised by the Israel–Palestine conflict. Arguably too, it is the main force driving sentiment in South Africa against the Zionist enterprise. In tracing evolving Muslim attitudes and growing politicisation, as well as escalating Manichaean fantasies, it is necessary to return to the early decades of apartheid and the ideological challenges faced by this minority (today less than two per cent of the total population) in its struggle against white minority rule, and its shifting options in a turbulent age of burgeoning global Islamism.

Islamic Resurgence

Historically regarded as a part of the Coloured and Indian populations, South Africa's Muslim minority are descendants of political prisoners brought to the Cape by the Dutch rulers from the Indonesian islands in the seventeenth century, as well as of ex-slaves, nineteenth-century Indian immigrants and the offspring of black–white miscegenation.[89] Residing mainly though not exclusively in the Western Cape, Gauteng and KwaZulu-Natal regions, Muslims interacted in the labour and economic spheres with South African whites, but in the social context the divide ran deep. It was only once rigid racial separation began to erode in the late 1980s that Jews began to sense Muslim hostility towards Zionism and Israel.[90] The geography of apartheid, coupled with state repression and the rather insular and non-challenging character of the conservative Muslim elite, had given Jews a false sense of harmony.⁹¹ While the mainstream 'white-owned' and Eurocentric media empathised with Israel, Muslims took a decidedly different view. For them, the creation of the Jewish state in 1948 was a catastrophe (*Nakba*),⁹² with the pain compounded by further Israeli victories against Arab forces, culminating in the Six Day War in 1967 and the occupation of the West Bank and reunification of Jerusalem.⁹³ South African Muslims shared in the humiliation of their Muslim 'brothers and sisters'. Indeed, at the time of the Six Day War in 1967, Al-Jihaad, a tiny Shiite-inclined Muslim group which had been founded in Cape Town four years earlier, sought to join the fight against the Jewish state, while at UCT the war 'generated anguish in the ranks of the Islamic Society'.⁹⁴ Six years later, Muslims again indicated a willingness to help – this time during the 1973 October War.⁹⁵ By then 'Zionism' was a term of opprobrium for most South African Muslims, and Israel considered an aggressor state.⁹⁶ Prominence had indeed long been given to 'The Tragedy of Palestine'.⁹⁷ Local Muslims were warned about 'Zionist designs' and *Muslim News* – a mainstream and widely circulated fortnightly newspaper (it became the monthly *Muslim Views* in 1986) – exhorted its readers to avail themselves of *The Protocols of the Elders of Zion*.⁹⁸

Signs of an Islamic resurgence in South Africa can be traced to the 1950s when a number of 'progressive' Islamic groups were established across the country: in the Transvaal, the Young Men's Muslim Association (1955) and the Universal Truth Movement (1958); in Natal, the Arabic Study Circle (1950) and the Islamic Propagation Centre International or IPCI (1957); and in the Cape Province, the Cape Muslim Youth Movement (1957) and the Claremont Muslim Youth Association (1958).⁹⁹ While emphasis in the Transvaal and Natal was on Islamic understanding, in the Cape Islamic resurgence was the primary focus, and the writings of the Indian philosopher Abul A'la al-Mawdudi (1903–79) and the Egyptian revolutionary Sayyid Qutb (1906–66), which targeted secularism, the West and deviant Arab regimes, were widely circulated.¹⁰⁰

The 1969 death in police custody of the Cape Town Islamist and anti-apartheid cleric Imam Abdullah Haron added fuel to Islamic politicisation.¹⁰¹ In particular, the silence of the Muslim clergy at the time led 'to a deep sense of betrayal and disillusionment on the part of young Muslims'.[102] In the words of the Muslim intellectual Farid Esack, they turned towards a more 'socially relevant Islam', epitomised in the formation of the Muslim Youth Movement (MYM) in 1970 and the Muslim Students Association (MSA) in 1974.[103] A range of Islamic activities was increasingly coordinated and guided by what was understood to be an authentic modern Islamic paradigm.[104] While the emphasis was not specifically on the South African political situation, that dimension was not ignored.[105] What was evident, however, was that the MYM rejected the West and, in calling for an 'Islamic way of life', reflected the Black Consciousness Movement's 'appeal to an authentic Black identity in South Africa'.[106]

Despite substantial opposition to this Islamic resurgence in the Muslim community itself (particularly among those consolidating 'revivalist' Deobandi thought in the Transvaal and Natal), the progressive forces gradually gained ascendancy.[107] *Muslim News* increasingly projected a more radical Islam, which intensified in the wake of the 1975 United Nations General Assembly resolution equating Zionism with racism. This was hailed as a victory for the PLO and a defeat for the United States and Israel.[108] For a community that was characterised by one Muslim commentator as 'Zionophobes', the UN resolution was an inspiring moment.[109] By the late 1970s, a Palestinian Islamic Solidarity Committee had been established in Durban,[110] and the MYM had embarked on a thorough training schedule that included *halaqat* (study circles), manuals and special camps, which were all intricately linked to international Islamic literature and audiotapes: Zionism, secularism, capitalism and communism were identified as threats,[111] and Zionists were accused of controlling the world's media.[112]

The success of the Iranian Revolution in 1979 further energised local Islamic resurgence, and the writings of the secularly educated Iranian sociologist Ali Shari'ati (1933–77) and the Ayatollah Ruhollah Khomeini were now included in MYM reading lists.[113] Although Iran was not seen as a model for Muslims in South Africa, Qibla, a radical Cape Town-based Islamist organisation (formally established in 1981 by Achmad Cassiem), was patently inspired by the overthrow of the Shah.[114] 'Islamic revolution in South Africa' became a popular slogan in Cape Town at Muslim demonstrations against Israel and Zionism, while UCT and Wits saw substantial upheavals at the time of the Sabra and Shatila massacres following Israel's invasion of Lebanon in 1982.[115]

Clashes between Jewish and non-Jewish students at both universities revealed an intensification of anti-Zionist sentiment among young Muslims and a new determination for action.[116] Anti-Zionist rhetoric rapidly escalated: Hitler was an amateur compared to what Israeli prime minister Menachem Begin was doing in Lebanon, editorialised *Muslim News*,[117] while at a Palestine Solidarity meeting (attended by AZAPO, which had ties to Qibla) called to discuss Israel's invasion of southern Lebanon, speakers referred to a genocide of the Palestinians.[118] Notably they expressed no objection to Jews, only to Zionists. Two weeks later, PLO slogans were daubed on the walls of a Waverley synagogue in Johannesburg and windows were broken at several other synagogues.[119]

Radicalisation and Division

Increasing anger and politicisation among the Muslim community were evident in the refusal of the MJC to support the tricameral constitution introduced by the National Party in 1983, which was widely seen as a form of co-optation.[120] But, when it came to joining the broad-based anti-apartheid United Democratic Front (UDF), the issues were more complex. Here the presence of non-Muslims, communists, 'amoral' secularists and Zionists raised issues of principle. For the conservative *ulama* or 'learned ones' who had built their clerical power on a modus vivendi with the apartheid state and wished to avoid *fitnah* or disorder, the UDF posed a threat to their authority; but the MJC did affiliate, as did the small Shia Al-Jihaad group.[121] The MYM and Qibla, however, refused to join on the grounds that the UDF lacked a revolutionary ideology, a view shared by *Muslim News*, which considered this movement dangerous and feared that affiliation would result in an erosion of Muslim identity: 'This is the WCC [World Council of Churches] cum Zionist and Stalinist politics which the MJC is playing at,' wrote one correspondent.[122] Basically, then, the UDF's composition was perceived – at least by some conservative Muslims – as a threat to Islam. They were not prepared to see Christians, Jews and the 'Other' as their brothers and sisters in the struggle: interfaith solidarity was considered sinful as it harboured the potential to 'reduce Islam to the level of a religion in the western sense of the word'.[123] Adil Bradlow, an exemplar of such thinking, argued that it would dilute and 'prevent the presentation of Islam [to the oppressed] as the major liberating power'. Acknowledging the concept of democracy as embodied in UDF objectives, warned Bradlow, 'is tantamount to an act of *shirk* [polytheism], associating others with Allah for He Alone is "Sovereign"'.[124]

Underpinning this opposition to interfaith solidarity, explains Esack, was the notion 'that non-Islam is necessarily void of virtue and that freedom outside the parameters of Islam is of no consequence'.[125] Self-styled 'progressive' Muslims, on the other hand, argued that Islam had space for all, and were determined to participate in the struggle with all elements, including Christians and Jews.[126] This is not to say that they jettisoned the religious basis of their opposition to apartheid but rather that they built on a more humanistic and inclusive tradition, including the writings of the Punjabi poet Muhammad Iqbal, Ali Shari'ati, and the Iranian cleric Mahmoud Taleghani.

In 1984 this 'progressive' wing broke away from the MYM and MSA to establish the Call of Islam, which specifically presented a 'South African' Islamic face within the UDF.[127] Its message, spread through mass rallies, pamphleteering and involvement in political funerals, directly challenged the Muslim establishment. One of the leaders, Ebrahim Rasool, Western Cape secretary of the UDF, argued that the UDF would 'create the conditions whereby Muslims will take their rightful place in the struggle'.[128] Most importantly, Rasool and others advocating interfaith solidarity drew upon Islamic tradition and Qur'anic texts to legitimise their stance. 'We find examples when the Prophet had co-operated with non-Muslims because there were objectives of justice which were involved,' noted Rasool. 'The Qur'an makes it clear that non-Muslims *per se* are not our enemy. An enemy of Islam must be defined by the way in which they undermine Islamic values. Values like justice. Those are the enemies of Islam, not just because he's a non-Muslim by name or belief.'[129]

Not all Muslims agreed with Rasool. In debates surrounding interfaith solidarity, the position of the 'Other', including the Jew, remained contentious. The Zionist question especially complicated matters.[130] Progressive South Africans at this time shared a powerful anti-colonialism embedded in a Third World *Weltanschauung*. Within this framework, the illegitimacy of Zionism was an important component. Added to that, South Africa had close ties with Israel. These had blossomed from 1976 after Prime Minister Vorster's visit to the Jewish state, which cemented technological, scientific and military bonds.[131]

Qibla was certainly quick to harness this anti-Zionism in framing its opposition to the UDF. Describing the organisation in classic conspiratorial terms as Zionist-controlled and acting at the behest of international Jewish financiers,[132] it was able to tap into a deep-rooted anger which identified Zionism as the 'citadel' of imperialism. Some observers even held Jewish and Zionist manipulation responsible for apartheid.[133] In short, a paranoid imagination identified a global and demonic Jewish plot, centring on Zionism. Such machinations were also frequently discussed in the Muslim press,[134] with mainstream newspapers perceived as being 'controlled by the Jews' – as MJC president Sheikh Nazeem Mohammed told an interviewer.[135] In control of 'a large stash of economic power in South Africa', Jews enjoyed substantial influence and political power, asserted Ebrahim Moosa, a former Muslim student leader turned journalist and academic. A 'set of elders within the Jewish community', he explained, looked after the interests of Jews. 'One finds that it dates back to the Elders of Zion and to the whole formation of Israel.'[136]

While liberation strategies (including interfaith alliances) and the question of Zionism had generated substantial contention within the Muslim polity, political action was not inhibited by dissenting views. Muslims regularly took to the streets in the late 1980s. State repression was fierce, but the Call of Islam's organising abilities, coupled with Qibla's 'revolutionary' fervour, ensured that resistance captured international headlines. Once President De Klerk lifted the ban on illegal organisations in February 1990, marches became even more frequent as local Muslims took to identifying with their co-religionists in Bosnia, Kashmir and 'Palestine'.[137] Placard-waving Muslims with their *kaffiyahs* (traditional Arab headdress) and Palestinian scarves conjured up images of protests in Iran, Algeria and the West Bank, and gave a distinct sense of Muslim 'fundamentalism' on the move. It is no wonder, writes Esack, 'that the BBC reported that the streets of Cape Town resembled those of Tehran'.[138] 'One Zionist, one bullet' was the common refrain heard at anti-Zionist protests, echoing the well-known PAC slogan 'One settler, one bullet'.[139]

Hard-Wired to the Middle East

In May 1990 the Call of Islam initiated a Muslim National Conference to mobilise a response to the changing political situation in South Africa. Islamic organisations from throughout the country attended, and although there were indications that more 'progressive' positions were being accepted, a powerful strain of anti-state discourse persisted.[140] Qibla, for example, rejected broader political participation in South Africa's transition and, at a subsequent inaugural conference of the Islamic Unity Convention (IUC) held in 1994, Muslims were called upon (without success) to boycott the country's first democratic election.[141] One year later the IUC established its own radio station, Radio 786, broadcasting on behalf of 250 regional and nationally based organisations.[142] Achmad Cassiem replaced Sheikh AK Toffar as chairman of the IUC, signalling a militant Islamist turn.

At the heart of Qibla (and the IUC) was an anti-Western sentiment and virulent hatred of Israel that often descended into fantasies about the malevolent Jewish state.[143] It saw the Zionist–United States coalition as determined to destroy Islam, an idea reinforced at the time of the Gulf War of 1990–1, when a US-led coalition drove the Iraqis out of Kuwait.[144] South African Muslims were exhorted to identify with the global Muslim struggle, at the centre of which many identified the Palestinian issue. *Muslim Views* captured this sentiment:

> What has made the relationship between Islam and the west even more problematic has been its role in the creation and preservation of the Jewish state of Israel. This factor alone is proving to be sufficient to eliminate the possibility of survival for collaborators (with the west) within a world of Islam which witnesses a return of western troops to its territory ... the present age, which has witnessed the Islamic

revolution in Iran, for example, is one in which Islam is fast becoming unshackled to a significant actor in world affairs.[145]

Indicative of Muslim political radicalisation and its focus on the Middle East were the frequent marches on the United States and Israeli embassies in Pretoria, where the US and Israeli flags were invariably burned in protest at injustices perpetrated against fellow Muslims abroad.[146] There were also calls to physically participate in the confrontation in the Gulf. A group of Muslims calling themselves the Islamic Mujahideen Foundation, for example, made themselves available to serve as soldiers 'against the USA and its allies'.[147] Qibla was particularly apoplectic in its condemnation of American aggression and racism, incorporating all dimensions of the Islamist anti-colonial and anti-Western worldview:

> The Muslims of Iraq and the neighbouring regions have our full support against the occupying imperialist and zionist forces of the great satan, USA. Muslims and the oppressed people condemn outright the presence of the USA and its confederates in Hijaz. We must prepare to counter any further acts of aggression that the forces of evil have planned against the Muslims and the oppressed people worldwide.
>
> The events unfolding in the Middle East must be seen as the great and inevitable confrontation between Islam and unbelief which will unfortunately but necessarily be a bloody one. Muslims and the oppressed must protect each other and cut off the hands of the oppressors.
>
> We note that the apartheid regime has sided with the USA against the Muslims. To this end they have deployed their security forces to counter Muslim offensives in the Cape and elsewhere. 'They plan and Allah plans ... and the best planner is Allah...
>
> America is a racist imperialist country. It is no champion of democracy and freedom. American democracy and freedom can only apply to white skinned people and not blacks and browns. America has rushed with its army to Vietnam, Korea, Haiti, Panama and other non-white countries.
>
> When it comes to white skinned countries like Russia in its wars against Afghanistan, America never sent its army to enforce UN Resolutions... in this war it is the duty of Muslims to support Iraq against American zionist aggression.[148]

As the Gulf War unfolded, Muslim protests, especially in Cape Town, gained momentum. President De Klerk was called upon to withdraw 'unmandated support for America and its allies' and South Africa was condemned for its 'strong trading links with the Zionist state'.[149] The Palestinian question remained integral to the invective against the United States, and Israel was identified as the 'arch-enemy of Islam' and the 'root cause' of problems in the Middle East. 'The zionists, through their servants, the Americans, have manipulated the situation in the Middle East to such an extent that they have succeeded in leaving the Middle East totally defenceless,' asserted *Muslim Views*.[150] 'The world's greatest evils today are zionism and imperialism,' noted a Qibla document. 'It is against those evils that Allah is warning us: the Jew with his bigoted Zionist racism and the exploitative selfish capitalism and the world devouring and dehumanising imperialist in the name of Christianity.'[151]

Hostility towards those perceived as enemies of the Muslim world intensified. Both Wits and UCT witnessed the burning of American and Israeli flags,[152] and the Muslim press was inundated with conspiratorial articles and letters that identified Zionism, the United States and the CIA as primary enemies.[153] Anger was subsequently fuelled by the visit of Yasser Arafat in 1994. Speaking in a mosque in Johannesburg, the PLO chairman called on South African Muslims to join the Palestinian struggle to liberate Jerusalem.[154] One year later, on *al-Quds* (Jerusalem) day, placards were displayed outside the Israeli Embassy in Cape Town reading 'Kill a Jew and kill an Israeli'.[155] Not surprisingly, the assassination of Israeli prime minister Yitzhak Rabin in 1996 was reported in *Muslim Views* (quoting Hezbollah, a militant Shia anti-Zionist movement based in Lebanon) as 'a miracle from God'.[156] By then the Israeli–Palestinian conflict had become a preoccupation of Muslims in South Africa, with the Jewish state identified as the incarnation of evil and the Zionist movement its conspiratorial centre. At an international Muslim conference 'Creating a New Civilisation of Islam' held in Pretoria in April 1996, speakers referred to Jews as 'a powerful economic force' and blamed Zionists for 'all evils in society'.[157] And a few months later, Jewish loyalty to South Africa was raised in *Muslim Views* after the Jewish Board of Deputies objected to a proposed visit of Iranian president Akbar Hashemi Rafsanjani. 'The Jewish community must begin to owe allegiance to this country and start to think like everyone else in this country,' ran an editorial. 'They must not support President Mandela when it suits them and turn their backs when they think of Israel.'[158]

These were age-old canards at the heart of which is the idea of an omniscient and omnipotent Jew. Fu'ad Rachman (a foreign journalist and one-time anti-apartheid activist) illustrated this in a response to 'The Threat of Islam' – an ANC document that had been drawn up in the wake of a Qibla-inspired Cape Town vigilante movement, People Against Gangsterism and Drugs (PAGAD), founded in 1996.[159] In a lengthy article riddled with paranoia, Rachman asserted that the document was a product of 'the Israeli intelligence network known as Mossad' and that the ANC government was 'heavily influenced and controlled by Zionists', while Mossad 'working hand in glove with the CIA (American intelligence) knew about PAGAD before PAGAD knew about PAGAD'. Rachman claimed that just as the 'Jewish' mining magnate Harry Oppenheimer and the American business grandee Rockefeller manipulated American policy, so South Africans in turn were being manipulated by Zionists, who controlled the Johannesburg Stock Exchange and 'infiltrated major ANC-government structures with so-called white liberals sitting in key positions'. Even the demise of the National Party was blamed on Zionists, who, claimed Rachman, would similarly render the ANC incapable of governing.[160]

It is clear that global events, strong local ties to Muslims in the Middle and Near East, and domestic contestations around PAGAD sharpened boundaries between Muslims and non-Muslims. According to Esack, PAGAD's self-publicised links with the Palestinian Islamic Resistance Movement (Hamas) and Hezbollah were 'misplaced bluster and bravado' rather than 'strategic earnestness' on its part, but they were indicative of psychological connections to the *ummah* (the universal Muslim community).[161] They were also indicative of an overwhelming belief in sinister Israeli power. Members of the Muslim community even blamed Israel's Mossad intelligence agency for a bomb blast at a mosque in the small town of Rustenburg; this led to a vociferous Qibla-organised march on the Israeli Embassy, culminating in the by now ritual burning of an Israeli flag. A similar march took place in Johannesburg, organised by the IUC. A few months later, Muslims held pro-Hamas demonstrations outside a Pretoria mosque and placed a full-page advertisement in the *Pretoria News* criticising that newspaper's 'biased and one-sided version of events in the Middle East'. The advertisement appealed to President Nelson Mandela to take account of the 'facts' of hostile attacks on the people of Palestine.[162] The infamous 'pig poster' incident in Hebron in which the Prophet Muhammad was depicted as a pig trampling on the Koran also led to heated protests in Pretoria and Cape Town.[163] A home that housed a Jewish book centre in Cape Town was firebombed and phone threats were made against a Jewish aged home and a synagogue.[164] Despite widespread condemnation of that bombing, the MJC was silent – perhaps an indication of grassroots radicalisation and fear.[165]

Anti-Zionist hostility intensified following the collapse of the Israeli–Palestinian Oslo peace process, which had begun so optimistically with Israeli prime minister Yitzhak Rabin and PLO chairman Yasser Arafat shaking hands in the White House rose garden. In this polarised atmosphere, an invitation to the Reverend William Bantom, New National Party mayor of the Cape Metropolitan Council, to attend an international mayoral conference in Israel in May 1998, was greeted with outrage by Muslim organisations, supported by the ANC provincial caucus. Given such tensions, it was not surprising that the Israeli Jubilee celebrations in Cape Town saw Qibla-led demonstrators chanting 'One Zionist one bullet' and 'Viva Hezbollah and Hamas' outside the venue, where placards equating Zionism with apartheid were also held aloft.[166]

The anti-Zionist mood was again apparent when the South African government refused to issue a visa to Sheikh Ahmed Yassin, spiritual leader of Hamas.[167] A telephone interview with Yassin from Kuwait in which he denounced all Zionists as terrorists was broadcast on a Cape Town Muslim radio station and relayed live to a public meeting in Gatesville, a predominantly Muslim suburb in Cape Town. Qibla also organised a protest outside the gates of parliament, decrying the government's decision to ban Yassin. Once again, an Israeli flag was burned while other Israeli flags were hurled into the street for protesters to 'clean their shoes'. Marchers chanted slogans such as 'Death to Israel' and 'One Zionist one bullet'.[168]

It is notable that many Muslim activists continued to express their views on Jews and Zionism in terms of conspiracy theories built upon notions of a 'New World Order' and the scapegoating of Muslims.[169] Following the outbreak of the Second Intifada in the Occupied Territories in 2000, about a thousand Muslims – including many women and children – marched on the United States and Israeli embassies in Pretoria. This 'Free Palestine Campaign' demanded that the South African government sever ties with Israel and that the United States end its support for the Jewish state. Protesters carried placards calling for an end to Israeli 'apartheid' and 'the Holocaust and genocide of the people of Palestine'.[170] Demonstrations also took place at Wits and UCT, and a McDonald's outlet – probably viewed as a symbol of the United States – was attacked in Cape Town.[171]

Crossing the Line between Anti-Zionism and Antisemitism

Anti-Zionist outrage reached its zenith just prior to and during the United Nations World Conference Against Racism, Racial Discrimination, Xenophobia and Related Intolerance (WCAR) in Durban in August 2001. The conference turned into 'an extension of the Arab–Israeli conflict' and presented opportunities 'to insert wording into draft resolutions portraying Israel and Zionism as racist and minimising Jewish suffering and anti-Semitism', opined the *South African Jewish Report*.[172] The weekly was quite correct. Jewish representatives at the conference were the targets of threatening taunts, and a Syrian delegate openly described the Holocaust as 'a Jewish lie', while Israel was portrayed as the world's 'central locus of evil'.[173]

This mood was already apparent in the build-up to the WCAR. Cape Town had witnessed a 15,000-strong Muslim march to parliament to protest against what was termed atrocities committed against the Palestinians by Israel. The march brought the city to a standstill and banners bore the slogan 'Zionism is racism'. The Israeli prime minister Ariel Sharon was depicted as a war criminal and Hamas was praised for its role in the united struggle against Zionism. Sheikh Achmat Sedick appealed to the South African government to restore the 'Zionism is racism' resolution (overturned by the UN in 1991) to the agenda of the WCAR and called for South Africans to 'take immediate action against Israel by breaking off all diplomatic and trade relations'.[174]

At the preliminary NGO Forum at the Durban conference, Israel was lambasted, and pamphlets disseminated by the Arab Lawyers Union depicted Jews in the most horrific fashion. Attempts by Jewish delegates to present a positive view of Zionism were drowned out by hecklers chanting 'Jew, Jew, Jew' and proclaiming that Zionism was racism and Israel an apartheid state.[175] At the official WCAR meeting that followed the NGO Forum, swastikas were on display and *The Protocols of the Elders of Zion* was on sale at the stand of the Arab Lawyers Union. The *Protocols* was also distributed at other venues together with antisemitic flyers emanating from the Shia-Muslim-run Ahlul Bait Foundation of South Africa, known for Holocaust denial and ties to Iran.[176] One of these flyers had a picture of Hitler accompanied by the following question: 'What would have happened if I had won. The Good things. There would have been no Israel and no Palestinian's [sic] bloodshed. The rest is your guess.'[177] Hostile anti-Jewish caricatures were also on display, with one depicting a rabbi wearing an Israeli army cap on his head holding *The Protocols of the Elders of Zion*. Another poster described how Passover bread was made with the blood of Muslims.[178] This was 'anti-Semitism in the guise of anti-Zionism', commented Marlene Bethlehem, national president of the Jewish Board of Deputies. 'The onslaught on Israel and the Jewish people is an absolute scandal and it is racism and anti-Semitism of the worst kind,' stated Mervyn Smith, a former president of the Board.[179] The internationally respected American journalist Charles Krauthammer described the WCAR as 'a universal conference whose overriding objective was to brand one country and one people as uniquely, transcendently evil'. Its objective was 'to rekindle the Arab campaign to delegitimize the planet's single Jewish state – and thus prepare the psychological and political ground for its extinction'.[180]

Significantly, it was not only Jews who were outraged at the turn of events. In response to one of the cartoons distributed by the Arab Lawyers Union, the UN Human Rights commissioner, Mary Robinson, stated: 'When I see something like this, I am a Jew.' Prominent ANC leader Pallo Jordan also found the disruptions 'disgraceful',[181] while South Africa's deputy minister of foreign affairs, Aziz Pahad, lamented some months later that the conference 'was hijacked and used by some with an anti-Israel agenda to turn it into an anti-Semitic event'.[182] Twenty years later, Mary Kluk, national president of the Board of Deputies, similarly recalled the horror of Durban. 'I grew up there and to see copies of the blood libel the *Protocols of the Elders of Zion* being sold openly on those streets; the violence, the thuggery and the naked hatred was deeply unnerving. I remember the pamphlets, the so-called Hitler Handbill, being handed out on the streets – paid for, we found out afterwards, by the Bin Laden family; the Jihadist banners, literally calling for the extermination of Jews.'[183]

A Cosmological and Manichaean Struggle

Only a few days after the Durban gathering – and perhaps even inspired by the event – Sheikh Mogamat Faaik Gamieldien of Cape Town wrote a letter to the *Cape Argus* entitled 'The Golden Calf of Judaism' in which he quoted with approbation *The Protocols of the Elders of Zion*. Readers were reminded that this publication had been banned under the apartheid regime (a form of endorsement presumably) and that it clearly provided an explanation for Zionist and Israeli actions. Gamieldien did his best to deprecate the idea of Jewish self-determination and claimed that the Durban conference had 'succeeded in exposing Zionism, the golden calf of Judaism, as actively pursuing the genocide of the Palestinian people'.[184]

Similarly conspiratorial ideas were taken even further in the wake of the September 11 attacks on the World Trade Center in New York and the Pentagon. Mossad was accused of masterminding the strikes and it was claimed that New York Jews had been warned in advance not to go to work on that day.[185] According to *Muslim Views*, Western hysteria masked any realisation of the real reason that America had been attacked and prevented any serious reflection 'on what their government is really doing in the world'.[186] Tellingly, the 9/11 events were located within a conspiratorial framework in which the United States and Israel colluded against Islam and sought global domination.

Some years later, this collusion was forcefully expressed by one Mustafa Jonker during an interview that followed his arrest for terrorism in Cape Town. Jonker's detailed account is worth quoting at length in so far as his sentiments illustrate the intersection of global and domestic worldviews, the religious mindset, and the power of historical memory, as well as the conspiratorial imagination with Israel at its centre:

> I, like thousands of Muslims am concerned at the plight of the oppressed in general and the Muslim Ummah in particular which over the last century has witnessed an unprecedented onslaught from global disbelief. I realised from an early age that America is the main source of this global tyranny by her directly invading Muslim lands and killing their people and also by supporting apostate governments that subdue their people on her behalf. We returned to South Africa in 1999 [from Saudi Arabia] and I soon realised that while the racist apartheid regime had been removed, this new 'democracy' had come about by the ANC [African National Congress] selling South Africa to multi-national corporations. The ANC has a history of concern for only the middle- and upper-class blacks. The result of this treachery is a symbolic multicultural government which is dictated to by and passes laws on behalf of mainly European and American companies, the same Crusader nations pillaging Afghanistan and Iraq today. Today South Africa has the biggest gap between rich and poor in the world; a direct result of the government's neoliberal capitalist policies. A wealthy elite owns South Africa's wealth, while thirty million people suffer from poverty. Resulting from this poverty is crime of which South Africa has the highest statistics in the world as well. I began advocating as Allah commanded direct action against the Crusader–Zionist alliance and her pawns in power and this is the background behind my being labelled a terrorist. As far as this word goes, it is a label placed on anyone challenging the greedy bloodthirsty agenda of the West and I therefore take a pride in it. Ours is a blessed terror that desires to see an end to America's oppression ... it is a fact that the Jews around the world using the Crusaders are the main benefactors of the global campaign against Islam ... Jews like the Oppenheimers have a monopoly over South Africa's resources and their banks ensure that the 'goyim' as they call the suffering masses are kept in a state of debt slavery. They use Usury which Allah forbade them from practicing, to turn free people

into slaves. Africa in particular is suffering from great debts owed to these prophet murderers and it is therefore not surprising that the bulk of attacks on Jews outside the Holy Land have been in Africa. Over the last few years, Mujahideen have attacked the Jews in Mombasa in East Africa, they attacked them in Tunisia and Egypt in North Africa and they attacked the Israeli embassy in Mauritania in west Africa and we don't consider the Muslims here in South Africa to be any less determined to punish the Jews for spreading corruption over Allah's earth. The Muslims in South Africa hold a special place in their hearts for their suffering brethren in Palestine and perhaps among them are those who pledged to fight until the Bastard State of Israel is eradicated and have pledged to pray in Masjid al-Aqsa as conquerors or to meet Allah on the way...[187]

It is apparent – and not only in Jonker's anti-American, anti-Zionist and anti-Jewish repertoire – that what is essentially a political conflict over disputed territory has for many Muslims become a cosmological and Manichaean struggle wrapped in a giant conspiracy. The Jew is at its centre, with anti-Zionism often morphing into, or being informed by, classic antisemitism: this is especially apparent in Holocaust denial, as illustrated in the Radio 786 interview with the historian Yaqub Zaki noted earlier. Besides claiming that the 'million plus' Jews who died in the Second World War had succumbed to infectious diseases, Zaki spent much of his time engaged with elaborate Jewish conspiracies, including a bizarre connection between Jewish financiers, the Anglo-Boer War, Alfred Milner and Zionism. In addition, Zaki claimed that the Third Republic in France 'fell into the hands of Jews'; the Bolshevik Revolution was funded by Kuhn, Loeb & Co., the great Jewish bank of New York; President Woodrow Wilson was an adulterer whom Jews threatened to expose in order to promote their nefarious goals; and the Freemasons, controlled by Jewish finance, persuaded Milner and Balfour (both initiates of the Grand Lodge of Great Britain) to issue the Balfour Declaration. In an uncanny echo of Rudman, Schoeman, Benson and Brown, Zaki claimed communism and Zionism were two sides of the same coin.[188]

Significantly, claims that the Holocaust (or its scale) is an invention serve to delegitimise the Jewish state in so far as the birth of Israel is commonly – albeit incorrectly – tied to the destruction of European Jewry.[189] Often referred to as 'negationism', Holocaust denial is undoubtedly a form of antisemitism, invariably tied to the struggle against Zionism. It is not surprising that Jamiel McWilliams – who, as noted earlier, raised questions about the veracity of the Holocaust following the opening of the Cape Town Holocaust Centre in 1999 – accused Zionists of creating a guilt syndrome and repeating 'the "Six Million" like a mantra, the chanting of which becomes more intense with the passing of time'.[190]

Worrying Developments

A more disturbing trend in recent years has been the growing expressions of anti-Zionism – comfortably conflated with classic Jew-hatred – at the highest level in the South African government. At the time of Operation Cast Lead in 2008–9 (the Israeli response to barrages of rockets fired from Gaza), South Africa's deputy foreign minister, Fatima Hajaig, told a mainly Muslim audience in the Johannesburg suburb of Lenasia that the United States and most Western countries were 'in the hands of Jewish money and when Jewish money controls … you can expect anything'.[191]

This conflation of Jews and Israeli actions persisted well after Israel's Gaza operation.[192] In 2012 the deputy foreign minister, Ebrahim Ebrahim, called on South Africans not to visit Israel,[193] while COSATU went so far as to describe the South African Zionist Federation as having hands 'dripping with blood'.[194] Similar accusations were articulated during Operation Protective Edge (another Israeli incursion into Gaza) in August 2014. In a particularly illiberal and ugly communication, Tony Ehrenreich, a trade unionist and senior ANC politician in the Western Cape, called on Jewish leaders supporting Zionism to leave the country. 'If the Jewish Board of Deputies wants to advance a Zionist agenda, they should leave South Africa and go and advance their agenda elsewhere,' advised Ehrenreich, who, in addition, threatened Jewish-owned businesses.[195] 'What is at stake here', wrote former Oxford don RW Johnson, 'is that Mr Ehrenreich – and those like him – are seeking to demonise and bully a whole section of the country's population in clear defiance of our constitution and all our laws and values.'[196] In another hostile statement, the ANC secretary-general, Gwede Mantashe, described Israel as a state founded on the basis of apartheid, 'which according to international law and several UN conventions is a crime against humanity'.[197] There was even talk (albeit denied) of the ANC considering far-reaching changes to South African citizenship laws, the specific purpose of which was to place restrictions on ties between South Africans and Israel and impose punitive sanctions on South African companies that conducted business with Israel.[198] In response to an Israeli missile destroying a building in Gaza in 2016, COSATU also raised the possibility of trade unions targeting specifically Jewish businesses in South Africa.[199] Zionist and Jew have clearly been conflated, supporting the argument that anti-Zionist rhetoric is an attack on all Jews.[200]

Tensions with Israel have continued to the present day. Indeed, in 2017, the ANC passed a resolution at its national conference calling for the downgrading of ties with Israel and the permanent withdrawal of the South African ambassador from Tel Aviv. It is within this context of the conflation of Zionist and Jew, and of Zionism and apartheid, that the BDS movement has had such resonance in South Africa. Fully aware that it is the lynchpin in an international movement, BDS South Africa (as well as its breakaway, since 2020, Africa4Palestine) stresses the 'apartheid Israel' critique and has succeeded in keeping the issue alive.[201] This message resonates easily with many of those who struggled for liberation in South Africa and broadly share an anti-Western worldview that sympathises with the Palestinians. South African Jews are popularly accused of having sided with the apartheid regime and now with 'apartheid Israel'. During 'Israel Apartheid Week' in 2013, protesters led by the South African chapter of the BDS movement disrupted a concert at Wits featuring a visiting Israeli pianist.[202] Later in the year, demonstrators chanted 'Dubula e Juda' (Shoot the Jews, in Zulu) outside a concert intended to compensate for the earlier disruption.[203] BDS and Africa4Palestine deny antisemitism as a driving force and frame their case in a human rights discourse. The same cannot be said for some anti-Zionist extremists who betray crass Jew-hatred embedded in ugly tropes and fantasies.

For all that, it should be noted that labelling all criticism of Israel as antisemitic has serious problems. In fact, the Board of Deputies effectively discounts manifestations of anti-Zionism in its annual analysis of domestic antisemitism, and it refuted the 2019 ADL findings referred to earlier that South Africa ranked just below Poland in the antisemitic stakes. In a statement issued immediately after the ADL release, the Board claimed that local surveys revealed 'that the great majority of South Africans either have no knowledge at all about Jews or hold no opinion of them one way or another'. The statement pointed out that South Africa was in fact a world leader in promoting 'tolerance and respect for diverse religious beliefs'. To the extent that Jew-hatred existed, it was restricted to far-right supremacists, a tiny fringe among whites. Most importantly, noted the Board, South Africa has 'consistently recorded amongst the lowest rate of antisemitism in terms of actual attacks on Jews in the world'.[204]

It is certainly true that South Africa has experienced few anti-Jewish incidents. In 2019 only 36 were logged by the Board, a more than 40 per cent decline from 2018 and almost 50 per cent lower than the annual average recorded since 2006. David Saks, associate director of the Board, attributed this to the absence of major conflict between Israelis and Palestinians. Annual local incidents, noted Saks, escalated only when Israel was at war with Hamas. But Saks – a seasoned observer of South African antisemitism – did not dismiss out of hand the earlier ADL findings and stressed that these might indicate 'thinking bad things about Jews without necessarily ever expressing or acting on such beliefs'. Acknowledging that it 'may well be that there is more anti-Semitic sentiment out there than we realise', Saks nevertheless insisted that it was 'obviously not at a rate of nearly one in two South Africans'.[205]

This might well be so, but we do know that a very significant proportion of Jews in South Africa are concerned about anti-Israel sentiment and antisemitism. South African opinion surveys have consistently reported widely held anti-Jewish stereotypes, with opponents of the Zionist idea often peddling conspiracies and employing unvarnished anti-Jewish tropes in their critiques of Israel.[206] Indeed, we saw this once again in May 2021 during Israel's Operation Guardian of the Walls against Hamas and Islamic Jihad in Gaza. A massive spike in incidents, including violence, was reported to the Board, while social media was abuzz with vitriolic and unexpurgated Jew-hate, illustrating the slippery slope from anti-Zionism to antisemitism.[207] 'I'm starting to wonder if the Holocaust was a blessing,' wrote Nazeem Hartey Jumbo, to which Sarah Achmad replied, 'Me too, they never learnt their lesson.'[208] Importantly and disturbingly – and again affirming the slippage between anti-Zionism and antisemitism – the ANC acting secretary-general, Jessie Duarte, during a protest outside the Israeli Embassy in Pretoria, spoke in conspiratorial terms of Israel colonising Africa. 'If we do not stop this imperialism in Israel, one day they will move into Africa and start dispossessing our land here,' she stated. 'They will become the next imperialists.'[209]

Despite such rhetoric from a high-ranking ANC official, we know classic anti-Jewish fantasies and propaganda have not had much traction since 1948. Even the Covid-19 crisis that began in 2020 has failed to evoke sustained conspiratorial blame on Jews for the virus.[210] Jews as such are today an issue only for those on the fringes of South African political life, who for most part operate online.[211] Importantly, hate speech is unconstitutional and, given the ANC's opposition to racism, the climate for opposing Jew-hatred in present-day South Africa is more favourable than it has been in the past.[212]

And what about prospects for the future? Here we need to reflect upon the features and characteristics of antisemitism in South Africa over the *longue durée*. This will enable us to appreciate its aetiology and tenacity, its ebbs and flows, its continuities, discontinuities and its contingencies.

Afterthoughts

> *It is an obvious, if frequently forgotten, rule that anti-Jewish feeling acquires political relevance only when it can combine with a major political issue, or when Jewish group interests come into open conflict with those of a major class in society.*
> Hannah Arendt, *The Origins of Totalitarianism*, 1951

Continuities, Discontinuities and Contingencies

At the start of this study it was pointed out that 'private' or 'ideational' hostility towards Jews only transforms into 'programmatic' antisemitism under specific conditions. These did not exist after 1948 in apartheid South Africa; neither have they been present in post-apartheid South Africa. Programmatic antisemitism – or at least attempts to bring the 'Jewish question' into party politics – operated only in the 1930s and early 1940s, when an exclusivist *völkisch* Afrikaner nationalism emerged at a time of 'poor white' unemployment and political and social instability, which coincided with the threat of substantial Jewish immigration and Jewish upward mobility. Under these circumstances, antisemitism acquired what Hannah Arendt has termed 'political relevance'.[1] The Jew helped consolidate an all-embracing Afrikaner identity, understood in terms of cultural unity, national roots, and opposition to the foreigner, with antisemitism serving to blur class divisions and antagonisms within Afrikaner society. By employing the discourse of 'race' to exclude and denigrate Jews, the Afrikaner's inferior status in society and his poverty could be explained in 'racial' or national terms.[2] Consequently, despite the upturn in the economy from the mid-1930s, it is no coincidence that antisemitism continued to suffuse specifically right-wing Afrikaner political discourse and programmes. And it is also no coincidence that the 'Jewish question' continued to be tied to internecine Afrikaner struggles, and utilised according to prevailing political needs, cultural ambitions and power games.[3]

Notwithstanding the importance of contingencies and context, the transformation of 'private' into 'public' antisemitism in the 1930s and early 1940s would not have been possible without the emergence and consolidation of an anti-Jewish stereotype that had long penetrated the national consciousness. Without this, white radical right propaganda in the 1930s would not have been embraced at the popular level. There is, in other words, a connection and a continuity between anti-Jewish sentiment as manifest in images of and ideas about the Jew before 1930, and the anti-Jewish political programmes of the 1930s and early 1940s, but it was the specific circumstances of the 1930s that enabled the earlier sentiments to be translated into party-political policy.[4]

This analysis is confirmed by the rapid decline in anti-Jewish hostility after 1948, despite sporadic incidents of Jew-hatred and antisemitic propaganda disseminated by fringe actors and groups. Fantasies persisted, but the crude and popular animosity of earlier decades largely withered away. Vulgar Hoggenheimer cartoons, for example, were used only very occasionally and then with diminishing returns. Upwardly mobile Afrikaners no longer perceived the Jew as a threat, and there was little need to utilise the Jew to further *völkisch* ends. Within a few years, an emergent Afrikaner bourgeoisie, well-educated and more self-assured than its forebears, enjoyed the economic fruits of racist exploitation and political power. Afrikaners developed a new-found respect for enterprise and material success and, as they began to experience power and mobility themselves, their sense of inferiority and fear of the Jew (now unequivocally part of the dominant and privileged white population) began to evaporate. Simply put, prosperity blunted resentment.

In some quarters, however, Jews were still associated with money and sharp business practices, and the scent of grand Jewish conspiracies lingered, albeit with little traction. Even the disproportionate involvement of Jews in the Treason and Rivonia trials of the 1950s and early 1960s failed to ignite party-political action. However, notions of the liberal and communist Jew persisted and, as political deviants, they were seen to threaten the apartheid project. Perceptions of subversion were reinforced and intensified by Israel's hostile stance towards South Africa in the early 1960s when the Jewish state supported the African bloc against the apartheid regime in international forums.

Yet attempts to propagate and mobilise around anti-Jewish conspiracies had little success. Even pristine neo-Calvinist exclusivism – resurrected under the HNP after 1970 and the CP and AWB in the 1980s – failed to galvanise action. By then, writes Jonathan Hyslop, Afrikaner identification with 'the modernist statist project of apartheid' had given way to rampant individualism and consumerism.[5] Nevertheless, Jews continued to be associated with liberalism and communism. Of course, a kernel of truth underpinned these notions: Jews *were* over-represented on the white radical left and *were* prominent among liberal opponents of the National Party, and Israel *was* vocal in its opposition to apartheid in the early 1960s.[6] On the other hand, chimerical or irrational fantasies about Jews – arguably, the hallmark of antisemitism – seemingly served psychological and social needs and were demonstrably connected to centuries of antisemitic pathology.[7] The continuing circulation of *The Protocols of the Elders of Zion* illustrates this. For 'the losers' its message is especially appealing, writes Stephen Bonner, as blame for political failure could be shifted onto the 'alien' outsider.[8] More generally, however, fantasies, including Holocaust denial and the belief that Israel serves as the locus of international Jewish power (a sort of Jewish Vatican), suggest 'paranoia'.[9] In the final analysis, it seems that fabrications and conspiratorial fantasies offer simple explanations for what the historian David Nirenberg calls 'fearful complexity'.[10] So-called facts can be shoehorned into a supposedly logical consistency, and hatred or anger – whatever its aetiology – projected onto a chosen target.

This is certainly the case for remnants of the white radical right and for those Muslims who disseminated *The Protocols of the Elders of Zion* and denied the Holocaust. In the search for simple answers to complex issues, the anti-Zionist left and the radical right indeed share an image of an omnipotent Jew – one undermining, the other embracing, apartheid (as manifest in the Pretoria–Jerusalem axis of the 1970s and 1980s). Convergence in the sense of a shared image of the all-powerful Jew is also apparent in the use of antisemitic tropes: Israel – the Jew writ large – is seen as the centre of a vast conspiracy, nefariously manipulating global and South African politics and finance. In the words of Martin Jansen, a prominent member of the Palestine Solidarity Committee, 'the powerful tentacles of Zionist power and influences reach into the commanding heights of our economy and the ANC government through business arrangements and patronage, including President Zuma and family members'.[11] This kind of statement connects seamlessly to a long history of Jew-hatred, facilitated in today's world by ubiquitous social and electronic media (particularly the internet's hate-filled sites), which include South African locations.[12] Speed and connectivity are everything, explains Robert Wistrich: 'The "new" Judeophobes can take the age-old anti-Semitic narrative, link it to highly inflammatory images of real conflict (Iraq, Palestine, Lebanon), and spread a toxic message of fanaticism and Jew-hatred that can reach millions of people at the click of a mouse.'[13]

Israel has now become the locus of hate. In South Africa this is driven primarily, but not exclusively, by Muslims. Many human rights-oriented elites – both black and white, Christian and Muslim – consider Zionism (essentially a nineteenth-century ethnonational movement) to be illegitimate.[14] There is little empathy for ethnic polities in South African thought today, which, as Giliomee puts it, is informed by 'a dogmatic or intransigent universalism'. 'Its point of departure', he writes, 'is that race or ethnicity as a principle of social organization is essentially irrational and ephemeral and that there is no need to make any concessions to it. What this boils down to is the unshakeable conviction that there is not much more to racial or ethnic identification than the legacy of apartheid classification.'[15] Such views were widely shared in progressive circles. Certainly, the ANC, dating back to its formative policy document, the Freedom Charter of 1955, has little time for ethnic politics or what it sees as 'tribalism'. It has always viewed such politics as a means to divide and rule, manifest in the apartheid project with its proposed puppet ethnic 'homelands'.[16] Archbishop Desmond Tutu went so far as to declare 'native' cultural identities as little more than an excrescence of colonial racism – something a democratic nation should not countenance.[17]

For the critics of Zionism, historic ties between Jews and the 'land of Israel' are of no consequence. An important dimension of Jewish identity is thereby fundamentally challenged. The reality of Zionism as a Jewish liberation movement is discarded; the term has been mangled and has become associated with exclusivism, oppression and expansionism. 'It's a policy that to me looks like it has very many parallels with racism,' said Tutu.[18] Jewish suffering in the diaspora and the dramatic rebirth of a legitimate, United Nations-sanctioned Jewish state are not acknowledged. Even South Africa's celebration of cultural diversity – enshrined in its Constitution – seemingly cannot entertain space for its Jewish minority which overwhelmingly (albeit not uncritically) shares the Zionist dream.[19]

In power since 1994, the ANC has effectively separated 'good' from 'bad' (Zionist) Jews. Its chief representative at the United Nations, Dr Neo Mnumzana, put it as follows in 1988:

> Jews in South Africa come in many different political colours. There are those who belong to the Zionist movement and represent the same reality which is concretised in the state of Israel, and we disapprove of those members of the Jewish community who have these Zionist affiliations. There are also Jews who belong to the broad struggle against apartheid. We see such members of the Jewish community in a positive light. There are also Jews who belong to the African National Congress, which is the national liberation movement of the South African people. We see them in an even more positive light.[20]

A Changing Cast: Jew-Hatred in South Africa

Over time the identity of the purveyors of Jew-hatred in South Africa has changed. Anti-alienism (or hostility towards the eastern European Jewish immigrants in the late nineteenth and early twentieth centuries) emanated essentially from the white English-speaking merchant class and rural Afrikaners, and was rooted in upheavals wrought by the 'mineral revolution', the demonstrable power of mining capital, and the economic recession in the wake of the Anglo-Boer War. By the 1930s and early 1940s, the 'Jewish question' was driven by the white (mainly Afrikaner) radical right and was embedded in the nativism of the 1920s and the socio-economic instability and political tensions at a time of burgeoning *völkisch* Afrikaner nationalism. Since the 1970s, a 'Zionist question' has replaced the 'Jewish question' as a younger Muslim generation, operating in the oppressive apartheid political milieu, sought meaning and explanations in radical Islamist literature and conspiratorial texts.[21] More recently, the anti-Western and post-colonial intellectual turn has brought in other 'progressives' beyond the Muslim community.[22]

In each of these different phases it is apparent that attitudes have been informed – at least in part – by ideas and intellectual traditions emanating from beyond South Africa. This is hardly surprising. The period of anti-alienism in early twentieth-century South Africa was an age of increasing literacy, improved communications and large population migrations, notably from Britain to South Africa. The penetration of European ideas was inescapable, and a vaguely racial definition of 'Jewishness' ensured that those traits traditionally associated with Jews abroad would be ascribed to their co-religionists in South Africa. The impact of European ideas was also apparent in the 1930s when the radical right imported fascist ideas, as evident in the 'shirtist' movements, the Ossewabrandwag and Pirow's New Order. The penetration into South Africa of *The Protocols of the Elders of Zion*, a foundational text for modern Jew-hatred, forcefully illustrates this. One of those charged in the 1934 Grahamstown *Protocols* or 'Greyshirt' trial, Johannes von Strauss von Moltke, specifically claimed he was inspired by Hitler's 'revolution' and was deeply influenced by Henry Hamilton Beamish, a well-known Irish-born antisemite. A one-time resident of the Cape Colony, Beamish subsequently founded the antisemitic Judaic Publishing Company (renamed the Britons Publishing Company) in England in 1922.[23] Von Moltke was acquainted with Beamish's writings and, as noted earlier, the Irishman gave supporting testimony at the *Protocols* trial.[24] Post-war radical right conspiracists, including Holocaust deniers, were similarly informed by global networks and publications. By way of example, we know that Ray Rudman, SED Brown and Ivor Benson were very familiar with the works of international Jew-haters and had personal connections with neo-Nazis and fantasists abroad, while Johan Schoeman dipped widely into the world of conspiracy literature. Obsessive anti-Zionists on the left similarly connected to a print and, later, an electronic global network, fuelled by a post-colonial anti-Zionist discourse.[25]

In more recent times this hostility has evolved into the global Boycott, Divestment, Sanctions (BDS) movement in which South Africa has been described as the 'linchpin'.[26] Accusations of American imperialistic 'machinations' in the Middle East, with Israel identified as the handmaiden of the United States, resonate widely, as do other conspiracy theories.[27] Living as second-class citizens under a centrally controlled authoritarian apartheid regime has probably encouraged South African Muslim conspiratorial fantasies. Here Fred Halliday's observations on the Arab world may well be pertinent: 'The very condition of being oppressed, in a collectivity as much as in an individual, is likely to produce its own distorted forms of perception: mythical history, hatred and chauvinism towards others, conspiracy theories of all stripes, unreal phantasms of emancipation.'[28]

For each cast of haters, the Jew has been identified as a source of evil in South Africa: at the turn of the century, it was for fomenting war, corroding business ethics, and corrupting society; in the 1930s and early 1940s, for pulling the political and economic strings of society; and in recent decades (in the form of anti-Zionism), for malevolently orchestrating global politics and financial affairs in a quest for world domination. In this sense the radical right and the contemporary anti-Zionist left share much with the left-liberal JA Hobson, whose work on imperialism deeply influenced Lenin.[29] Writing at the end of the nineteenth century and informed by the so-called logic of capitalism and its ties to imperialism, Hobson saw Jews as orchestrating the Anglo-Boer War for financial gain. Like the Hobsonians on the left and the radicals on the right, some anti-Zionists today have constructed a fantasy world with the malevolent and manipulative Jew at its centre.

It is tempting to note that Hobson's explanation for the Anglo-

Boer War, von Moltke's advocacy of *The Protocols of the Elders of Zion*, and the global Jewish conspiracies purveyed by Islamists each have a bearing on what Daniel Pipes refers to as the great 'radical utopian ideologies' of the twentieth century: Leninism, fascism and Islamism. Each is informed by a world conspiracy and each attempts to 'disrupt the very premises of human life', writes Pipes.[30] Yet ironically, each of these ideologies sees 'the Other' – and more specifically the Jew – as conspiring to dominate the world. Thus Hobson's understanding of financiers (chiefly Jewish) driving imperialism captivated Lenin, who refined the idea of 'monopoly capitalism' and its threat as a part of the communist worldview; the *Protocols* in turn informed Hitler and Nazism and served – in the classic phrase of Norman Cohn – as a 'warrant for genocide'; while Islamists focus on an apocalyptic struggle in which Israel – the collective Jew – serves as the focal point of fantasy.[31] The historical hand may have moved on, but the 'hidden hand' of the Jew remains.

Accounting for the Ebb and Flow of Antisemitism

Accounting for the ebb and flow of antisemitism is complicated, and anti-Jewish hostility cannot be reduced to a single cause. The structural position of Jews and the timing of their entry into society are, in the South African case, important factors. One certainly sees a significant increase of antisemitism during times of economic and social stress. This was apparent on the Witwatersrand in the mid-1890s and in Cape Town during the economic depression which followed the Anglo-Boer War. It was particularly the case in the 1930s, when, in the wake of the Wall Street crash, South Africa grappled with social, political and economic instability. Some would argue that it was the alien nature of the Yiddish-speaking immigrants that underpinned much of the hostility. Jews were seen to be ineradicably different and set apart by specific cultural and religious predilections and, according to their detractors, by a racial otherness. But to account for antisemitism in terms of the conspicuousness of the victims – or, for that matter, their structural position within the economy and society – is too simplistic. Prevailing discourses, as Bryan Cheyette has argued in the British context, are inclined to construct the Jew within a pre-set frame, and no account of antisemitism can ignore the historical evolution of an anti-Jewish discourse.[32] Here one must consider the Christian *adversus Judaeos* legacy and Islamic anti-Jewish religious texts and narratives, as well as the mutations of Jew-hate during the Enlightenment and post-Enlightenment, including social Darwinism and the racialisation of the Jew.

Christian religious antisemitism in South Africa certainly cannot be entirely discounted. In the decades prior to apartheid, religious framing undoubtedly played a role and continued to do so in the post-1948 period when neo-Calvinism powerfully informed the cultural agenda under the National Party and its offshoots. Religious differences may well have reinforced the alien or outsider status of the Jew, but, in the main, Jews in South Africa have not been perceived through a theological prism. General perceptions have been rooted largely in the context of South Africa's own historical reality and intellectual traditions. In this regard, nativism and ethnonationalism in the 1920s and 1930s heightened and sharpened differences. Here there are instructive parallels to be drawn with Quebec in the interwar years, where fascist groups, such as Adrien Arcand's Parti National Social Chrétien, similarly highlighted the allegedly negative role of Jews – a useful means of bolstering a francophone identity founded in confession and notions of race. The source of this hostility lay in a hostile anti-modernist ethnonationalism, which had striking similarities to Afrikaner interwar nationalism. French-Canadian nationalists, supported by the Roman Catholic Church, saw the Jews and other so-called foreigners as an obstacle to this project.[33] As we have seen, neo-Calvinist Afrikaners similarly saw their lifestyle threatened by English speakers, who dominated the urban centres, and among whom the Jew emerged as a convenient symbol. Anti-modernist ethnonationalism of both the Quebecois and the Afrikaner in the 1930s employed the 'Other' to enhance self-definition and to deflect divisions within the group. Insular and backward-looking, ethnonationalists focused on the Jew as an exemplar of the despised modern. The danger inherent in ethnonationalism – be it Quebecois or Afrikaner or any Other – was even more apparent in interwar Europe.[34] It is also arguable that black–Jewish tensions in the United States are the outcome of a variant of black nationalism combined with religious hatred of the sort expounded by Louis Farrakhan's Nation of Islam – an explosive mixture.[35]

Given the inherent danger of exclusivist nationalism, it is particularly significant that the character of nationalism in South Africa today is, at least formally, inclusive in orientation and non-racial in content. Pluralism, multiculturalism and 'rainbowism' – the very antithesis of ethnonationalism – take the sharpness out of ethnic conflict and militate against antisemitism. South Africa's 'rainbow' nation celebrates diversity and difference. Cultural rights and religious freedom are enshrined in the new South African Constitution, while Church and State are separated.[36] In 1998 the provincial affairs and constitutional development minister, Mohammed Valli Moosa, spoke in parliament of the government's endeavour to protect the rights of cultural, religious and linguistic communities in the context of mutual respect and universalist humanism. Speaking in the same debate, the deputy speaker of the National Assembly, Baleka Mbete-Kgositsile, emphasised the need for South Africans to promote and enjoy their diverse cultures. No one culture, language or religion was superior to another. 'This is important to understand', she stressed, 'because if we do not understand this, we then give a superior status to some in our society because the cultures, religions and languages we regard as superior are theirs.'[37]

Such sentiments are far removed from the exclusivist and triumphalist character of Afrikaner nationalism in the 1930s and 1940s. Equally important is the condemnation of antisemitism by political leaders in recent years. Unlike the Nationalists of the 1930s, the ANC has not manipulated whatever anti-Jewish sentiment exists for political gain. One of its Western Cape executive members who chanted during a protest march on the Israeli Embassy in Cape Town that Hitler should have killed more Jews was severely sanctioned.[38] Similarly, the industrial disputes referred to earlier that specifically accused 'Jewish capitalists' were condemned. In fact, COSATU emphasised that such slogans were racist and contrary to its policy of non-racialism. Recently, however, condemnations of antisemitism have become more tepid. There are, indeed, disturbing signs that many South Africans have turned away from non-racism and multiculturalism.[39]

More concerning is a burgeoning anti-Zionism, which for some provides a fig leaf for simple Jew-hatred. Much of this is driven by a radicalised Muslim minority that is well connected to a global network. Some of this hatred is tied to historically contingent factors. For example, in the Western Cape, where most Muslims reside, some of the anger is underpinned by historical landlord–tenant relations in the inner city, encounters between employers and employees in the textile industry (where Jews were prominent as employers and Muslims as employees) and, of course, a general anger at white privilege with which Jews are associated. Ebrahim Rasool captured some of these perceptions: 'the Jewish community is also by and large the business community, the owners of the big shops, the factories. More often than not, our relationship with the Jewish community is one where we are around negotiating tables with them. Our workers are striking at their factories and so forth.'[40] Farid Esack put it even more bluntly when discussing Muslim attitudes towards Jews that were embedded in a particular relationship:

> All the normal prejudices that Jews are misers, the longnosed ones, the sellouts, that you can't trust the Jews and this, that and the other. All those prejudices are in the Muslim community. There is a very intense hostility towards Jews amongst Muslims. The one is the ordinary contact that our mothers and fathers had with Jews. The contact with Jews was that the Jew was the debt collector or the money lender. There is this ongoing antagonism between the money collector and the person who has to pay the money, which I guess would be this way in any kind of society. Muslims, however, would know that this guy was a Jew. The black Christian neighbour in the community would consider this man as just another white man.[41]

A dialectical relationship thus operates between negative stereotyping embedded in historical encounters, religious differences, radical teachings and specific realities. In other words, even without the close ties between the apartheid state and Israel from the late 1960s until 1990, tensions would have been unavoidable. Importantly, however, a decidedly anti-Jewish tone has crept into anti-Zionist rhetoric. Taj Hargey, a Muslim academic, explains this in terms of an 'incompetent clergy' which was unable to deal with Zionism on an 'intellectual and rational basis' and was thus obliged to resort to 'sheer emotive' antisemitism: 'So they go onto *The Protocols of the Elders of Zion*, they mention other scurrilous material, usually long noses, being stingy – the Shylock type imagery of Jews.'[42]

Hargey's observations are important: patently anti-Jewish motifs are often embedded in Muslim anti-Zionist discourse and propaganda. This informs the rhetoric associated with *al-Quds* day during the Muslim holy month of Ramadan and the propaganda disseminated by, for example, the Indian-born author Ahmed Deedat, who was head of the missionary-oriented Islamic Propagation Centre International (IPCI) in Durban, a well-funded organisation that for decades disseminated anti-Hindu, anti-Christian, anti-Zionist and antisemitic leaflets to thousands of households.[43] With regard to Jews, IPCI propaganda emphasised their power, cunning and duplicity – indicative of the easy shift from criticism of Israeli behaviour to something more sinister.[44]

It should be noted that some Jews consider the ANC's pro-Palestinian policy in the Middle East to be a form of antisemitism, but this view needs to be carefully evaluated. The ANC is fully entitled to maintain close ties with the PLO and support the Palestinian struggle. These ties date back to the ANC's years in exile when it had every reason to look askance at Pretoria's cosy relationship with Jerusalem. Jews will have to accept the paradox that some of the people whose struggle for freedom they overwhelmingly supported are hostile to the Zionist idea and genuinely sympathetic to the Palestinians. Certainly, Mandela saw Yasser Arafat and Muammar Gaddafi as comrades-in-arms, loyal friends who helped the ANC with funds, training and international support; but applauding notions such as 'Zionism is racism' (as happened in an address to parliamentarians during Arafat's visit in 1998) raises serious questions for most Jews.

The Future

Although there can be little doubt that antisemitism in South Africa has waned since 1948, it has not disappeared. Its latest incarnation is obsessive hostility to Israel which utilises well-worn anti-Jewish tropes such as Holocaust denial and affirmation of *The Protocols of the Elders of*

Zion.⁴⁵ Importantly, hostility towards Israel has substantial resonance in a country whose intelligentsia all too easily frame the Israeli–Palestinian conflict through a South African prism. That conflict has undoubtedly harmed relations between Jews and Muslims. But it is important to remember that the Muslim community is not a monolith.⁴⁶ As we have seen, various intellectual discourses operate and compete. Some are innovative and progressive, with an emphasis on Islamic humanism, universalism and interfaith co-operation; while others such as Qibla and the IUC, heavily influenced by Khomeinism and some of the more radical schools of Islamic thought, are conservative and at odds with religious pluralism and ecumenism.⁴⁷ However, a hostile critique of Zionism is common to both the progressive and conservative strands.⁴⁸ In some cases, this hostility is separated from antisemitism; in others, Zionism and Jews are conflated into a combination that incorporates fantasies about Jewish financial machinations and manipulative imperialism. Notably, much sentiment emerging from hostility towards Zionism and Israel has overflowed into vulgar antisemitism. This was noted decades ago by Farid Esack. 'Nothing that the Jews do will be enough for Muslims,' explained a concerned Esack in response to a question asking whether Jews would be accepted by the Muslim community if they renounced all recognition and support for Israel.⁴⁹

For all that, when we reflect on the future, Muslim hostility towards Jews should be put in perspective. In the first instance, the Muslim population – although relatively large in the Western Cape, KwaZulu-Natal and Gauteng – numbers less than two per cent of the total South African population, and only a small minority are intent on dragging the Middle East conflict with all its toxicity into local politics. It cannot be said that a 'Jewish problem' exists in today's South Africa. When ethnic violence does occur, targets have been black African foreigners, usually in the context of competition over resources and desperate domestic poverty.⁵⁰ Xenophobia in that sense is currently not directed at whites, let alone Jews. Certainly, the South African Jewish Board of Deputies (the official voice of the community) does not see Jews threatened in any serious way.⁵¹ This is not to say that the Jewish community is devoid of concerns, but these are shared with all South Africans and are related primarily to crime, the economy, education and health care.⁵² Even hostility towards Israel needs to be put in perspective. It is not without significance that a Pew poll conducted in South Africa in 2007 revealed greater support for the Israeli Jews than for the Palestinians.[53] It should also be noted that the ANC and its allies COSATU and the SACP alone will not define attitudes to Zionism for all time. Several South African black African leaders have visited Israel and have spoken highly of its achievements. Furthermore, most black Africans are Christians, with a deep attachment to the Holy Land. If Israelis and Palestinians should ever resolve their differences, it is possible that tensions surrounding South African Zionism could dissipate substantially.

Nevertheless, South African Jews cannot afford to be complacent. As we have seen, a range of surveys over five decades have shown a sustained level of anti-Jewish stereotyping. We also know that history has demonstrated unequivocally that ideas precede action. For now, however, the possibility of hostile ideas mutating into public policy is highly unlikely. And that is the litmus test. But it should also be appreciated that historians are notoriously poor at predicting the future. 'Life, unlike science, is simply too full of surprises,' writes Richard Evans when reflecting on historians as prophets. After all, maintains Evans, Paul Kennedy – with all his prodigious learning – predicted in his 1987 bestselling book, *The Rise and Fall of Great Powers*, that the Soviet Union was far from collapse.[54]

Despite this cautionary warning, it is fair to assert that at present Jews are not central to broader cultural and political concerns. But things can change. Black swans do appear. For one thing, if viewed historically, the current politics of pessimism could conceivably provide fertile ground for the targeting of Jews. *Fin de siècle* Austria and Germany stand out as classic examples of mobilisation around resentment, as does the rise of the radical right in Europe today.[55] It may indeed be prudent to heed the wise words of Hugh Trevor-Roper cited in the preface to this study: 'History teaches us that even the most tenuous phantoms can come to life if objective circumstances change. The fantasies of one generation can provide the mental furniture, even the life-blood, of another.'[56]

Notes

Preface

1. See Milton Shain, *The Roots of Antisemitism in South Africa*, University Press of Virginia, Charlottesville, VA, and Witwatersrand University Press, Johannesburg, 1994; and Milton Shain, *A Perfect Storm: Antisemitism in South Africa, 1930–1948*, Jonathan Ball Publishers, Cape Town, 2015.
2. Private antisemitism in this view refers 'to expressions of contempt or discrimination outside the realm of public life' while public antisemitism refers to the 'eruption of anti-Semitism in political life – the injection of anti-Semitism into matters of policy and the manipulation of anti-Semitism for partisan political ends'. See Todd M Endelman, 'Comparative Perspectives on Modern Anti-Semitism in the West', in David Berger (ed.), *History and Hate: The Dimensions of Anti-Semitism*, Jewish Publication Society, Philadelphia, 1986, p. 104.
3. HR Trevor-Roper, 'The Phenomenon of Fascism', in SJ Woolf (ed.), *Fascism in Europe*, Methuen, London, 1981, p. 23.
4. See Shain, *A Perfect Storm*, chapter 6.
5. Black African foreigners have been a primary target in xenophobic conflict for the last two decades.
6. See Richard J Evans, *The Hitler Conspiracies: The Third Reich and the Paranoid Imagination*, Allen Lane, London, 2020, p. 216.
7. This is an estimated figure. Since 2006 'religion' has not been included in the South African census. In 2016, however, an intercensal census that included religious affiliation revealed that Jews numbered 49,470 out of a total population of 55,653,654. See Stats SA, *Community Survey 2016: Report 03-01-06*, https://www.statssa.gov.za/publications/03-01-06/03-01-062016.pdf. In 2019 the Jewish population was estimated at 52,300. See David

Graham, *The Jews of South Africa in 2019: Identity, Community, Society and Demography*, Institute for Jewish Policy Research and the Isaac and Jessie Kaplan Centre for Jewish Studies and Research, University of Cape Town, 2020, p. 12.

8   It is hoped that scholars will in time productively locate and 'entangle' (to use a term employed by Jonathan Judaken) parallel and overlapping hatreds of others in South Africa. See Jonathan Judaken, 'Introduction', in 'Rethinking Anti-Semitism', AHR Roundtable, *American Historical Review*, October 2018. It is certainly the case that hatred of Jews is often shared with hatred of blacks in South Africa.

9   It should be noted that comment focuses mainly on the collective 'Jew', with a bias towards the male stereotype that perhaps reflects sexist assumptions. The reader will also note that extensive use has been made of direct quotations from the sources. Paraphrasing often dilutes the sentiments, tone and temper of the times. In addition, the reader should appreciate that although opinions about and attitudes towards the Jew are inferred by and large from the literate middle classes, it is reasonable to assume that the sources used do not seriously distort popular views.

10   For the origins of the *Protocols*, see Norman Cohn, *Warrant for Genocide: The Myth of the World Jewish Conspiracy and the Protocols of the Elders of Zion*, Harper and Row, New York, 1969; Michael Hagemeister, 'The Protocols of the Elders of Zion: Between History and Fiction', *New German Critique*, 103, vol. 35, no. 1, Spring, 2008; and Evans, *The Hitler Conspiracies*, pp. 15–25.

Introduction

1   Richard Hofstadter, *Social Darwinism in American Thought*, rev. edn, Beacon Press, Boston, 1955, pp. 203–4.

2   See Mark Lilla, *The Once and Future Liberal: After Identity Politics*, HarperCollins, New York, 2017, p. 23.

3   See Shain, *The Roots of Antisemitism in South Africa*.

4   *Volk* translates as 'people' but also refers to an ethno-culturally defined nation.

5   For the Quota Act, see Shain, *The Roots of Antisemitism in South Africa*, pp. 137–41.

6   See Shain, *A Perfect Storm*, chapters 5 and 6.

7   See ibid., chapters 4 and 5.

8   For the Ossewabrandwag, see Christoph Marx, *Oxwagon Sentinel: Radical Afrikaner Nationalism and the History of the Ossewabrandwag*, University of South Africa Press, Pretoria, 2008; P de Klerk, 'Die ideologie van die Ossewabrandwag', in PF van der Schyff (ed.), *Die Ossewa-brandwag: Vuurtjie in droë*

gras, Potchefstroom, 1991; and Shain, *A Perfect Storm*, chapter 6. For the New Order, see FA Mouton, *The Opportunist: The Political Life of Oswald Pirow, 1915–1959*, Protea Book House, Pretoria, 2020, chapter 13.

9   For the impact of National Socialism, see William Henry Vatcher, *White Laager: The Rise of Afrikaner Nationalism*, Frederik Praeger, New York, 1965, pp. 69–75; and Patrick J Furlong, *Between Crown and Swastika: The Impact of the Radical Right on the Afrikaner Nationalist Movement in the Fascist Era*, Wesleyan University Press, Hanover, NH, and Witwatersrand University Press, Johannesburg, 1991, chapters 8–10.

10 Four population groups were defined according to the Population Registration Act No. 30 of 1950: black, white, Coloured and Indian. (Coloureds were people of mixed descent.) The literature sometimes refers to blacks as Africans, while blacks, Coloureds and Indians are sometimes collectively referred to as 'blacks' or (historically) 'non-whites'. To avoid confusion, I shall when necessary use the term 'black African' to distinguish black Africans from Coloureds and Indians.

11 Sally Peberdy, *Selecting Immigrants: National Identity and South Africa's Immigration Policies, 1910–2008*, Witwatersrand University Press, Johannesburg, 2009, p. 82.

12 Abraham Kuyper, the Dutch theologian and statesman, argued that organic social groups existed within wider society.

13 See Saul Dubow, *Apartheid, 1948–1994*, Oxford University Press, Oxford, 2014, pp. 9–16; and 'Afrikaner Nationalism, Apartheid and the Conceptualization of Race', *Journal of African History*, vol. 33, 1992.

14 See Saul Dubow, 'A Definitive Study of the Ossewabrandwag', *Historia*, vol. 1, May 2010, p. 158.

15 Hansard, 10 February 1930.

16 See Shain, *A Perfect Storm*, pp. 203 and 229.

17 Ibid., pp. 194–211.

18 Ibid., pp. 272–8.

19 *Die Burger*, 15 January 1948.

20 *Zionist Record*, 7 May 1948; see also *Zionist Record*, 14 May 1948.

21 See 'Editorial Comment: The "Jewish Question" in SA Politics', *Jewish Affairs*, May 1949.

22 On Malan's political opportunism as regards the Jews, see Milton Shain, 'Paradoxical Ambiguity: DF Malan and the "Jewish Question"', *Transactions of the Royal Society of South Africa*, vol. 72, no. 1, 2017.

23 *Die OB*, 12 November 1947.

24 See Newell M Stultz, *Afrikaner Politics in South Africa, 1934–1948*, University of California Press, Berkeley, 1974, pp. 113 and 136–43; and Lindie Koorts, *DF Malan and the Rise of Afrikaner Nationalism*, Tafelberg, Cape Town, 2014, pp. 376–8.

25 Stultz, *Afrikaner Politics in South Africa*, p. 130.
26 See Atalia Ben-Meir, 'The South African Jewish Community and Politics, 1930–1978, with Special Reference to the South African Jewish Board of Deputies', PhD thesis, University of Natal, 1995, p. 149.
27 See 'Editorial Comment: The Government and the Jews', *Jewish Affairs*, July 1948, p. 2; Gideon Shimoni, *Jews and Zionism: The South African Experience, 1910–1967*, Oxford University Press, Cape Town, 1980, p. 207; Edgar Bernstein, 'Union of South Africa', in Harry Schneiderman and Morris Fine (eds), *American Jewish Year Book 1948–1949*, vol. 50, American Jewish Committee, Jewish Publication Society of America, Philadelphia, 1948–9, p. 304; and South African Jewish Board of Deputies: Report of the Executive Council, August 1947 to May 1949.
28 See Edgar Bernstein, 'Union of South Africa', in Morris Fine (ed.), *American Jewish Year Book*, vol. 51, American Jewish Committee, Jewish Publication Society of America, Philadelphia, 1950, p. 291.
29 Ibid., p. 292.
30 Israel Abrahams, *The Birth of a Community: A History of Western Province Jewry from Earliest Times to the End of the South African War, 1902*, Cape Town Hebrew Congregation, Cape Town, 1955, pp. xii–xiii.
31 At its zenith in 1970, the Jewish population numbered 118,200 or 3.1 per cent of the white population and 0.52 per cent of the total population. See Allie A Dubb, *The Jewish Population of South Africa: The 1991 Sociodemographic Survey*, Jewish Publications–South Africa, Isaac and Jessie Kaplan Centre for Jewish Studies and Research, University of Cape Town, 1994, p. 7.
32 See Jan Hofmeyr, *Christian Principles and Race Problems*, Hoernlé Memorial Lecture, South African Institute of Race Relations, Johannesburg, 1945.
33 *Die Burger*, 11 October 1944.
34 HG Stoker, *Die stryd om die ordes*, Caxton Drukkery, Pretoria, 1941, pp. 117–18, 157–8.
35 See Sheila Patterson, *The Last Trek: A Study of the Boer People and the Afrikaner Nation*, Routledge and Kegan Paul, London, 1957, p. 77.
36 For the Sauer Commission, see 'Kleurvraagstuk-Kommissie van die Herenigde Nasionale Party', African Studies Pamphlet Collection, Special Collections, University of Cape Town Libraries. On the racialisation of the Jew in the first half of the century, see Milton Shain, 'From Undesirable to Unassimilable: The Racialization of the "Jew" in South Africa', in Shirli Gilbert and Avril Alba (eds), *Holocaust Memory and Racism in the Postwar World*, Wayne State University Press, Detroit, MI, 2019.
37 See Vicki Caron, *Between France and Germany: The Jews of Alsace-Lorraine, 1871–1918*, Stanford University Press, Stanford, CA, 1988, pp. 2–5.
38 See Yuri Slezkine, 'The USSR as a Communal Apartment, or How a Socialist State Promoted Ethnic Particularism', *Slavic Review*, vol. 53, no.

2, Summer 1994, p. 415.
39 See Patterson, *The Last Trek*; and Gwendolen M Carter, *The Politics of Inequality: South Africa since 1948*, rev. edn, Frederick A Praeger, New York, 1959.
40 Carter, *The Politics of Inequality*, p. 250.
41 See Daniel Silke, 'The Broadcasting of Politics in South Africa', MSocSc thesis, University of Cape Town, 1989.
42 *Die Burger*, 7 June 1948.
43 Gus Saron, 'After the Election', *Jewish Affairs*, June 1948, p. 9.
44 *Zionist Record*, 21 May 1948.
45 *Die Burger*, 28 December 1948. Holm subsequently obtained a senior position in the Department of Education. Later he published *Man en standpunt*, Morester en Noordtransvaler, Potgietersrus, 1960, a book which praised Nazism and included antisemitic statements. See *Sunday Times*, 10 January 1960.
46 See *Die Burger* and *Volksblad*, 1 February 1949.
47 See, for example, the 'Honiball' cartoons in *Die Burger*, 7, 14 and 31 January, and 14 February 1953; also 'Hoggenheimer is Back', *Sunday Times*, 25 February 1951. For the origins and evolution of the caricature, see Milton Shain, 'Hoggenheimer: The Making of a Myth', *Jewish Affairs*, September 1981.
48 See Hansard, 19 February 1952.
49 The change was welcomed by both *Die Vaderland* (19 September 1951) and *Die Transvaler* (19 September 1951).
50 See Ben-Meir, 'The South African Jewish Community and Politics', p. 162; and Shimoni, *Jews and Zionism*, pp. 210–11. The Transvaal ban was only lifted when the Afrikaner Party and NP merged in 1951.
51 See René de Villiers, 'Afrikaner Nationalism', in Monica Wilson and Leonard Thompson (eds), *The Oxford History of South Africa*, vol. 2, Clarendon Press, Oxford, p. 399.
52 See Phyllis Lewsen, 'The Threat of "Christian National" Education', *Jewish Affairs*, February 1949.
53 See Education League, *Blueprint for Blackout: A Commentary on the Education Policy of the Instituut vir Christelik-Nationale Onderwys*, Education League, Johannesburg, n.d., p. 23.
54 See Hansard, 3 May 1949; *Die Kerkbode*, 16 March 1949; and DC Coetzee, 'C.N.O.: Beleid – toegelig en verdedig', *Inspan*, March 1949. See also Carter, *The Politics of Inequality*, pp. 261–6; and Graham Leach, *The Afrikaners: Their Last Great Trek*, Macmillan, London, 1989, pp. 43–5.
55 Ten years after *Blueprint for Blackout* was published, the Education League published another booklet condemning CNO and noting that what was initially 'unofficial policy' had become formal National Party policy. See

Education League, *Blackout: A Commentary on the Education Policy of the Institut vir Christelik-Nasionale Onderwys*, Education League, Johannesburg, 1959, p. 8.

56 See Shimoni, *Jews and Zionism*, p. 255.
57 Hansard, 3 May 1949.
58 Effectively CNE separated English and Afrikaans pupils, thus ending a long tradition of single-medium bilingual education. For an example of long-standing Afrikaner fears of Catholicism, see *Die Kerkbode*, 29 September 1951. See 'Die gewetensklousule', by Professor DH Cilliers of the University of South Africa (*Bulletin van die Suid-Afrikaanse Vereeniging vir die Bevordering van Christelike Wetenskap*, vol. 20, pp. 30–10S), where Roman Catholics and Jews appear embroiled in the liberal impulses of the conscience clause.
59 Hansard, 22 February 1967. Vegkop and Bloedrivier were sites of historic Boer military victories.
60 Only Potchefstroom University was ultimately able to modify its conscience clause in line with that institution's historical theological origins. See Gustav Saron, 'A University's "Private Affair" or State Policy?', *Jewish Affairs*, January 1962.
61 See Edgar Bernstein, 'Union of South Africa', in Morris Fine (ed.), *American Jewish Year Book 1951*, vol. 52, American Jewish Committee, Jewish Publication Society of America, Philadelphia, 1951, p. 265.
62 See South African Jewish Board of Deputies, Executive Council Minutes, 14 November 1966. It should be noted that there was substantial opposition across the political divide to the abolition of the conscience clause.
63 Problems remained. A Jew or Roman Catholic, for example, would not be considered appropriate for the Chair of Philosophy at RAU on the grounds that it would detract from the Afrikaans spirit of the university. See South African Jewish Board of Deputies, Executive Council Minutes, 2 October 1968.
64 See *Main Report of the Commission of Inquiry into Universities*, Department of National Education, Pretoria, n.d., p. 71.
65 *Sunday Times*, 16 May 1980.
66 Hansard, 15 April 1932.

Chapter 1

1 See *Rand Daily Mail*, 29 August 1968; and *Die Vaderland*, 29 August 1968. For the 'Mafeje Affair', see Howard Phillips, *UCT under Apartheid: From Onset to Sit-In, 1948–1968*, Jacana Media, Johannesburg, 2019, pp. 318–23; and, for the 'Muller Affair', see Ben-Meir, 'The South African Jewish Community and Politics', pp. 366–75, and Shimoni, *Jews and Zionism*, pp. 296–7.

2   See Shimoni, *Community and Conscience*, pp. 115–16. Importantly, the Report of the Sauer Commission of 1947 identified both liberalism and communism as threats to the survival of whites in South Africa. See 'Kleurvraagstuk-Kommissie van die Herenigde Nasionale Party'.
3   Hansard, 19 August 1948.
4   *Rand Daily Mail*, 2 June 1948.
5   See Carter, *The Politics of Inequality*, p. 253; and Aletta J Norval, *Deconstructing Apartheid Discourse*, Verso Books, London, 1996, chapters 1–3.
6   See 'Grondbeginsels van die Calvinisties-Christelike staatkunde' (Fundamental principles of Calvinist-Christian political science) in *Handelinge van die twee-en-twintigste vergadering van die Raad van die Kerke: Gehou in Bloemfontein op 16 May 1951 en volgende dae*, Voortrekkerpers, Johannesburg, pp. 52–75, Dutch Reformed Church Archives in South Africa, Stellenbosch. See also Johann Kinghorn, 'Modernization and Apartheid: The Afrikaner Churches', in Richard Elphick and Rodney Davenport (eds), *Christianity in South Africa: A Political, Social and Cultural History*, James Currey, Oxford, and David Philip, Cape Town, 1997, pp. 143–4.
7   *Sunday Express*, 1 September 1968.
8   See, for example, *Cape Argus*, 29 August 1968.
9   *Beeld*, 1 September 1968.
10 See Ben-Meir, 'The South African Jewish Community and Politics', p. 375.
11 This is illustrated by the substantial opposition expressed by Parktown residents in Johannesburg when it was announced that a synagogue was to be built in their neighbourhood. The 'people in the neighbourhood do not want a "nuisance" in the shape of Jews who come and worship in that area in large numbers at certain times,' said the National Party MP for North Rand, Barzillai ('Blaar') Coetzee, Hansard, 3 April 1957. Blackballing persisted well into the 1980s if not beyond. See, for example, *Sunday Star*, 23 August 1987.
12 See Richard Mendelsohn and Milton Shain, *The Jews in South Africa: An Illustrated History*, Jonathan Ball Publishers, Cape Town, 2007, chapter 3.
13 Hansard, 19 August 1948.
14 *Dagbreek en Sondagnuus*, 11 October 1964.
15 The 'apartheid project', writes Posel, 'was pervaded by a neo-Fichtean idealisation of a divinely inspired Afrikaner nation as the political vanguard of the white race'. See Deborah Posel, 'The Apartheid Project, 1948–1970', in Robert Ross, Anne Kelk Mager and Bill Nasson (eds), *The Cambridge History of South Africa*, vol. 2, *1885–1994*, Cambridge University Press, Cambridge, 2012, p. 325. Notwithstanding scholarly debates regarding the depth of its missionary and religious motivations, the power of the Church as a locus of guidance cannot be minimised. See FA van Jaarsveld, 'The Idea of the Afrikaner on His Calling and Mission', in *The Afrikaner's Interpretation*

of South African History, Simondium Publishers, Cape Town, 1964.
16 See Norval, *Deconstructing Apartheid Discourse*, pp. 67–76.
17 Hansard, 19 August 1948.
18 See *Die Burger*, 24 January 1949.
19 Evangelos Mantzaris, 'Radical Community: The Yiddish-Speaking Branch of the International Socialist League, 1918–1920', in Belinda Bozzoli (ed.), *Class, Community and Conflict: South African Perspectives*, Ravan Press, Johannesburg, 1987; and Tom Lodge, *Red Road to Freedom: A History of the South African Communist Party 1921–2021*, Jacana Media, Johannesburg, 2021, chapter 1.
20 See Bernard Sachs, *Multitude of Dreams*, Kayor Publishing House, Johannesburg, 1949, p. 132; and Shain, *The Roots of Antisemitism in South Africa*, pp. 82–6.
21 See Shain, *The Roots of Antisemitism in South Africa*, pp. 92–9; and Wessel Visser, 'The Production of Literature on the "Red Peril" and "Total Onslaught" in Twentieth-Century South Africa', *Historia*, vol. 49, no. 2, November 2004, pp. 106–7.
22 See Shain, *A Perfect Storm*, pp. 90 and 205; and Irina Filatova and Apollon Davidson, *The Hidden Thread: Russia and South Africa in the Soviet Era*, Jonathan Ball Publishers, Cape Town, 2013, p. 201.
23 See Visser, 'The Production of Literature on the "Red Peril"', p. 111.
24 Norval, *Deconstructing Apartheid Discourse*, p. 82.
25 *SAJC*, 11 November 1938; and *Die Volkstem*, 8 November 1938.
26 See Koorts, *DF Malan*, pp. 363–4; and *Die Transvaler*, 25 June 1941.
27 See, for example, *Die OB*, 10 May 1944 and 19 July 1944.
28 See Shain, *A Perfect Storm*, chapter 6; and Filatova and Davidson, *The Hidden Thread*, chapters 6 and 7.
29 See Filatova and Davidson, *The Hidden Thread*, chapters 6 and 7.
30 *Die OB*, 28 August 1946.
31 Filatova and Davidson, *The Hidden Thread*, p. 170.
32 Hansard, 27 January 1943.
33 Eric Louw, *The Communist Danger*, Publications of the Enlightenment Service of the Reunited Nationalist Party, no. 5, 1943.
34 Hansard, 22 February 1945.
35 *New Era*, 20 September 1945.
36 *New Era*, 22 August 1946.
37 See Visser, 'The Production of Literature on the "Red Peril"', pp. 111–12; and SJ Botha et al., *Bewaar jou erfenis: Simposium oor kommunism*, Antikom, Port Elizabeth, 1968, pp. 11–15.
38 See Visser, 'The Production of Literature on the "Red Peril"', pp. 111–12.
39 See Reinier Willem Louw, 'Die vormingsjare van die kerkleier JD (Koot) Vorster 1909–1956', MA thesis, University of South Africa, 1994. For

Vorster's hostility to communism, see Daniël Johannes Langner, 'Teen die hele wêreld vry: JD Vorster as 'n neo-Calvinis in die Nederduitse Gereformeerde Kerk 1935–1980', Doctor Theologiae thesis, University of the Free State, 2004, pp. 172–84.
40 See Vatcher, *White Laager*, pp. 63–4.
41 See Marx, *Oxwagon Sentinel*, p. 377.
42 See *New Era*, 26 April 1945.
43 *Die Transvaler*, 9 April 1938; and Bruce K Murray, *Wits: The Open Years; A History of the University of the Witwatersrand, Johannesburg 1939–1959*, Witwatersrand University Press, Johannesburg, 1997, p. 102.
44 See Shain, *A Perfect Storm*, p. 262.
45 *Die Burger*, 19 September 1945.
46 *Die OB*, 28 August 1946.
47 JFJ van Rensburg, *Their Paths Crossed Mine: Memoirs of the Commandant-General of the Ossewa-Brandwag*, Central News Agency, Johannesburg, 1956, p. 242.
48 See Hansard, 26 January 1950.
49 See *Die Burger*, 28 August 1945.
50 See Koorts, *DF Malan*, p. 376.
51 See Edward Shills, *Tradition*, Chicago University Press, Chicago, 1981, esp. p. 39.
52 Hansard, 17 May 1949. In his autobiography, Morris Kentridge noted that 'whatever the reaction and extremism of the new Government may be, I must bear testimony to the fact that at no time has it raised the Jewish question, and that it continued Dr Malan's policy of friendship to the State of Israel and helpfulness to South African Zionism'. Morris Kentridge, *I Recall: Memoirs of Morris Kentridge*, Free Press Limited, Johannesburg, 1959, p. 392.
53 Kahn was often taunted in the House by Nationalists with calls of 'Jood, Jood' (Jew, Jew). I am indebted to Benjamin Pogrund for this recollection.
54 See Ben-Meir, 'The South African Jewish Community and Politics', p. 244.
55 See, for example, Alex Hepple (MP for Rosettenville) and Hyman Davidoff (MP for Edendale and then Johannesburg City), Hansard, 14 June 1954. In 1953 the CPSA re-emerged as the underground South African Communist Party (SACP).
56 In a debate on unions, for example, a veritable flood of Jewish names was mentioned: Hansard, 26 May 1952. Having been elected as a Native Representative to parliament following the passing of the Riotous Assemblies and Suppression of Communism (Amendment) Bill, Ray Alexander was forcibly blocked from taking her seat in 1954. See HJ and RE Simons, *Class and Colour in South Africa 1850–1950*, Penguin Books, Harmondsworth, 1969, p. 594.
57 See Report by the Investigation Officer of the South African Police into

the Activities of Communist Party of South Africa 1947, cited in Hansard, 13 June 1952. See Ben-Meir, 'The South African Jewish Community and Politics', pp. 167–70.

58 Koot Vorster raised the Harmel issue in an address to an International Symposium on Communism in Chicago in 1967 (see South African Jewish Board of Deputies: Report of Executive Council Minutes, 22 May 1967). See later reiterations in PJ Venter, 'Michael Harmel en die Joodse Raad', *Die Afrikaner*, 9 July 1976; and Johann Vorster, 'Hier is feite oor Joodse Raad en kommuniste', *Die Afrikaner*, 30 July 1976.

59 See Hansard, 29 April 1952 and 11 February 1954.

60 See Hansard, 19 February 1963.

61 For the fiery debate, see Hansard, 15 April 1952.

62 See Glenn Frankel, *Rivonia's Children: Three Families and the Cost of Conscience in White South Africa*, Farrar, Straus and Giroux, New York, 1999, p. 56.

63 See FR Metrowich, *Africa and Communism: A Study of Successes, Set-Backs and Stooge States*, Voortrekkerpers, Johannesburg, 1967, chapter 9.

64 See, for example, Eric Louw's attack on liberals and communists in *The Forum*, 1 April 1950; PJ Meyer, *Die hand van Moskou in Suid-Afrika: 'n Sonderlinge geskiedenis van ongelooflike gebeurtenisse*, Antikommunitiese Aksiekommissie, c.1950; and FA Mouton, '"Beyond the Pale": Oswald Pirow, Sir Oswald Mosley, the "Enemies of the Soviet Union" and Apartheid, 1948–1959', *Journal of Contemporary History*, vol. 43, no. 2, 2018.

65 Hansard, 18 February 1954.

66 Hansard, 13 May 1957.

67 Cited in Roy Isacowitz, *Telling People What They Don't Want to Hear: A Liberal Life under Apartheid*, Kibbitzer Books, Tel Aviv, 2019, p. 305. For Congress of the People, see p.32

68 Constitution and other documentation regarding the Sons of South Africa Movement; 'A Conception of South Africanism', by SED Brown, 1945–1947, EG Jansen Papers, PV 94, Number 11577, Archives for Contemporary Affairs, University of the Free State, Bloemfontein.

69 See *South African Observer*, 'Death of SED Brown', January 1991; Michael Cobden, 'The Invisible Mr. Brown', *Rand Daily Mail*, 2 September 1967; and JHP Serfontein, 'McCarthy's Friend was Given Secret Job as Captain in S.A. Army: S.E.D. Brown with the Lid Off', *Sunday Times*, 28 August 1966. For the League of Gentiles, see Shain, *The Roots of Antisemitism in South Africa*, pp. 121–5.

70 This was evident in the *South African Observer* from the start. Jews were associated with communism, while Zionism/Israel and 'international Judaism' were of major concern. See, for example, *South African Observer*, December 1955.

Notes

71 SED Brown to EG Jansen, 31 May 1946: Constitution and other documentation regarding the Sons of South Africa Movement; 'A Conception of South Africanism' by SED Brown, 1945–7, EG Jansen Papers.
72 See *Die Transvaler*, 20 November 1950.
73 See *Die Vaderland*, 11 May 1955; and Hansard, 26 February 1960.
74 *Die Transvaler*, 21 August 1954.
75 *Die Transvaler*, 31 August 1956.
76 *Die Transvaler*, 11 September 1956. The Black Sash was a non-violent anti-apartheid South African human rights organisation founded in 1955 by liberal white women.
77 *Die Transvaler*, 29 February 1956.
78 *South African Jewish Times*, 17 February 1956.
79 See Shain, *A Perfect Storm*, pp. 280–1; and Ben-Meir, 'The South African Jewish Community and Politics', pp. 260–1.
80 See Ben-Meir, 'The South African Jewish Community and Politics', pp. 262–3.
81 See David Welsh, *The Rise and Fall of Apartheid*, Jonathan Ball Publishers, Cape Town, 2009, p. 113.
82 *South African Observer*, February 1957.
83 *Die Transvaler*, 28 July 1958.
84 See Helen Suzman, *In No Uncertain Terms*, Jonathan Ball Publishers, Johannesburg, 1993, p. 41.
85 *Natal Witness*, 18 June 1959.
86 De Klerk, *The Last Trek*, p. 38. The ANC was in fact outlawed in April 1960.
87 *Sunday Express*, 15 September 1963.
88 Mandela was in jail at the time of the arrest.
89 Lionel (Rusty) Bernstein, Denis Goldberg, James Kantor, Alexander (Bob) Hepple, Harold Wolpe and Arthur Goldreich.
90 See *South African Observer*, August 1963.
91 *Rand Daily Mail*, 22 August 1963.
92 See Gordon Winter, *Inside Boss: South Africa's Secret Police*, Penguin, Harmondsworth, 1981, pp. 86–8; and Graham Macklin, 'The British Far Right's South Africa Connection: A.K. Chesterton, Hendrik van den Bergh, and the South African Intelligence Services', *Intelligence and National Security*, vol. 25, no. 6, 2010, pp. 838–40.
93 See, for example, *Die Burger*, 17 November and 22 November 1962; *Die Vaderland*, 22 November 1962; *Die Transvaler*, 15 May 1964 and letter from 'Nabob'.
94 *Die Oosterlig*, 20 September 1963.
95 The questions were also published in *Dagbreek en Sondagnuus*, 1 September 1963.

96 See SA Rochlin Archives, Executive Council Minutes, 4 September 1963.
97 See South African Jewish Board of Deputies: Executive Council Report, 16 April 1962.
98 Hansard, 7 March 1963.
99 *Die Oosterlig*, 8 March 1963.
100 *The Star*, 14 September 1963.
101 *Sunday Times*, 23 August 1964.
102 See *Christian Civilisation Against Communism: Papers Read at the National Congress to Combat Communism*, 31 March – 2 April 1964, National Congress to Combat Communism, Pretoria, 1964, p. 231; see also *Sunday Times*, 6 April 1964.
103 *Die Transvaler*, 18 June 1964.
104 See, for example, *Die Transvaler*, 17 June 1964.
105 *Die Vaderland*, 16 June 1964.
106 These sensitivities were vividly on display in the brouhaha that had broken out two months prior to the Rivonia judgment when Etienne Leroux's novel *Sewe dae by die Silbersteins* (Seven Days at the Silbersteins) was awarded the Hertzog Prize for prose – a book condemned by its critics as 'the best propaganda for communism'. See Dan O'Meara, *Forty Lost Years: The Apartheid State and the Politics of the National Party, 1948–1994*, Ohio University Press, Athens, OH, and Ravan Press, Johannesburg, 1996, p. 124.
107 See *Eastern Province Herald*, 2 and 13 June 1964.
108 *South African Observer*, July 1964.
109 Froneman might have added that the state prosecutor, Percy Yutar, was also Jewish. See *Die Burger*, 16 June 1964. The notion of Jewish incitement of the black majority remained deeply embedded in South African memory as did the arrests at Rivonia.
110 See *Antikom* newsletter, 8 August 1964. For a global examination of the Jewish–Bolshevik canard, see Paul Hanebrink, *A Spectre Haunting Europe: The Myth of Judeo-Bolshevism*, Harvard University Press, Cambridge, MA, 2018.
111 See *Sunday Times*, 11 October 1964.
112 *South African Jewish Times*, 16 October 1964; *Evening Post*, 5 November 1964; and South African Jewish Board of Deputies: Executive Council Minutes, 12 October 1964. According to the *Sunday Times* (11 October 1964), *Antikom* was issued by the Inter-Church Commission of the NGK.
113 See South African Jewish Board of Deputies: Executive Council Minutes, 21 October 1964.
114 For criticism of Vorster see, for example, *Die Burger*, 6 November 1964.
115 *Die Oosterlig*, 9 November 1964.
116 *Die Burger*, 10 November 1964.
117 See, for example, letters from Andries Breytenbach (*Die Transvaler*, 16

November 1964) and W Tweer (*Die Transvaler*, 9 December 1964).
118 See *Eastern Province Herald*, 2 June 1964.
119 *Die Kerkbode*, 18 November 1964.
120 Under the 90-day detention clause, the police were empowered to detain without judicial procedure a person suspected of a politically motivated crime and hold them incommunicado for ninety days, which could be continually extended.
121 *Dagbreek en Sondagnuus*, 26 September 1965.
122 See, for example, *Dagbreek en Sondagnuus*, 17 October 1965.
123 *Dagbreek en Sondagnuus*, 10 October 1965.
124 *Dagbreek en Sondagnuus*, 17 October 1965.
125 *Dagbreek en Sondagnuus*, 31 October 1965.
126 *Sunday Times*, 2 October 1966.
127 See *Rand Daily Mail*, 28 September 1966; and *Die Transvaler*, 1 October 1966.
128 Visser, 'The Production of Literature', pp. 112–13.
129 *Rand Daily Mail*, 30 September 1966.
130 *Die Transvaler*, 1 October 1966. See also *Sunday Times*, 9 October 1966; and Shimoni, *Community and Conscience*, p. 72.
131 *South African Observer*, April 1966.
132 Winter, *Inside Boss*, p. 87.
133 For examples of this view, see *South African Observer*, March 1956, October 1963 and November 1974.
134 *Dagbreek en Sondagnuus*, 31 March 1968.
135 See *Die Transvaler*, 29 June 1967.
136 See John Matisonn, *God, Spies and Lies: Finding South Africa's Future through Its Past*, Ideas for Africa and Missing Ink, Cape Town, 2015, p. 27.
137 Associated Press communiqué, 13 July 1961, cited in Shimoni, *Jews and Zionism*, p. 305.
138 For a judicious and full account, see Shimoni, *Jews and Zionism*, chapter 10; and *Community and Conscience*, pp. 46–54.
139 See *Die Transvaler*, 13 July 1961.
140 *Sondagblad*, 26 November 1961.
141 Shimoni, *Jews and Zionism*, p. 307.
142 *Die Oosterlig*, 27 November 1961.
143 Verwoerd's comments were made in a letter to former Cape Town city councillor Sydney East after East had written to the prime minister condemning Israel's behaviour. See *Sunday Express*, 19 November 1961.
144 Parallels too were drawn with the idea of 'Chosenness'. See *Huisgenoot*, Bob van Wyk, 'Apartheid in Israel', 1 April 1966; and 'Waarom staan die Jood', *Huisgenoot*, 6 May 1966.
145 See Shimoni, *Jews and Zionism*, p. 317.

146 Zionist Federation, Minutes of Hon. Officers Fed. and Board, 23 March 1962: Report on Interview with Minister of Finance, 23 March 1962. Cited in Shimoni, *Jews and Zionism*, p. 319.
147 Of concern for the government was the official silence of local Jewry.
148 *Die Transvaler*, 30 September 1963.
149 *Die Burger*, 20 September 1963.
150 *Die Vaderland*, 19 September 1963.
151 See for example, 'Pro-patria', *Die Burger*, 17 September 1963.
152 Shimoni, *Jews and Zionism*, p. 341; and *South African Observer*, January 1966.
153 *Die Transvaler*, 3 May 1967.
154 *Die Transvaler*, 5 May 1967.
155 See *S. African Jewish Times*, 6 November 1964; and South African Jewish Board of Deputies: Executive Council Minutes, 4 November 1964.
156 *Rand Daily Mail*, 13 September 1965.
157 *Rand Daily Mail*, 25 March 1964; see also *Die Burger*, 7 December 1964.
158 *Dagbreek en Sondagnuus*, 19 December 1965.
159 *Beeld*, 10 July 1966.
160 *Die Kerkbode*, 1 February 1967.
161 See Interview: Raymond Suttner, in Immanuel Suttner (ed.), *Cutting through the Mountain: Interviews with South African Jewish Activists*, Viking Penguin, London, 1997, p. 507.
162 See Welsh, *The Rise and Fall of Apartheid*, pp. 131–2.
163 See Hansard, 16 May 1969.
164 See Norval, *Deconstructing Apartheid Discourse*, pp. 185–6.
165 *South African Observer*, October 1967.
166 Sasha Polakow-Suransky, *The Unspoken Alliance: Israel's Secret Relationship with Apartheid South Africa*, Jacana Media, Johannesburg, 2010, p. 46.
167 Suzman, *In No Uncertain Terms*, p. 115.
168 See Edgar Bernstein, 'South African Jewry', in Morris Fine and Milton Himmelfarb (eds), *American Jewish Year Book 1968*, vol. 69, American Jewish Committee, Philadelphia, 1968, p. 534.
169 See Johann van Rooyen, *Hard Right: The New White Power in South Africa*, IB Tauris, London, 1994, pp. 17–20.
170 *Die Vaderland*, 15 April 1969.
171 See Van Rooyen, *Hard Right*, p. 19.
172 Afrikaners had other things to think about. *Völkisch* exclusivism was receding, and the National Party began to grapple with petty apartheid (or the cruder aspects of separate development) and to seek new political frameworks.
173 See Michael Cobden, 'Anti-Semitism: Its Sources and Extent', *Rand Daily Mail*, 20 May 1967.
174 See Bernard Sachs, *Mists of Memory: An Autobiography*, Vallentine,

Mitchell, London, 1973, p. 210.
175 *Sunday Times*, 8 August 1965.
176 See Shimoni, *Jews and Zionism*, p. 354; and *Die Vaderland*, 30 October 1967.
177 These ties had in fact developed beneath the radar from the early 1960s, notwithstanding the political noise around Israel's anti-apartheid stance. See Polakow-Suransky, *The Unspoken Alliance*, pp. 43–4.
178 See ibid., p. 53.
179 *Die Vaderland*, 14 April 1969.
180 This opposition included 'progressive Jews' who believed Israel had lost its moral compass.
181 See, for example, *South African Observer*, November 1970 and July 1967.

Chapter 2

1. See *Die Transvaler*, 25 February 1948. Weichardt was appointed a Union organiser for the National Party (seemingly focused on Natal) in 1950. See *Rand Daily Mail*, 20 September 1950. He then turned away from anti-Jewish activism in the interest of common white concerns.
2. See Daniel Pipes, *Conspiracy: How the Paranoid Style Flourishes and Where It Comes From*, Free Press, New York, 1997, pp. 52–9.
3. Richard Hofstadter, 'The Paranoid Style in American Politics', in *The Paranoid Style in American Politics and Other Essays*, Vintage Books, New York, 1967, p. 3.
4. See Cohn, *Warrant for Genocide*.
5. See Shain, *A Perfect Storm*, chapter 2. Von Moltke was one of four found guilty.
6. Ibid.
7. See Shain, *The Roots of Antisemitism in South Africa*, pp. 38–44. For the Jameson Raid as a *coup d'état*, see Charles van Onselen, *The Cowboy Capitalist: John Hays Hammond, the American West and the Jameson Raid*, Jonathan Ball Publishers, Jeppestown, 2017.
8. Fritz Stern, *Dreams and Delusions: The Drama of German History*, Yale University Press, New Haven, 1999, p. 106. For Hoggenheimer, see Shain, *The Roots of Antisemitism in South Africa*, pp. 62–3.
9. See Shain, 'Hoggenheimer: The Making of a Myth'.
10. See Shain, *The Roots of Antisemitism in South Africa*, chapters 5 and 6.
11. See Shain, *A Perfect Storm*, pp. 269–70.
12. See *Die Transvaler*, 18 October 1939.
13. SA Rochlin Archives, Press Digest, 1946, p. 7.
14. See Archives for Contemporary Affairs, University of the Free State, RK Rudman Collection, PV 160: 1/16/21/1; and OB Archive, North West University: Interview with RK Rudman, Tape 104, 24 October 1975. For

biographical details, see Archives for Contemporary Affairs, RK Rudman Collection, PV 160: file 33; SA Rochlin Archives, Rudman Collection, Correspondence 1946 and 1947; and *Golden City Post*, 6 September 1959.

15 See Shain, *A Perfect Storm*, pp. 49–50.
16 Ibid., p. 50.
17 See Izak Hattingh, 'Nasionaal-Sosialismus en die Gryshemp-beweging in Suid-Afrika', DPhil thesis, University of the Orange Free State, 1972, pp. 157–8.
18 See Shain, *A Perfect Storm*, pp. 268–9.
19 For Rudman's war years, see OB Archive: Interview with RK Rudman, Tape 104, 24 October 1975.
20 See *Evening Post*, 29 August 1959; SA Rochlin Archives, Rudman Collection, Newspaper Clippings, 1950s. The Maritz connection was noted on the masthead of *Die NS Boerenasie*.
21 See Dennis Eisenberg, *The Re-emergence of Fascism*, Macgibbon and Kee, London, 1967, pp. 304–5.
22 Ibid., p. 304 and n. 30.
23 Archives for Contemporary Affairs, Rudman Collection, PV 160: 1/16/20/1, Ray Rudman to Secretary, World Aryan Union, 16 April 1953.
24 The title related to the biblical King David; see 2 Samuel 11:25.
25 See Archives for Contemporary Affairs, Rudman Collection, PV 160: 1/16/20/1 and 1/16/14/1.
26 Archives for Contemporary Affairs, Rudman Collection, PV 160: 1/16/14/1 and 1/16/20/1. Archives for Contemporary Affairs, Rudman Collection, PV 160: 1/16/12/1.
27 Archives for Contemporary Affairs, Rudman Collection, PV 160: 1/16/1/2.
28 Rudman's papers (housed at the University of the Free State) are replete with anti-Jewish clippings, both local and international, as well as propaganda and articles. He collected hundreds of articles on Jews both in South Africa and abroad, and read huge amounts of antisemitic material.
29 Rudman's connections are reflected in his wide-ranging correspondence. See Archives for Contemporary Affairs, Rudman Collection, PV 160: 1/51/22/1; and SA Rochlin Archives, Rudman Collection, Correspondence 1946 and 1947.
30 Editor, *Common Sense*, to Editor, *Inside Out*, 16 May 1949, SA Rochlin Archives, Rudman Collection, Correspondence 1948–9.
31 NS Boerenasie in fact sent a representative to attend several international fascist conferences in Europe in 1962. See Eisenberg, *The Re-emergence of Fascism*, p. 305.
32 Archives for Contemporary Affairs, Rudman Collection, PV 160: 1/17/14/1.
33 See Thomas Linehan, *British Fascism, 1918–1939: Parties, Ideology and Culture*, Manchester University Press, Manchester, 2000, pp. 246–7.

Notes

34 See Cobden, *Rand Daily Mail*, 20 May 1967.
35 According to Rudman, Atilhan (the author of *Zionism: The Danger That Faces Islam*) had been fighting Jews for twenty-five years. See Ray Rudman to Herr G Teitz, 6 December 1952, Archives for Contemporary Affairs, RK Rudman Collection, PV 160: 1/27/1/1. Atilhan in fact said thirty-five years. See Cevat Rifat Atilhan to RK Rudman, 16 November 1952, Archives for Contemporary Affairs, RK Rudman Collection, PV 160: 1/17/14/1.
36 From Martin Hughes, Archives for Contemporary Affairs, RK Rudman Collection, PV 160: 1/69/1/1.
37 Bradley J Smith to Ray Rudman, 21 March 1971, Archives for Contemporary Affairs, RK Rudman Collection, PV 160: 1/97/1/1.
38 See R Rudman to R Harwood, 25 October 1974, Archives for Contemporary Affairs, RK Rudman Collection, PV 160: 1/51/24/1. Rudman's private papers reveal ongoing correspondence with the radical right across the world, while his book collection, now housed at the University of the Free State, betrays an obsession with conspiracies, Nazis and fascists.
39 Gus Saron to Mr Caminsky, 11 October 1948, SA Rochlin Archives, Rudman Collection, Correspondence 1948–9.
40 E Tannenbaum, South African Jewish Board of Deputies, to Sydney Salomon, Board of Deputies of British Jews, 13 September 1948, SA Rochlin Archives, Correspondence 1948–9.
41 G Kellman (New York) to SA Jewish Board of Deputies, 22 December 1948, SA Rochlin Archives, Rudman Collection, Correspondence 1948–9. Rudman's wide-ranging connections were confirmed by the Board of Deputies of British Jews. See Sydney Salomon to Gus Saron, 31 August 1948, SA Rochlin Archives, Rudman Collection, Correspondence 1948–9.
42 Stetson Kennedy to Editor (*Common Sense*), 28 March 1949, SA Rochlin Archives, Rudman Collection, Correspondence 1948–9.
43 Editor (*Common Sense*) to Stetson Kennedy, 16 May 1949, SA Rochlin Archives, Rudman Collection, Correspondence 1948–9.
44 Ray Rudman to Herr G Teitz, 23 May 1953, Archives for Contemporary Affairs, RK Rudman Collection, PV 160: 1/27/1/1.
45 See, for example, Archives for Contemporary Affairs, RK Rudman Collection, PV 160: 1/70/4/1.
46 Archives for Contemporary Affairs, RK Rudman Collection, PV 160: 1/51/22/1. Rudman was referring to the Aliens Act of 1937.
47 Archives for Contemporary Affairs, RK Rudman Collection: PV 160: 1/51/1/1.
48 Archives for Contemporary Affairs, RK Rudman Collection, PV 160: 1/97/1/1.
49 See *Die Burger*, 25 August 1962; and SA Rochlin Archives, Rudman Collection, Correspondence & Memoranda, 1960s. SONOP was in fact

another name for the Suid-Afrikaanse Blanke Werkersbond (South African White Workers' League), established by Rudman in September 1962.

50   See Eisenberg, *The Re-emergence of Fascism*, p. 305; and SA Rochlin Archives, Rudman Collection, Correspondence & Memoranda, 1960s.
51   ee Shain, *A Perfect Storm*, chapter 2.
52   See PC du Plessis, 'SA se stroomopste vegter', *Die Huisgenoot*, 28 October 1957.
53   Johan Schoeman, a teenager at the time of his father's death, was surely scarred and eventually wrote a book in defence of his father. See Johan Schoeman, *Generaal Hendrik Schoeman: Was hy 'n verraaier?*, Pretoria, 1950. For events surrounding the incarceration of Hendrik Schoeman, see Albert Grundlingh, *The Dynamics of Treason: Boer Collaboration in the South African War of 1899–1902*, Protea Book House, Pretoria, 2006, pp. 95–7.
54   *Union Review*, 1949. Barnett had edited the *Natal Witness* from 1931 to 1935.
55   See RC Hargreaves to Johan Schoeman, Office of the Governor General, 4 January 1927, National Archive, Pretoria, GG Athlone 2288, 11/82.
56   See Du Plessis, 'SA se stroomopste vegter'.
57   Mr Rich to Public Relations Dept, 11 January 1954, SA Rochlin Archives, South African Jewish Board of Deputies.
58   Johan Schoeman, *Vistas 59: Die krisis in Suid-Afrika*, Pretoria and Broederstroom, 1959, p. 150.
59   See ibid.
60   See ibid. For Schoeman's oeuvre and Jew-hatred, see *Hear the Other Side: The Afrikaner Side and the German Side*, Kroonstad and Broederstroom, 1946.
61   See SA Rochlin Archives, Executive Council Minutes, 3 July 1963.
62   SA Rochlin Archives, Executive Council Minutes, 23 April 1956.
63   Sarg in fact warned Rudman against dealing with Schoeman until he cast off Schlesinger. See Archives for Contemporary Affairs, RK Rudman Collection: Wolfgang Sarg to Rudman, 28 December 1953, PV 160: 1/70/5/1.
64   *Sunday Times*, 26 June 1966.
65   See SA Rochlin Archives, South African Jewish Board of Deputies, Executive Council Minutes, 21 May 1962, 11 February 1963, 6 June 1963, 8 and 20 September 1965, and 12 September 1966.
66   See, for example, *Adv. Pirow se Nuusbrief*, 31 January 1958. For the Pirow relationship with Mosley, see Robert Skidelsky, *Oswald Mosley*, Macmillan, London, 1975, p. 486; Alex Mouton, '"Beyond the Pale"'; and Mouton, *The Opportunist*, pp. 206–8.
67   See *Adv Pirow se Nuusbrief*, 26 September 1952.

Notes

68 See SA Rochlin Archives, Executive Council Minutes, 13 June 1966, 6 July 1966, 23 January 1967, and 13 February 1967. For *Boomerang*'s links with the Patriots Society for Race Friendship in Pretoria, see South African Jewish Board of Deputies, Executive Council Minutes, 6 July 1966.

69 See, for example, 'Pseudo-Liberals Strategy of War', by Noel Crowd; 'Internationalism', by Count Rev; 'World Opinion: Fact or Fiction' (which embodied the first two and a new section 'Iron Curtain of the Press'). The pamphlets were issued by P de Beer and printed by V and R Printing, Paul Kruger Street, Pretoria. See South African Jewish Board of Deputies, Executive Council Minutes, 5 November 1969.

70 Noel Crowd and Count Revo, *The Pattern of Assassination*, Boomerang Publications, Pretoria, 1967.

71 See SA Rochlin Archives, Executive Council Minutes, 13 June 1966.

72 See Cobden, *Rand Daily Mail*, 20 May 1967. Importantly, at this time Brown served on the South African Censorship Board.

73 See, for example, *South African Observer*, 6 December 1955.

74 *South African Observer*, 7 January 1956.

75 See *South African Observer*, January 1956 and April 1971.

76 *South African Observer*, May 1970.

77 See, for example, *South African Observer*, December 1970.

78 *South African Observer*, September 1973.

79 *South African Observer*, May 1976.

80 Benson edited *Behind the News: A Southern African Bulletin* from 1969 to 1972 and again as *Behind the News* (under his National Forum, the South African chapter of the World Anti-Communist League, an international collection of antisemites and neo-fascists) from 1977 to 1983. See 'Right Wing Directory', Independent Board of Inquiry, March 1996, Historical Papers, University of the Witwatersrand, Independent Board of Inquiry Records (IBI) 1989–96, AG 2543: 2.3.7.

81 See Ivor Benson, *The Opinion Makers*, Dolphin Press, Pretoria, 1967. For Benson's controversial appointment in Rhodesia, see Elaine Windrich, 'Rhodesian Censorship: The Role of the Media in the Making of a One-Party State', *African Affairs*, vol. 79, no. 313, 1979.

82 See Benjamin Pogrund, *War of Words: Memoir of a South African Journalist*, Seven Stories Press, New York, 2000, p. 158.

83 His work for the World Anti-Communist League (WACL) is referred to by Geoffrey Stewart-Smith, who, in the early 1980s, headed the British branch of the WACL. See David Lethbridge, 'Jew-Haters and Red-Baiters: The Canadian League of Rights', *Antifa Info-Bulletin*, 2 February 1999, http://www.hartford-hwp.com/archives/44/087.html.

84 It will be recalled that he served on the Antikom committee which convened an anti-communist congress in 1964.

85 See Pogrund, *War of Words*, p. 53.
86 *Behind the News*, April 1972. Benson shared much with Oswald Pirow and Oswald Mosley, both of whom, as mentioned earlier, wished to racially divide the African continent into black and white.
87 See chapter 4.
88 *Behind the News*, October 1970.
89 For the 'money power', see *Sunday Times*, 8 March 1970; and *Behind the News*, October 1971.
90 SA Rochlin Archives, 'Anti-Jewish and Neo-Nazi Activities in the Republic', Executive Council Minutes, 7 June 1967.
91 SA Rochlin Archives, Executive Council Minutes, 5 April 1967.
92 *Candour* began as a magazine of the League.
93 Cobden, *Rand Daily Mail*, 20 May 1967. Chesterton spent time in South Africa to deal with his emphysema; here he established tight bonds with Hendrik van den Bergh. See Macklin, 'The British Far Right's South Africa Connection'.
94 See Cobden, *Rand Daily Mail*, 20 May 1967; Eisenberg, *The Re-emergence of Fascism*, p. 308; and Visser, 'The Production of Literature on the "Red Peril"', pp. 103–5. In turn Chesterton expected supporters of the League to provide him with information on communist subversion which he would relay to the South African security police. See Graham Macklin, *Failed Führers: A History of Britain's Extreme Right*, Routledge, London, 2020, p. 217.
95 See *Rand Daily Mail*, 31 March 1965; and Cobden, *Rand Daily Mail*, 20 May 1967. Kleist was an executive member of Friends of Cairo Organisation. In March 1967 it was resolved to form the Deutscher Arbeitskreis Volkstreuer Verbände in Südafrika (German Work Group of Nationally Loyal Associations in South Africa) under Sheffler. See Brian Bunting, *The Rise of the South African Reich*, Penguin Books, Harmondsworth, 1969, pp. 72–3.
96 Cobden, *Rand Daily Mail*, 20 May 1967.
97 *Personality*, 4 December 1969. Journalist Bob Hitchfield estimated the presence of two hundred neo-Nazis in 'Southern Africa'. See *Sunday Times*, 7 May 1967.
98 See *South African Observer*, 11 October 1960. For further comment on controversies around Butler's visits to South Africa, see *Rand Daily Mail*, 4 July 1964; and *Dagbreek en Sondagnuus*, 5 July 1964.
99 See *Die Afrikaner*, 15 May 1970.
100 *Cape Times*, 22 April 1965.
101 See SA Rochlin Archives, 'Anti-Jewish and Neo-Nazi Activities in the Republic', Executive Council Minutes, 7 June 1967.
102 See Giliomee, *The Afrikaners*, p. 491.
103 See *Rand Daily Mail*, 27 September 1962.
104 Cobden, *Rand Daily Mail*, 20 May 1967.

105 See SA Rochlin Archives, Executive Council Minutes, 11 June 1962. This might also have been related to the General Law Amendment Bill (the 'Sabotage Bill') which was being debated in parliament. See SA Rochlin Archives, Executive Council Minutes, 13 February 1967; and *Rand Daily Mail*, 21 January 1964.
106 See SA Rochlin Archives, Executive Council Minutes, 10 May 1967. A vivid account of the celebration is provided by Tony Hillhouse, a South African journalist, writing in the ANC monthly, *Sechaba*, July 1967.
107 See Bernard Moses Casper, *A Decade with South African Jewry*, H Timmins, Cape Town, 1972, p. 20.
108 Hansard, 9 May 1967.
109 *Rand Daily Mail*, 10 May 1967.
110 See *Beeld*, 24 May 1970; *Sunday Express*, 30 April 1972 and 21 May 1972.
111 *Sunday Express*, 25 April 1971.
112 *The Star*, 21 April 1975.
113 Cobden, *Rand Daily Mail*, 20 May 1967; SA Rochlin Archives, Executive Council Minutes, 10 February 1969.
114 See *Hoofstad*, 31 December 1969; and *Die Transvaler*, 27 December 1969.
115 *The Star*, 22 May 1970.
116 See, for example, *Die Vaderland*, 26 September 1972. Of course the Rockefellers were not Jewish but were nonetheless commonly identified as Jews.
117 See *Argus*, 6 October 1972; *The Star*, 21 November 1972; and *Rand Daily Mail*, 23 November 1972.
118 *Sunday Tribune*, 9 September 1973. Although the institute was unknown, the fact that the note was posted from a mystery man in Wartburg, Natal, suggests it was Rudman.
119 *South African Observer*, November 1974.
120 See Robert S. Wistrich, *A Lethal Obsession: Anti-Semitism from Antiquity to the Global Jihad*, Random House, New York, 2010, pp. 663–4.
121 *Die Afrikaner*, 23 January 1976.
122 See Shain, *A Perfect Storm*, pp. 269–70; and Milton Shain and Andrew Lamprecht, 'A Past That Must Not Go Away: Holocaust Denial in Apartheid and Post-Apartheid South Africa', in John K Roth and Elizabeth Maxwell (eds), *Remembering the Future: The Holocaust in the Age of Genocide*, vol. 1, Palgrave, New York, 2001, pp. 858–69.
123 See Johan Schoeman, *Small Essays on Big Subjects*, QVS Press, Kroonstad, 1952; *Zionist Record*, 4 May 1956.
124 Schoeman, *Hear the Other Side*; *Goering's Last Letter! Field-Marshal Hermann Goering Speaks from His Grave to His Accuser, Prosecutor, Judge, Hangman – Winston Churchill and the World Christian Conscience*, Kingdom Press of Pretoria, Pretoria, 1949; *In Gods naam! ontwaak: As Duitsland sterf*

(of verplig word Stalin te steun) sterf die Christendom!, Broederstroom, 1948. See Du Plessis, 'SA se stroomopste vegter'.

125 *The Star*, 20 March 1959.
126 *The Star*, 14 March 1961.
127 See SA Rochlin Archives, Johan Schoeman, *Eichmann Is Not Guilty*, Broederstroom, pp. 4–13. The Eichmann trial in Jerusalem had substantial coverage in South Africa.
128 *Dagbreek en Sondagnuus*, 12 September 1965.
129 *Die Transvaler*, 5 April 1965.
130 *Daily Dispatch*, 1 November 1966.
131 *Die Vaderland*, 26 May 1965; see *Common Sense*, 1 March 1965.
132 SA Rochlin Archives, Executive Council Minutes, 2 June 1965,
133 'The Falsehood about the Six Million Jews Said to Be Gassed by Hitler Exposed', Archives for Contemporary Affairs, RK Rudman Collection, PV 160: 1/51/25/1. See SA Rochlin Archives, Executive Council Minutes, 19 April 1971.
134 See 'Siek en sat', *Op en Wakker*, 3 April 1970.
135 See H Viedge, *Daily Dispatch*, 5 January 1971.
136 *Brandwag*, 14 May 1971; see also *Sunday Tribune*, 23 May 1971.
137 See *Rapport*, 21 November 1971.
138 *Hoofstad*, 2 December 1971.
139 *Ster*, 8 June 1973.
140 *Ster*, 13 April 1973.
141 *Die Afrikaner* was founded in 1970, soon after the HNP was established. The HNP also had its own newspaper, *Veg* (Fight).
142 See *Die Afrikaner*, 23 July 1971.
143 See *Die Afrikaner*, 13, 20, 27 February, 5, 12, 19, 26 March and 2, 9, 16, 23, 30 April 1976. For the *Historikerstreit*, see Richard Evans, *In Hitler's Shadow: West German Historians and the Attempt to Escape the Nazi Past*, IB Tauris, London, 1989.
144 Richard Harwood [Richard Verrall], *Did Six Million Die? The Truth at Last*, Richmond, Surrey, 1974; and Arthur R. Butz, *The Hoax of the Twentieth Century*, Richmond, Surrey, 1974. For the Brown review, see *South African Observer*, September 1976.
145 *Die Afrikaner* (6 August 1976) reported that the decision would be appealed.
146 Arthur Suzman and Dennis Diamond, *Six Million Did Die: The Truth Shall Prevail*, South African Jewish Board of Deputies, Johannesburg, 1977. The book was based on the material acquired for the court action.
147 Shirli Gilbert, 'Nazism and Racism in South African Textbook', in Gilbert and Alba (eds), *Holocaust Memory and Racism in the Postwar World*, p. 363.
148 See, for example, *Rand Daily Mail*, 3 April 1976.
149 *The Star*, 23 March 1976.

150 *Beeld*, 17 May 1976.
151 *Cape Times*, 17 May 1976.
152 *Cape Argus*, 17 May 1976.
153 *The Star*, 19 May 1976; see also *Tempo*, 21 May 1976.
154 *The Star*, 20 May 1976.
155 *Rand Daily Mail*, 19 May 1976.
156 See *Tempo*, 21 May 1976.
157 *Die Afrikaner*, 21 May 1976.
158 See *Die Vaderland*, 19 May 1976, which included an extract from *Did Six Million Really Die?*
159 *South African Observer*, June 1976. Significantly, Vorster had visited Israel six weeks earlier, much to the chagrin of the radical right.
160 *South African Observer*, June 1976.
161 *Rand Daily Mail*, 31 May 1976.
162 *Sunday Tribune*, 23 May 1976. Notably, leaflets denying the Holocaust were placed under the windshield wipers of cars parked outside a Johannesburg hotel where the producer of *The World at War*, Jeremy Isaacs, was giving a public lecture.
163 See *Rand Daily Mail*, 31 March 1976.
164 See *Rand Daily Mail*, 22 March 1976; and *Sunday Express*, 4 April 1976.
165 *Sunday Express*, 6 June 1976.
166 WD Chalmers, *The Conspiracy of Truth*, Dolphin Press, Durban, 1978. Notably, the book was published by Ivor Benson. See *Sunday Times*, 6 May 1978. Importantly, Chalmers claimed most Jews were oblivious to the plotting of the cabal.
167 'This booklet ought to be widely distributed,' wrote Vorster, 'for whoever reads it will be enriched and well equipped to carry on the good fight.' Chalmers, *The Conspiracy of Truth*, p. vi.
168 See, for example, *The Citizen*, 4 May 1979.
169 Hansard, 25 May 1979.
170 *Sunday Times*, 14 October 1979.
171 *Sunday Times*, 21 December 1975.
172 In 1982, Roeder was arrested in Germany for bombing Vietnamese refugee hostels. He made a visit to South Africa in 1993 and was well connected to far-right groups and international neo-Nazi groups.
173 *Sunday Times*, 21 December 1975.
174 See *Rand Daily Mail*, 13 December 1975.
175 Frequent letters to the press and the distribution of anti-Jewish flyers demonstrated this. See, for example, *Die Vaderland*, 19 December 1975, letter from IJ Ingram questioning murder of the Jews of Europe.
176 *The Star*, 20 December 1975.
177 *Rand Daily Mail*, 22 December 1975.

178 Doussy was regarded as a prominent neo-Nazi in South Africa who joined the application of Brown in the attempt to ban the screening of 'Genocide' by the SABC. Doussy owned the Hansa restaurant in Pretoria and the building in which it was housed. Other tenants included a bookshop managed by a former Nazi SS officer who had spent time in a Russian detention camp. See *Mail & Guardian*, 9 September 1994.
179 *Beeld*, 11 August 1976.
180 See *Sunday Times*, 18 November 1979; and *Rand Daily Mail*, 21 November 1979.
181 According to the *Sunday Express*, 29 March 1981, all far-right groups in South Africa were internationally connected, although the British National Front denied any ties to the SANF.
182 SA Rochlin Archives, Executive Council Minutes, 22 January 1979. National Front anti-Jewish pamphlets were distributed in Hillbrow.
183 See *Sunday Express*, 29 March and 5 April 1981.
184 See South African Jewish Board of Deputies, Executive Council Minutes, 20 February 1978.
185 *Natal Mercury*, 17 May 1979.
186 *Rapport*, 18 November 1979.
187 See 'Nazi Victory Feast', *Sunday Times*, 19 October 1980; and *Rand Daily Mail*, 16 October 1980.
188 See *The Friend*, 29 April 1980.
189 *Rand Daily Mail*, 23 February 1982.
190 *Sunday Times*, 24 August 1980.
191 See *Pretoria News*, 31 July 1980.
192 *Sunday Times*, 6 September 1981.
193 *Pretoria News*, 11 November 1980.
194 *Daily Dispatch*, 16 December 1981
195 *The Star*, 16 August 1982.
196 See *Rand Daily Mail*, 18 August 1982.
197 See Welsh, *The Rise and Fall of Apartheid*, chapter 6.
198 See *Natal Mercury*, 17 May 1979.
199 See *The Star*, 14 June 1979.
200 *Rapport*, 2 December 1979.
201 *Rand Daily Mail*, 31 May 1976.

Chapter 3
1 See Norval, *Deconstructing Apartheid Discourse*, pp. 185–6.
2 The report is no longer extant but is noted in the Broederbond Archives.
3 See Martin Schöteich and Henri Boshoff, *In 'Volk', Faith and Fatherland: The Security Threat Posed by the White Right*, ISS Monograph Series, no. 81, March 2003, Pretoria, p. 16.

Notes

4 The terms '*verlig*' and '*verkramp*' had been coined by academic and journalist 'Wimpie' de Klerk in 1966 to capture the battle within the National Party between those resisting change to apartheid and those wishing to reform or adapt apartheid to new circumstances.

5 Albert Grundlingh, '"Are We Afrikaners Getting Too Rich?": Cornucopia and Change in Afrikanerdom in the 1960s', *Journal of Historical Sociology*, vol. 21, nos. 2/3, 2008, p. 143.

6 *South African Observer*, November 1974. A prominent right-winger, Chris Beyers had been approached to lead the AWB at its inception in 1973. See Arthur Kemp, *Victory or Violence: The Story of the AWB*, Forma Publishers, Pretoria, 1990, pp. 56–7.

7 https://africanelections.tripod.com/za.html.

8 *Die Afrikaner*, 13 April 1970.

9 See *Die Transvaler*, 17 March 1970. These sentiments were confirmed by a number of HNP candidates. See *Sunday Express*, 22 March 1970; and *Die Burger*, 14 March 1970.

10 *Rand Daily Mail*, 6 March 1970; and *Die Afrikaner*, 13 March 1970.

11 See, for example, *Die Kerkbode*, 5 December 1962.

12 See *South African Jewish Times*, 23 October and 6 November 1964; *Sunday Express*, 30 May 1971; and *Rapport*, 23 May 1971.

13 Evangelising was a longstanding issue. In 1931 a storm had broken out following comments in two reports on evangelising submitted to the NGK. See *South African Jewish Chronicle*, 24 April 1931; and *Die Transvaler*, 2 May 1970.

14 See SA Rochlin Archives, Executive Council Minutes, 4 November 1979. For the *adversus Judaeos* tradition, see, for example, Marcel Simon, *Verus Israel: A Study of the Relations between Christian and Jews in the Roman Empire AD 135–425*, Littman Library of Jewish Civilization, London, 1996; and Rosemary Radford Ruether, *Faith and Fratricide: The Theological Roots of Anti-Semitism*, Seabury Press, New York, 1974.

15 See *The Star*, 15 February 1967; and *Sunday Times*, 7 May 1967.

16 See, for example, *The Friend*, 28 November 1958; and SA Rochlin Archives, Executive Council Minutes, 19 January 1959.

17 See SA Rochlin Archives, Executive Council Minutes, 9 February 1959,

18 SA Rochlin Archives, Executive Council Minutes, 11 May 1959.

19 See *Rand Daily Mail*, 6 March 1970; and *Die Afrikaner*, 13 March 1970.

20 *Volksblad*, 7 September 1973. A year later, Clase was elected MP for Virginia and was appointed minister of education from 1985 to 1991.

21 See Hermann Giliomee, 'The Development of the Afrikaner's Self-concept', in Hendrik W van der Merwe (ed.), *Looking at the Afrikaner Today*, Tafelberg, Cape Town, 1975.

22 *Sunday Times*, 18 April 1971.

23 See *Sunday Express*, 27 May 1973; and *Sunday Times*, 3 June 1973. For Botes's comments at NGK Synod, see *Volksblad*, 20 September 1975.
24 See *Volksblad*, 20 September 1975.
25 *To the Point*, 16 May 1975.
26 See SA Rochlin Archives, Executive Council Minutes, 2 September 1970.
27 *The Star*, 5 November 1970 and 16 November 1972.
28 See *The Argus*, 6 October 1972; *The Star*, 21 November 1972; and *Rand Daily Mail*, 22 September 1971 and 23 November 1972. For pamphlets and daubings, see *The Argus*, 6 October 1972; *The Star*, 21 November 1972; and *Rand Daily Mail*, 22 September 1971 and 23 November 1972.
29 See *Sunday Times*, 26 November 1972; and *Sunday Express*, 8 October 1972.
30 See CN van der Merwe, *Breaking Barriers: Stereotypes and the Changing of Values in Afrikaans Writing 1875–1990*, Rodopi, Amsterdam, 1994, pp. 20–3; and Marcia Leveson, *People of the Book: Images of the Jew in South African English Fiction 1889–1992*, Witwatersrand University Press, Johannesburg, 1996, chapter 7.
31 See Ilana Hitner Klevansky and Alan H Levine, *The Kugel Book*, Jonathan Ball Publishers, Johannesburg, 1982.
32 *Rapport*, 18 May 1972. For subtle othering, note a study undertaken by Henry Lever four years before Arthur Suzman made his optimistic assessment. Lever's study revealed that pupils in Afrikaans schools looked askance at Jews – a 'social distance' inversely related to status; but this was of marginal significance. See Henry Lever, *Ethnic Attitudes of Johannesburg Youth*, Witwatersrand University Press, Johannesburg, 1968, p. 90.
33 See, for example, *Die Afrikaner*, 11 July 1980.
34 *Die Afrikaner*, 29 August 1980.
35 *Die Afrikaner*, 5 September 1980.
36 *Die Afrikaner*, 13 April 1983.
37 See *Die Afrikaner*, 22 June 1988.
38 See *Die Afrikaner*, 26 April 1989.
39 See, for example, *Die Afrikaner*, 6 March 1981.
40 See *Die Afrikaner*, 27 June 1980.
41 See *Die Afrikaner*, 12 January 1983.
42 *Die Afrikaner*, 9 February 1983.
43 *Die Afrikaner*, 13 February 1985. For Beetge, see Bunting, *The Rise of the South African Reich*, pp. 77–8.
44 *Die Afrikaner*, 4 November 1987. In 1988 Stoffberg was linked to the racist White National Movement (WNM), well known for promoting anti-Jewish conspiracy theories.
45 *South African Observer*, March 1980.
46 *South African Observer*, February 1980.
47 *South African Observer*, September 1982. Kissinger had long been portrayed

by the radical right as a bogeyman and a symbol of Jewish machinations See, for example, *Die Afrikaner*, 7 September 1973, 11 and 18 April 1975; and *South African Observer*, February 1974.
48. For example, *Die Hervormer*, June 1983, published a letter from WHJ Breytenbach which called the murder of Europe's Jews a 'great lie'.
49. *South African Observer*, November 1980.
50. *Sunday Times*, 2 June 1985. The AV had been established in 1984 by Carel Boshoff, who had resigned from the Broederbond.
51. See Saul Dubow, 'Racial Irredentism, Ethnogenesis, and White Supremacy in High-Apartheid South Africa', *Kronos*, vol. 41, no. 1, 2015.
52. TEW Schumann, *The Abdication of the White Man*, Tafelberg, Cape Town, 1963, pp. 8–9.
53. Ibid., p. 42.
54. Ibid.
55. See, for example, Robert Faurisson, 'Myth of the Six Million,' *Behind the News*, March 1982.
56. *Behind the News*, March 1985.
57. *The Star*, 13 November 1972.
58. JA Hobson, *The War in South Africa: Its Causes and Effects*, James Nisbet & Co., London, 1900, p. 189. Hobson's book was riddled with ugly references to Jews.
59. See Ivor Benson, 'The Siege of South Africa', *Journal of Historical Review*, vol. 7, no. 1, 1986.
60. Ivor Benson, 'Russia 1917–1918: A Key to the Riddle of an Age of Conflict', *Journal of Historical Review*, vol. 10, no. 3, 1990.
61. Ivor Benson, *The Opinion Makers*, Dolphin Press, 1967; *The Worldwide Conspiracy*, New Times Limited and Dolphin Press, 1972; *The Battle for South Africa*, Dolphin Press, 1979; and *The Zionist Factor: The Jewish Impact on Twentieth Century History*, rev. edn, Noontide Press, 1992 [1986].
62. Benson, *The Zionist Factor*.
63. Benson, *The Battle for South Africa*, p. 31.
64. Douglas Reed, *The Controversy in Zion*, Dolphin Press, Durban, 1978. The manuscript was completed in 1956. In all likelihood, Benson had established a relationship with the controversial English journalist (who was persona non grata in Fleet Street) after Reed had settled in Durban in 1952. Benson's Dolphin Press also published *Behind the Scene* (1975) and *The Grand Design of the 20th Century* by Douglas Reed (1977). See Richard Thurlow, 'Anti-Nazi Antisemite: The Case of Douglas Reed', *Patterns of Prejudice*, vol. 18, no. 1, 1984.
65. Reed, *The Controversy in Zion*, pp. 138–64.
66. *Sunday Tribune*, 29 September 1980.
67. *Sunday Tribune*, 22 March 1981.

68 O'Meara, *Forty Lost Years*.
69 https://africanelections.tripod.com/za.html.
70 FA Mouton, '"Dr No": A.P. Treurnicht and the Ultra-Conservative Quest to Maintain Afrikaner Supremacy, 1982–1983', *South African Historical Journal*, vol. 65, no. 4, December 2013, p. 583.
71 Hansard, 1 March 1982.
72 For the political drama, see Alf Ries and Ebbe Dommisse, *Broedertwis: Die verhaal van die 1982-skeuring in die Nasionale Party*, Tafelberg, Cape Town, 1982, pp. 156–79.
73 See Grobbelaar, 'Ultra-Rightwing Afrikaners', pp. 292–3.
74 Notably, the leaders of these breakaway groups were, for the most part, not composed of *déclassé* Afrikaners. Rather, they were intellectuals and cultural entrepreneurs who projected ethnic and moral fears.
75 See, for example, *Hoofstad*, 2 December 1971.
76 *Hoofstad*, 18 July 1981.
77 *The Star*, 15 July 1983.
78 Andries Treurnicht: Interview, in Tzippi Hoffman and Alan Fischer, *The Jews in South Africa: What Future?*, Southern Book Publishers, Johannesburg, 1988, p. 193.
79 Ibid., p. 193.
80 Ibid., p. 195.
81 Ibid., p. 194.
82 Ibid., p. 193.
83 For details of the meeting and the early years of the AWB, see Kemp, *Victory or Violence*; and Myda Marista Visser, 'Die ideologiese grondslae en ontwikkeling van die blanke fascistiese bewegings in Suid-Afrika, 1945–1995', MA thesis, University of Pretoria, 1999, pp. 109–14.
84 *Rand Daily Mail*, 20 April 1970.
85 *Beeld*, 11 October 1974. Ruiterwag (literally, horse carriage or mounted rifleman guard; the junior wing of the Broederbond); Rapportryers (literally, report riders; a service organisation for prominent Afrikaans men).
86 See Kemp, *Victory or Violence*, pp. 156–7; *Beeld*, 11 October 1974; PW Bingle, *Grondwet*, Afrikaner-weerstandsbeweging, Grondwetkomitee, Pretoria, 1987; PW Bingle, *The AWB: Program van beginsels*, Afrikaner Weerstandsbeweging, Pretoria, 1988.
87 Kemp, *Victory or Violence*, p. 157.
88 *Die Transvaler*, 21 November 1975.
89 *Die Vaderland*, 26 November 1975.
90 *Die Transvaler*, 21 November 1975.
91 *Sunday Times*, 23 November 1975.
92 *Rand Daily Mail*, 22 December 1975.
93 *Rand Daily Mail*, 23 December 1975. Of course, the 'British professor'

referred to was not a professor, but Richard Verrall of the British National Front.

94 *The Star*, 12 March 1976. The Third Republic relates to the two earlier Boer Republics of the nineteenth century, while the Vierkleur was the flag of the South African Republic, which existed from 1852 to 1877 and from 1881 to 1902.

95 *The Star*, 12 March 1976. See also Amos van der Merwe and Eugène Terre'Blanche, *Eugène Terre'Blanche: My storie*, Griffel Media, Cape Town, 2010, p. 13.

96 Leach, *The Afrikaners*, p. 100. 'The leader of the AWB Eugène Terre'Blanche has modelled himself into a Hitler figure and within a year, if he polishes his speaking technique, he will become a great orator,' said Irving, a frequent visitor to South Africa. See *Pretoria News*, 25 September 1986.

97 See Grobbelaar, 'Ultra-Rightwing Afrikaners', p. 301.

98 *The Star*, 12 March 1976. It has been suggested that the triple seven (likened to a swastika) related to the date of the AWB's formation (7/7/73). At one AWB rally, Jan Groenewald, the movement's full-time secretary, said the insignia's three bent legs were three 7s, the perfect number. It symbolised the final victory of the white man and the Christian. See *The Star*, 12 March 1976. Many years later Terre'Blanche claimed that 7 was a number from the Bible representing goodness and purity. The 777 was the number used to counter the 666 'beast' or anti-Christ in the Book of Revelation. Regarding their colours, the black represented courage; the white circle represented the love and purity of Jesus Christ; and the red background represented the blood of Jesus Christ, spilt for the salvation of mankind. See *Saturday Star*, 12 March 1988.

99 See Kemp, *Victory or Violence*, pp. 18–19.

100 See, for example, *Beeld*, 13 April 1979; and *The Star*, 12 April 1979.

101 *Eastern Province Herald*, 9 April 1979; and *Die Oosterlig*, 15 May 1979.

102 *Sunday Tribune*, 15 April 1979.

103 See editorial, *Diamond Fields Advertiser*, 5 July 1979.

104 *Rand Daily Mail* and *Beeld*, 13 June 1979.

105 *Rapport*, 9 September 1979; and *Beeld*, 13 November 1979.

106 *Sunday Times*, 25 November 1979. For the relationship between Jews and Freemasons, dating back to the eighteenth century, see Jacob Katz, *Jews and Freemasons in Europe, 1723–1939*, Harvard University Press, Cambridge, MA, 1970.

107 See *Sunday Times*, 20 April 1980; *The Citizen*, 11 August 1981; and Van Rooyen, *Hard Right*, pp. 47–9. In fact, the BVP never contested elections, although it came close to doing so in 1989. It did, however, help the HNP and NCP in the general election of 1981.

108 *The Argus*, 25 April 1980.

109 See *Sunday Express*, 19 April 1981.
110 *Sunday Express*.
111 *Sunday Express*, 16 August 1981.
112 See Visser, 'Die ideologiese grondslae en ontwikkeling van die blanke fascistiese bewegings in Suid-Afrika', p. 118.
113 See Welsh, *The Rise and Fall of Apartheid*, pp. 214–23.
114 *Sunday Times*, 22 November 1981.
115 In 1982 Terre'Blanche was charged with the illegal possession of weapons. In June 1987, Professor Willem Lubbe, now with the University of South Africa (Unisa), broke from the NGK and founded the Afrikaanse Protestantse Kerk (Afrikaans Protestant Church, or APK). See Helen Zille, 'The Right Wing in South African Politics', in Peter Berger and Bobby Godsell (eds), *A Future South Africa: Visions, Strategies and Realities*, Human and Rousseau, Cape Town, 1988, p. 68.
116 Grobbelaar, 'Ultra-Rightwing Afrikaners', p. 168.
117 See *Sunday Times*, 15 May 1983.
118 The liberal opposition was also opposed to the initiative, albeit for different reasons.
119 *Weekly Mail*, 2–8 August 1985.
120 *Natal Mercury*, 8 May 1986; and *Frontline*, June 1986.
121 *Sunday Express*, 11 April 1982.
122 See Kemp, *Victory or Violence*, pp. 72–3.
123 See *The Star*, 29 April 1987; *The Citizen*, 30 April and 5 May 1987.
124 Kemp, *Victory or Violence*, p. 73.
125 See JP Oberholzer and AG van Aarde, 'Studie en besluit oor AWB ruim onduidelikhede uit die weg', *Die Hervormer*, August 1987.
126 *Saturday Star*, 12 March 1988.
127 Eugène Terre'Blanche: Interview, in Michel Albeldas and Alan Fischer, *A Question of Survival: Conversations with Key South Africans*, Jonathan Ball, Johannesburg, 1987, p. 178.
128 *Sunday Star*, 12 March 1988.
129 Eugène Terre'Blanche: Interview, in Hoffman and Fischer, *The Jews in South Africa*, p. 188.
130 The society took its name from House of Orange in the Netherlands. It had 2,500 members and sought a *volksland* (national state).
131 Vermeulen maintained worldwide contacts with Nazi sympathisers. See Kemp, *Victory or Violence*, p. 78. In 1987 he launched the World Apartheid Movement, an initiative to gain international support for apartheid. Vermeulen was involved in the tarring and feathering of Floors van Jaarsveld.
132 Schabort relinquished his well-established academic career at the age of 49 in 1986 to pursue full-time politics. Till then he had a fine reputation as a scholar, having been appointed a full professor fourteen years earlier. Prior

Notes

to establishing the BBB, Schabort had been a member of the HNP.

133   The Boerestaat Party seems to have grown out of another radical group, Die Boerevolk, under Robert van Tonder.

134   It is unclear when Smith, a scientist, established the KvS. Three dates have been identified: 1979, 1984 and 1986. See Visser, 'Die ideologiese grondslae en ontwikkeling van die blanke fascistiese bewegings in Suid-Afrika', p. 147.

135   See Zille, 'The Right Wing in South African Politics', pp. 58–9. David Irving was a guest of the Stallard Foundation and Clive Derby-Lewis in 1986. See *Business Day*, 11 September 1986.

136   See Zille, 'The Right Wing in South African Politics', p. 61.

137   There were many more groups than those identified above. For a list at the mid-1990s, see 'Right Wing Directory', Independent Board of Inquiry, March 1996, Historical Papers, University of the Witwatersrand, Independent Board of Inquiry Records (IBI) 1989–1996, AG 2543: 2.3.7.

138   *Sunday Star*, 29 November 1987. Several well-known radical rightists were drawn to the movement, including Theunis Stoffberg, who was named honorary leader of the HNP. *Pretoria News*, 8 December 1988. In 1988 the BBB was banned by the South African government. In response, it changed its name to the Blanke Nasionale Beweging (White National Movement, or BNB) but was again banned. See *Business Day*, 17 January 1989.

139   Boers were defined as descendants of the Voortrekkers, citizens of the nineteenth-century Boer Republics and combatants in the Anglo-Boer War.

140   See *Sunday Times*, 2 June 1985.

141   *Die Stem van die Boerevolk*, July 1987.

142   This is evident in his voluminous writings. See, for example, B Klassen, *The White Man's Bible*, p. 123, cited in Visser, 'Die ideologiese grondslae en ontwikkeling van die blanke fascistiese bewegings in Suid-Afrika', p. 149.

143   See Visser, 'Die ideologiese grondslae en ontwikkeling van die blanke fascistiese bewegings in Suid-Afrika', p. 147; *The Citizen*, 12 September 1987; and Historical Papers, University of the Witwatersrand: AG 2543-2-3-7,   http://www.historicalpapers.wits.ac.za/inventories/inv_pdfo/AG2543/AG2543-2-3-7-01-jpeg.pdf.

144   See Eisenberg, *The Re-emergence of Fascism*, chapter 15.

145   See *The Citizen*, 21 August 1987; and *Sunday Times*, 23 September 1987.

146   *Pretoria News*, 21 April 1988.

147   *Business Day*, 26 August 1987.

148   *Die Vaderland*, 1 September 1987.

149   *Business Day*, 25 August 1987. In October 1987 the *Pretoria* News (13 October 1987) reported antisemitic daubing's in Pretoria as did *The Star* (1 December 1987) regarding Johannesburg. A year later *The Citizen* (21 April 1988) reported that, according to Koos Vermeulen, leader of the ANS, Hitler's birthday had been celebrated with screened guests. Another

celebratory function had been organised by Dr Pol Hyacinth Jozef Doussy. See *Pretoria News*, 21 April 1988.
150 https://africanelections.tripod.com/za.html.
151 See, for example, *South African Observer*, July 1984, where the Nkomati Accord, a non-aggression agreement between Mozambique and South Africa, was a product of Zionist manipulation. Similarly, the *South African Observer* (February 1987) alleged that 'world Jewry' was 'pressurising all the peoples of the world to gang up on one small nation, South Africa, and to get them to take a hand in the destruction of the last remaining stable government in Africa'.
152 See *Sunday Times*, 11 February 1990; and *Sunday Star*, 11 February 1990.
153 See *The Citizen*, 17 April 1990 and 16 April 1990.
154 See, for example, *The Citizen*, 12 March 1990 and 16 April 1990.
155 Hansard, 19 April 1990.
156 *Volksblad*, 24 April 1990.
157 See SA Rochlin Archives, Meeting of the National Executive Council, 27 May 1990.
158 At an HNP meeting in Boksburg anti-Jewish pamphlets were distributed by two unknown men and an anti-Jewish poster was brought into the meeting. According to the editor of *Die Afrikaner*, this was against the wishes or knowledge of the HNP, which distanced itself from such actions. See SA Rochlin Archives, Meeting of the National Executive Council, 27 May 1990.
159 *The Citizen*, 18 November 1993. The Commission was named after Justice Richard Goldstone.
160 *The Citizen*, 14 April 1994.
161 Ibid.

Chapter 4
1 According to the South African Census of 1991, black Africans made up approximately 75 per cent of the total population, while Coloureds and Indians made up 9 and 2.6 per cent respectively.
2 For an early and unfavourable view of Jews, see JK Masike letter in Part Mgadla and Stephen Volz (eds), *Words of Batswana: Letters to Mahoko a Becwana, 1883–1896*, Van Riebeeck Society, Cape Town, 2006, p. 315. In some cases, images were decidedly favourable. See, for example, Benjamin Pogrund, *How Can Man Die Better: The Life of Robert Sobukwe*, rev. edn, Jonathan Ball Publishers, Cape Town, 2006, pp. 233 and 291–2.
3 Stuart Buxbaum, 'The Social Distance Attitudes of a Sample of African and Coloured Matriculation Pupils: A Preliminary Analysis', Honours dissertation, University of the Witwatersrand, 1970, p. 94.
4 Melville Edelstein, 'The Urban African Image of the Jew', *Jewish Affairs*, vol. 27, no. 2, 1972, pp. 6–8. For the full study, see Melville Edelstein,

What Do Young Africans Think?, South African Institute of Race Relations, Johannesburg, 1972.

5   Interaction between black Africans and Jewish immigrants in the concession stores on the mines must have impacted on the image of the Jew. See Joseph Sherman, 'Serving the Natives: Whiteness as the Price of Hospitality in South African Yiddish Literature', *Journal of Southern African Studies*, vol. 26, no. 3, September 2000.

6   See Marcia Leveson, 'The Jewish Stereotype in Some South African Fiction: A Preliminary Investigation', in Reuben Musiker and Joseph Sherman (eds), *Waters out of the Well: Essays in Jewish Studies*, Wits University Library, Johannesburg, 1988, pp. 278–82; and Leveson, *People of the Book*, chapter 9.

7   Saths Cooper: Interview, in Hoffman and Fischer, *The Jews in South Africa*, p. 42. AZAPO was a Black Consciousness movement.

8   'The Attitude of White and Black Elites towards Anti-Semitism', in 'Opinion Surveys: Research for a New South Africa', Pretoria, 8–14 August 1990. A mimeographed report of this study was made available to the author by Jeremy Hayman (Information Officer, South African Zionist Federation, Johannesburg) three decades ago. This was a methodologically questionable survey, and it must be noted that surveys should not be equated axiomatically with actions.

9   Jocelyn Hellig, *Antisemitism in South Africa Today*, Project for the Study of Anti-Semitism, Tel Aviv University, 1996, p. 21.

10 Ibid.

11 Ibid.

12 SA Rochlin Archives, Executive Council Minutes, December 1994.

13 Saths Cooper: Interview, in Hoffman and Fischer, *The Jews in South Africa*, p. 39.

14 SA Rochlin Archives, 'Antisemitism Report 2004'.

15 'South Africa', in *Antisemitism Worldwide 2000*, Stephen Roth Institute for the Study of Contemporary Antisemitism and Racism, Tel Aviv University, 2001. See also Hellig, *Antisemitism in South Africa Today*, p. 18.

16 See, for example, SA Rochlin Archives, 'Antisemitism Report, South Africa 2014'.

17 See SA Rochlin Archives, 'Antisemitism Report, South Africa 2013'.

18 See SA Rochlin Archives, 'Antisemitism Report, South Africa 2002 and 2003'.

19 SA Rochlin Archives, 'Antisemitism Report, South Africa 2014'.

20 See https://www.timeslive.co.za/politics/2014-07-29-ancyl-distances-itself-from-keep-calm-and-kill-jews-twitter-account/.

21 *South African Jewish Report*, 2 July 2020.

22 'PAYCO Spokesman Says Hitler Was Better than Mandela', eNCA, 18 June 2013, https://www.enca.com/south-africa/payco-spokesman-says-hitler-

was-better-mandela; and SA Rochlin Archives, 'Antisemitism Report, South Africa 2013'.
23. See SA Rochlin Archives, 'Anti-Semitism Report, 1999'.
24. SA Rochlin Archives, 'Antisemitism Report, South Africa 2015'.
25. See *South African Jewish Report*, 10–17 February; and *Business Day*, 3 February 2017.
26. See, for example, *The Star*, 7 May 1984; and SA Rochlin Archives, 'Antisemitism Report, South Africa 2014'. For the ubiquity of Hitler's hold on the South African imagination, see Thierry Rousset, Gavaza Maluleke and Adam Mendelsohn, *The Dynamics of Racism, Antisemitism and Xenophobia on Social Media in South Africa*, Konrad-Adenauer-Stiftung, Johannesburg, 2022, pp. 95–105.
27. See, for example, SA Rochlin Archives, 'Antisemitism Report, South Africa 2013' and 'Antisemitism Report, South Africa 2014'.
28. See SA Rochlin Archives, 'Antisemitism and Anti-Zionism in South Africa, 2009'. The Board took Masuku's threats to the South African Human Rights Commission (SAHRC), which upheld the complaint and directed Masuku to apologise. Because he failed to do so, the SAHRC took the matter to the Equality Court in February 2017. The court upheld its findings. Thereafter COSATU appealed and, in December 2018, the Supreme Court of Appeal overturned the Equality Court judgment. The SAHRC then approached the Constitutional Court, which, in a landmark 'hate speech' case, ruled in February 2022 that Masuku must tender an unconditional apology to the Jewish community within thirty days. See https://www.news24.com/news24/southafrica/news/former-cosatu-leader-bongani-masuku-ordered-to-apologise-to-jewish-community-for-2009-hate-speech-20220216.
29. SA Rochlin Archives, 'South Africa, 2008'.
30. See *Haaretz*, 12 February 2015; and *TimesLive*, 13 February 2015, https://www.timeslive.co.za/news/south-africa/2015-02-13-expel-all-jews-call-withdrawn/.
31. News24, 11 February 2015, https://www.news24.com/News24/DUT-SRC-want-Jews-who-dont-support-Palestine-out-20150211; see also *Washington Post*, 12 February 2015.
32. See, for example, SA Rochlin Archives, 'Antisemitism Report, 2001'.
33. See Vashna Jagarnath, 'Anti-Semitism at Wits', *Daily Maverick*, 3 November 2016, https://www.dailymaverick.co.za/article/2016-11-03-op-ed-anti-semitism-at-wits/.
34. SA Rochlin Archives, 'Antisemitism Report, 2015'; see also Riante Naidoo, 'Jewish Student Organisation Responds to Dlamini's Hitler Comments', *Witsvuvuzela*, 28 April 2015, https://witsvuvuzela.com/2015/04/28/jewish-student-organisation-responds-to-dlaminis-hitler-comments/.

35 'Dlamini in Hot Water Again over "Jews Are Devils" Comment', News24, 29 June 2015, https://www.news24.com/News24/Dlamini-in-hot-water-again-over-Jews-are-devils-comment-20150629. In December 2020 Dlamini issued a formal apology for his comments.
36 SA Rochlin Archives, 'Antisemitism Report, 2018'.
37 See Garth Abrahams, *The Catholic Church and Apartheid: The Response of the Catholic Church to the First Decade of National Party Rule 1948–1957*, Ravan Press, Johannesburg, 1989, chapter 4.
38 *The Star*, 16 October 2000.
39 *Eastern Province Herald*, 11 April 2002.
40 See Independent Online, 27 August 2007, https://www.iol.co.za/news/politics/chabaan-accused-of-slurs-against-jews-368051; and SA Rochlin Archives, 'Antisemitism Report, 2007'. It needs to be noted that Chaaban also made racist comments about black Africans and Coloureds.
41 SA Rochlin Archives, 'Antisemitism Report, 2013'.
42 Ibid.
43 Ibid.
44 News24, 27 February 2018, https://www.news24.com/news24/southafrica/news/sa-jewish-board-of-deputies-condemns-anc-mpls-jewish-mafia-statement-20180227.
45 See ibid.
46 See SA Rochlin Archives, 'Antisemitism Report, South Africa 2021'.
47 For 'the gas chamber fable', see *Die Afrikaner*, 3–9 February 1995.
48 The Board and the International Association of Jewish Jurists successfully appealed against the unbanning of *The Protocols of the Elders of Zion* by the Directorate of Publications in 1991.
49 See PJ Pretorius, *Volksverraad: Die geskiedenis agter die geskiedenis*, Libanon Uitgewers, Mossel Bay, 1996.
50 Peter Banks, *En Mammon het gesê: Laat ons geld maak*, Vaandel-Uitgewers, Mossel Bay, 1998.
51 See Shain, *A Perfect Storm*, pp. 230–1.
52 See Lauritz Strydom, *Rivonia Unmasked: The South African State's Case against Nelson Mandela*, Ostara Publications, 2018.
53 *Antisemitism World Report, 1998*.
54 See 'South Africa', in *Antisemitism Worldwide 1999*, Stephen Roth Institute for the Study of Contemporary Antisemitism and Racism, Tel Aviv University, 2000. Jani Allan distanced herself from Johnson's views two days after the show. See https://www.iol.co.za/news/south-africa/janis-name-not-on-cape-talks-line-up-22466.
55 See *Natal Witness*, 25 February 1992; and *Journal of Historical Review*, vol. 16, no. 3, 1996–7.
56 *Journal of Historical Review*, vol. 16, no. 3, 1996–7.

57   See Milton Shain, 'South Africa', in David Singer and Lawrence Grossman (eds), *American Jewish Year Book 2000*, vol. 100, American Jewish Committee, New York, 2000, p. 419.
58   Voice of the Cape, Interview, 10 September 2004; and 'South Africa', in *Antisemitism Worldwide 2004*, Stephen Roth Institute for the Study of Contemporary Antisemitism and Racism, Tel Aviv University, Israel, 2004, p. 133. Colby was criticised by *Al-Qalam* (December 2005) after Radio 786 was found guilty of hate speech.
59   SA Rochlin Archives, 'South Africa: Anti-Semitism Report, 2004, for Institute of Contemporary Anti-Semitism and Racism, Tel Aviv University'.
60   Channel Islam International, 9 July 2008. The transcript was provided by the South African Jewish Board of Deputies. Henry Ford, the motor-car magnate, had published a version of *The Protocols of the Elders of Zion* in the 1920s.
61   CII, 23 December 2008.
62   Steven Mitford Goodson, *Inside the South African Reserve Bank: Its Origins and Secrets Exposed*, Black House Publishing, UK, 2014.
63   See *Arutz Sheva: Israel National News*, 23 April 2012. Goodson stood unsuccessfully as a candidate for the fringe Ubuntu Party in South Africa in the 2014 general election.
64   The circulation of *Die Afrikaner* was low and not of great significance. However, its voice did coincide with a growth in Muslim conspiratorial thinking (see below).
65   *Die Afrikaner*, 13–19 November; 20–26 November; 27 November – 3 December; 4–10 December 1998.
66   *Die Afrikaner*, 12–18 and 19–25 October 2001.
67   Qibla, under the one-time Robben Island prisoner and member of the PAC, Achmad Cassiem, was behind the formation of Radio 786. See Farid Esack, *Qur'an, Liberation and Pluralism: An Islamic Perspective of Interreligious Solidarity against Oppression*, One World Books, Oxford, 1997, p. 226.
68   A Swiss-born financier and funder of Islamists, Huber converted to Islam in 1962. See Robert S Wistrich, *A Lethal Obsession: Anti-Semitism from Antiquity to the Global Jihad*, Random House, New York, 2010, p. 604; Radio 786: Interview, January 1997; South Africa', in *Anti-Semitism Worldwide 1997*, Stephen Roth Institute for the Study of Contemporary Antisemitism and Racism, Tel Aviv University, 1998. The Board of Deputies complained both to the minister of telecommunications and to the Broadcasting Complaints Commission (BCC) and an 'out of court' settlement was arrived at: the Board would withdraw its allegations and Radio 786 would publicise an apology in its newscasts.
69   Interview: 'Prime Talk', 8 May 1998. Also known as James Dickie, Zaki was a convert to Islam and directed the pro-Iranian Muslim Institute in

Notes

London.
70 *Muslim Views*, August 1999.
71 *Muslim Views*, January 2000.
72 Pew Global Attitudes Project, 'Unfavourable Views of Jews and Muslims on the Increase in Europe', 17 September 2008, https://www.pewresearch.org/global/wp-content/uploads/sites/2/2008/09/Pew-2008-Pew-Global-Attitudes-Report-3-September-17-2pm.pdf. Despite the title, eighteen countries surveyed were outside Europe. By way of comparison, Australia had only 11 per cent harbouring hostile sentiments.
73 Reported incidents were ten times higher in the UK, France and Argentina, fifteen times higher in Australia, and twenty times higher in Canada and Germany. These figures were arrived at by David Saks, the associate director of the Board. The figures were based on the previous ten years.
74 https://global100.adl.org/country/south-africa/2014.
75 The survey was conducted in Cape Town, eThekwini (Durban), and Johannesburg. See University of Cape Town's Kaplan Centre for Jewish Studies and Research, *Attitudes and Perceptions of Black South Africans towards Jewish People in Cape Town, Durban and Johannesburg*, Mthente Research and Consulting Services, Cape Town, 2016, pp. 35–8, http://www.kaplancentre.uct.ac.za/sites/default/files/image_tool/images/151/Reports/FINAL_%20NarrativeReport_FINAL_March2017.pdf.
76 https://global100.adl.org/country/south-africa/2019; https://eurojewcong.org/news/news-and-views/adl-attitudes-survey-poland-south-africa-ukraine-and-hungary-top-list-for-antisemitism/.
77 Notably racism and discrimination are, at least formally, frowned upon. For example, COSATU condemned the use of 'Jews' in protest placards.
78 See, for example, Peter Stevens, 'Zionism, South Africa and Apartheid', *Sechaba*, September 1971; (Editorial) 'Israel, Imperialism and the Arabs', *African Communist*, vol. 30, 1967; and Samuel Ben-Adam, 'Zionism and the Future of Israel', *African Communist*, vol. 31, 1967.
79 Dr Neo Mnumzana: Interview, in Hoffman and Fischer, *The Jews in South Africa*, p. 72.
80 *The Citizen*, 1 March 1990.
81 See *The Citizen*, 14 August 1998. For all that, a Pew survey conducted in 2007 found greater support in South Africa for Israel than for the Palestinians. See https://studylib.net/doc/11969271/pew-global-attitudes-project--spring-2007-survey-survey-o.
82 The occasion was a Webinar hosted by the *Jerusalem Post*. See https://www.jpost.com/opinion/the-chief-justice-mogoeng-and-his-support-of-israel-633340.
83 See *Daily Friend*, 4 July 2020.
84 https://www.news24.com/news24/southafrica/news/naledi-pandor-

views-chief-justices-comments-on-israel-with-great-dismay-20200701.
85 https://www.iol.co.za/news/politics/chief-justice-mogoeng-must-resign-if-he-stands-by-his-remarks-supporting-apartheid-israel-says-mandla-mandela-49966588. Some months later the Judicial Conduct Committee demanded that the chief justice withdraw and retract unreservedly his comments, which were deemed to breach the code of judicial conduct. See *Business Day*, 5 March 2021.
86 https://afropalforum.com/afro/2022/03/14/speech-by-nkosi-zmd-mandela-mp-on-the-occasion-of-the-pan-african-palestinian-solidarity-network/.
87 See Robert Wistrich, *Anti-Semitism: The Longest Hatred*, Thames Mandarin, London, 1992.
88 See Bernard Harrison, *Blaming the Jews: Politics and Delusion*, Indiana University Press, Bloomington, 2020, p. 9. For reflections on the complex relationship between antisemitism and anti-Zionism, see Bernard Lewis, *Semites and Anti-Semites: An Inquiry into Conflict and Prejudice*, Norton & Co., New York, 1986, pp. 97–8; and Harrison, *Blaming the Jews*, chapters 9 and 15.
89 See Ebrahim Moosa, 'Islam in South Africa', in Martin Prozesky and John de Gruchy (eds), *Living Faiths in South Africa*, David Philip, Cape Town, 1995. The Muslim community is, for the most part Sunni, although there has been an influx of Shia Muslims from South-east Asia since the 1990s. More recently a small number of black Africans have converted to Islam. Black Africans now make up about 12 per cent of the Muslim population. See G Vahed and S Jeppie, 'Multiple Communities: Muslims in Post-Apartheid South Africa', in J Daniel, R Southall and J Lutchman (eds), *State of the Nation*, HSRC Press, Cape Town, 2005, p. 253; and Nuraan Davids, 'Muslim Education in Democratic South Africa: Convergence of Divergence of Religion and Citizenship', *Journal of Education in Muslim Societies*, vol. 1, no. 1, 2019, p. 48.
90 By and large, the historiography of South African Jewry has ignored Muslim–Jewish relations. Only in the late 1980s did Gideon Shimoni draw attention to growing Muslim–Jewish tensions. For more recent observations see Hellig, *Anti-Semitism in South Africa Today*; Margo Bastos, 'Muslim Anti-Zionism and Antisemitism since the Second World War, with Special Reference to "Muslim News/Views"', MA dissertation, University of Cape Town, 2002; Gideon Shimoni, *Community and Conscience: The Jews in Apartheid South Africa*, University Press of New England, Lebanon, NH, 2003; and Milton Shain and Margo Bastos, 'Muslim Antisemitism and Anti-Zionism in Postwar South Africa', in Robert Solomon Wistrich (ed.), *Holocaust Denial: The Politics of Perfidy*, Hebrew University Magnes Press, Jerusalem, and De Gruyter, Berlin, 2012.

91 In the 1950 and 1960s issues of orthodoxy characterised Muslim politics. See Abdulkader Tayob, *Islamic Resurgence in South Africa*, University of Cape Town Press, Cape Town, 1995, chapter 2.
92 See Muhammed Haron, 'The Muslim News (1960–1986): Expression of an Islamic Identity in South Africa', in Louis Brenner (ed.), *Muslim Identity and Social Change in Sub-Saharan Africa*, Hurst & Co., London, 1993, pp. 222–3.
93 See the article 'Barbarity of the Jews', *Muslim News*, 14 July 1967.
94 See Matthew Palombo, 'The Emergence of Islamic Liberation Theology in South Africa', *Journal of Religion in Africa*, vol. 44, no. 1, 2014; CJB le Roux and HW Nel, 'Radical Islamic Fundamentalism in South Africa: An Exploratory Study', *Journal of Contemporary History*, vol. 23, no. 2, 1998, p. 6; and Howard Phillips, *UCT under Apartheid, Part 1: From Onset to Sit-In, 1948–1968*, Jacana Media, Johannesburg, 2019, p. 285.
95 *Sunday Times*, 14 October 1973.
96 See, for example, *Muslim News*, 28 July 1967 and 12 September 1975; and Tayob, *Islamic Resurgence*, p. 85.
97 *Muslim News*, 23 August 1963 and 22 September 1968.
98 See *Muslim News*, 10 April 1971.
99 See Tayob, *Islamic Resurgence*, pp. 82–3.
100 See Tayob, *Islamic Resurgence*, chapter 3; Desmond Charles Rice, 'Islamic Fundamentalism as a Major Religiopolitical Movement and Its Impact on South Africa', MA dissertation, University of Cape Town, 1987, pp. 438–52; Muhammed Haron and Imraan Buccus, '*Al-Qalam*: An Alternative Muslim Voice in the South African Press', *South African Historical Journal*, vol. 61, no. 1, 2009, pp. 122–3; and Palombo, 'The Emergence of Islamic Liberation Theology in South Africa'.
101 See Rice, 'Islamic Fundamentalism', p. 452.
102 See Esack, *Qur'an, Liberation and Pluralism*, p. 32.
103 Ibid., p. 33. For a detailed examination of the Muslim Youth Movement, see Tayob, *Islamic Resurgence*.
104 Tayob, *Islamic Resurgence*, chapter 4.
105 Ibid., pp. 118–19.
106 Ibid., p. 122.
107 See Tayob, *Islamic Resurgence*, chapter 4.
108 See Haron, '*The Muslim News*', pp. 222–3; *Muslim News*, 28 November 1975; and Bastos, 'Muslim Anti-Zionism and Antisemitism since the Second World War', pp. 46–7.
109 Ibrahim Moosa: Interview, in Hoffman and Fischer, *The Jews in South Africa*, p. 173. Subsequently Ibrahim Moosa became Ebrahim Moosa.
110 Haron, '*The Muslim News*', p. 223.
111 Tayob, *Islamic Resurgence*, p. 140.

112 See Hariz Ahmed Saeed letter (*Muslim News*, 23 March 1979).
113 Al-Jihaad took some sustenance from the Iranian Revolution, claiming it was the first and only Shiite movement in South Africa loyal to the Ayatollah. See Le Roux and Nel, 'Radical Islamic Fundamentalism in South Africa', p. 6.
114 Cassiem was aligned to the PAC. See Palombo, 'The Emergence of Islamic Liberation Theology in South Africa', p. 43; and Muhammed Haron, 'Qibla Mass Movement and Its Leadership: Engaging with the Quran in an African Setting', 10th International Conference on Quranic Researches, Qom, Iran, https://www.academia.edu/31722804/Qibla_Mass_Movement_and_its_Leadership_Engaging_with_the_Quran_in_an_African_Setting?email_work_card=thumbnail. Given Cassiem's political background, it is not surprising that Qibla had links with the PAC and later with AZAPO.
115 *Varsity: Official Student Newspaper of the University of Cape Town*, vol. 41, no. 9, August 1982; see also Shimoni, *Community and Conscience*, pp. 175–6.
116 See *Rand Daily Mail*, 5 August 1982; also *Muslim News*, 3 May 1985; and *Cape Times*, 21 May 1987.
117 *Muslim News*, 20 August 1982.
118 *Rand Daily Mail*, 29 July 1982.
119 *Rand Daily Mail*, 13 August 1982.
120 See Esack, *Qur'an, Liberation and Pluralism*, pp. 36–7; and Rabia Pandy, 'A Critical Look at the Role of the Muslim Judicial Council in the Struggle for Liberation in South Africa from 1960 to 1994', BA (Hons) research paper, University of Cape Town, 1994, pp. 34, 37–9.
121 Esack, *Qur'an, Liberation and Pluralism*, p. 254; Abdulkader I Tayob, 'Muslims' Discourse on Alliance against Apartheid', *Journal for the Study of Religion*, vol. 3, no. 2, September 1990; and Farid Esack, 'Three Islamic Strands in the South African Struggle for Justice', *Third World Quarterly*, vol. 10, no. 2, 1988. For the class interests underpinning Muslim conservatism, see Ebrahim Moosa, 'Muslim Conservatism in South Africa', *Journal of Theology for Southern Africa*, vol. 69, 1989.
122 See *Muslim News*, 13 July 1984.
123 See Moosa, 'Muslim Conservatism in South Africa', p. 79; and Adil Bradlow, 'United Democratic Front: An Islamic Critique', paper, 1984, p. 10, cited in Esack, *Qur'an, Liberation and Pluralism*, p. 41.
124 Bradlow, 'United Democratic Front', p. 41; and Pandy, 'A Critical Look at the Role of the Muslim Judicial Council', pp. 34–42.
125 Esack, *Qur'an, Liberation and Pluralism*, p. 41.
126 Clashes broke out between Jewish and Muslim students at UCT.
127 The Call of Islam referred to a public statement organised by Imam Haron in 1961 which condemned 'oppression, tyranny and *baasskap* (white domination)' and called on Muslims to 'stand firm with our brothers in fighting the evil monster that is about to devour us'. *Muslim News*, 12 May

1961. See Palombo, 'The Emergence of Islamic Liberation Theology in South Africa', p. 33.

128 Ebrahim Rasool, 'Muslims Mobilize', *New Era*, March 1988, cited in Esack, *Qur'an, Liberation and Pluralism*, p. 36.

129 Ebrahim Rasool: Interview, in Hoffman and Fischer, *The Jews in South Africa*, p. 112.

130 Esack, *Qur'an, Liberation and Pluralism*, pp. 36–44. For debates and challenges posed by the creation of the UDF for Muslims, see Jill E Kelly, '"It Is *Because* of Our Islam That We Are There": The Call of Islam in the United Democratic Front Era', *African Historical Review*, vol. 41, no. 1, 2009. The MYM also took an anti-apartheid stance but did not align itself to any political organisation.

131 See James Adams, *Israel and South Africa: The Unnatural Alliance*, Quartet Books, London, 1984, p. 17; and Polakow-Suransky, *The Unspoken Alliance*.

132 Ebrahim Rasool: Interview, in Hoffman and Fischer, *The Jews in South Africa*, p. 118.

133 *Ibid*. The myth of American–Zionist imperialism has in some ways replaced the myth of Judaeo-Bolshevism.

134 See, for example, *Muslim News*, 19 June 1981.

135 Nazeem Mohammed: Interview, in Hoffman and Fisher, *The Jews in South Africa*, p. 137.

136 Ibrahim Moosa: Interview, in Hoffman and Fischer, *The Jews in South Africa*, p. 172.

137 See Esack, *Qur'an, Liberation and Pluralism*, p. 224.

138 Esack, 'Three Islamic Strands', p. 486.

139 See *Cape Times*, 14 March 1994; and Shimoni, *Community and Conscience*, p. 254. Notably, Qibla was aligned to the PAC.

140 Tayob, *Islamic Resurgence*, pp. 182–3.

141 The IUC claimed to be a union of 200 groups. According to Esack, it was 'a front for marginalised religious figures and a few small organisations who accept the pre-eminence of Qibla and its leader Achmad Cassiem'. See Farid Esack, 'Pagad and Islamic Radicalism: Taking on the State?', *Indicator SA*, vol. 13, no. 14, Spring 1996, p. 9. Yet even if Qibla was a minority movement, many of its antisemitic and anti-Zionist ideas were widespread.

142 See Muhammed Haron, 'The South African Muslims Making (Air) Waves during the Period of Transformation', *Journal for the Study of Religion*, vol. 15, no. 2, 2002, pp. 127–30.

143 For fantasy and irrationality as the defining features of antisemitism, see Gavin I Langmuir, *Towards a Definition of Antisemitism*, University of California Press, Los Angeles, 1990, pp. 306–10 and 334–40.

144 See for example, letters to *Muslim Views*, August 1990; and 'US Is the Biggest Warlord', *Al-Qalam*, August 1993.

145 *Muslim Views*, September 1990; see also *Muslim Views*, August 1990.
146 One such demonstration was held outside the Israeli embassy in response to the killing of 22 Palestinians by Israeli forces at Masjid-al-Aqsa. See *Muslim Views*, October 1990.
147 *Muslim Views*, November 1990.
148 *Muslim Views*, January 1991.
149 Ibid.
150 Ibid.
151 *One Solution, Islamic Revolution*, n.d., p. 1, cited in Esack, *Qur'an, Liberation and Pluralism*, p. 225.
152 See Allie A. Dubb and Milton Shain, 'South Africa', in David Singer and Ruth Seldin (eds), *American Jewish Year Book 1994*, vol. 94, American Jewish Committee, New York, 1994, p. 375.
153 See Bastos, 'Muslim Anti-Zionism and Antisemitism since the Second World War', pp. 88–92; and *Al-Qalam*, August 1993.
154 'Jihad will continue ... you have to fight and start the jihad to liberate Jerusalem, your sacred shrine.' See Milton Shain, 'South Africa', in David Singer and Ruth Seldin (eds), *American Jewish Year Book*, vol. 96, American Jewish Committee, New York, 1996, p. 357; and https://iris.org.il/arafats-johannesburg-speech/.
155 Jocelyn Hellig, 'South Africa', in *Antisemitism World Report 1996*, Institute for Jewish Policy Research and American Jewish Committee, London, 1996, p. 311.
156 *Muslim Views*, December 1995.
157 See 'South Africa', in *Antisemitism World Report 1996*, Institute for Jewish Policy Research and American Jewish Committee, London, 1997, p. 356. The conference was organised by Crescent International. See Le Roux and Nel, 'Radical Islamic Fundamentalism in South Africa', p. 13.
158 *Muslim Views*, September 1996.
159 PAGAD presented Islam as the only solution to the escalating problems of crime, drugs, unemployment and poverty as the apartheid 'police state' unravelled. It marched on the homes of known drug dealers. According to Esack, several militant elements within Qibla formed the core of PAGAD. See Esack, 'Pagad and Islamic Radicalism', p. 9.
160 *Muslim Views*, March 1997.
161 See Esack, 'Pagad and Islamic Radicalism', p. 10. In 1996 there were reports that Hamas delegates were planning to attend a conference and meet key South African politicians. Although the report turned out to be erroneous, further reports that Hamas had training camps in South Africa were treated seriously (although never confirmed) by the ANC-led Government of National Unity. See Milton Shain, 'South Africa', in David Singer and Ruth Seldin (eds), *American Jewish Year Book 1997*, American Jewish Committee,

New York, 1997, p. 419.
162 Milton Shain, 'South Africa', in David Singer and Ruth Seldin (eds), *American Jewish Year Book 1998*, American Jewish Committee, New York, 1998, p. 402.
163 Ibid., pp. 403–4.
164 Ibid., pp. 403–4; see also *Mail & Guardian*, 18 July 1997.
165 Shain, 'South Africa', in Singer and Seldin, *American Jewish Year Book 1998*, pp. 402–4.
166 *South African Jewish Report*, 22 May 1998.
167 Minister of justice Dullah Omar and minister of provincial and constitutional affairs Valli Moosa met with Hamas spiritual leader Sheikh Ahmed Yassin while in Saudi Arabia in April 1998.
168 *South African Jewish Report*, 22 May 1998.
169 *Muslim Views*, August 1998.
170 See 'Press Items of Jewish Interest', Rochlin Archives, South African Jewish Board of Deputies, October 2000, pp. 5–7. For Israeli apartheid, see, for example, Mahomed Elmasry, 'Why Israeli Apartheid and South African Apartheid Are So Similar', *Al-Qalam*, April 2006.
171 *Business Day*, 16 October 2000.
172 *South African Jewish Report*, 13 July 2001.
173 See Gabriel Schoenfeld, *The Return of Anti-Semitism*, Encounter Books, San Francisco, 2004, pp. 146–8; and Arch Puddington, 'The Wages of Durban', *Commentary*, February 2002.
174 *South African Jewish Report*, 13 July 2001.
175 *South African Jewish Report*, 14 September 2001; Wistrich, *A Lethal Obsession*, p. 487; Harris O Schoenberg, 'Demonization in Durban: The World Conference Against Racism', in David Singer and Lawrence Grossman (eds), *American Jewish Year Book*, vol. 102, American Jewish Committee, New York, 2002.
176 See 'South Africa', *Antisemitism Worldwide 2001*, Stephen Roth Institute for the Study of Contemporary Antisemitism and Racism, Tel Aviv University, 2002.
177 See Wistrich, *A Lethal Obsession*, p. 486.
178 See Joëlle Fiss, *The Durban Diaries: What Really Happened at the UN Conference Against Racism in Durban (2001)*, American Jewish Committee and European Union of Jewish Students, New York, 2008, p. 7.
179 *South African Jewish Report*, 31 August 2001.
180 *Weekly Standard*, 17 September 2001, cited in Kenneth S Stern, *Antisemitism Today: How It Is the Same, How It Is Different, and How to Fight It*, American Jewish Committee, 2006, p. 38. For first-hand accounts, see Benjamin Pogrund, *Drawing Fire: Investigating the Accusations of Apartheid in Israel*, Rowman and Littlefield, Lanham, MD, 2014, pp. 157–61; and Tova Herzl,

Madame Ambassador: Behind the Scenes with a Candid Israeli Diplomat, Rowman and Littlefield, Lanham, MD, 2015, pp. 187–96.

181   *The Guardian*, 31 August 2001.
182   *Haaretz*, 27 March 2002.
183   https://www.politicsweb.co.za/opinion/durban-i-a-retrospective. Arguably, Durban linked the Zionism–racism trope of the 1970s with a maturing intersectionality that combined anti-globalism, radical feminism, post-colonialism and human rights warfare. This has set the tone for the twenty-first century. See David Hirsch and Hilary Miller, 'Durban Antizionism: Its Sources, Its Impact and Its Relation to Older Anti-Jewish Ideologies', *Journal of Contemporary Antisemitism*, vol. 5, no. 1, Spring 2022, https://static1.squarespace.com/static/5fd29a1f51ae5c1b3ea73a07/t/6261af23326b464ded57b935/1650568995923/02_JCA_5-1_Durban+preprint.pdf.
184   *Cape Argus*, 6 September 2001.
185   See *Muslim Views*, September, November and December 2001.
186   *Muslim Views*, September 2001.
187   Khadija A Qahaar, exclusive interview with Mustafa Jonker: 'Ours Is a Blessed Terror', cited in Hussein Solomon, 'Combatting Islamist Radicalisation in South Africa', *African Security Review*, vol. 23, no. 1, 2014, pp. 19–20. The charges against Jonker were dropped. For a fuller account, see De Wet Potgieter, *Black Widow, White Widow: Is Al-Qaeda Operating in South Africa?*, Penguin Books, Johannesburg, 2014, pp. 104–15.
188   Interview, Radio 786: 'Prime Talk', 8 May 1998.
189   For Europeans, Holocaust denial assuages deep psychological guilt. See Wistrich, *A Lethal Obsession*, chapter 19.
190   *Muslim Views*, January 2000.
191   For the full (alleged) comments, see Solomon, 'Combatting Islamic Radicalisation in South Africa', p. 20.
192   We saw this with CII, and especially in the words of Jon Qwelane, who effectively declared all Jews 'legitimate targets'. In 2011 the University of Johannesburg severed ties with Ben-Gurion University of the Negev. Archbishop Emeritus Desmond Tutu and other prominent figures also castigated Israel's actions, albeit not as crudely as Qwelane did.
193   Raphael Ahren, 'South Africa's Deputy Minister "Don't Visit Israel"', *Times of Israel*, 12 August 2012.
194   https://www.politicsweb.co.za/politics/sa-zionist-federations-hands-dripping-with-blood--.
195   Tony Ehrenreich, 'If the SAJBD Wants to Advance a Zionist Agenda It Should Leave SA – COSATU WCape', Politicsweb, 30 July 2014, http://www.politicsweb.co.za/news-and-analysis/if-the-sajbod-wants-to-advance-a-zionist-agenda-it-. In an interview on Radio 786 (20 August 2014), Ehrenreich ridiculed the charge that he is an antisemite. In 2018,

however, he was found guilty of hate speech by the South African Human Rights Commission and formally apologised in 2020.

196 RW Johnson, 'Tony Ehrenreichs's Blood Libel', Politicsweb, 31 July 2014, http://www.politicsweb.co.za/news-and-analysis/tony-ehrenreich-blood-libel.

197 See *Times of Israel*, 15 September 2014. Mantashe seems to have forgotten that the UN created the Jewish State. Eight years later, following the shooting of Al Jazeera journalist Shireen Abu Akleh, the EFF issued a statement that described Israel as an 'evil state' which 'must be destroyed as a matter of urgency'. See https://www.politicsweb.co.za/politics/israel-is-an-evil-state-which-must-be-destroyed-as.

198 See *South African Jewish Report*, 9 September 2015.

199 See 'Cosatu to Intensify Israeli Goods Boycott', News24, 24 August 2016, https://www.news24.com/South Africa/News/Cosatu-to-intensify-Israeli-goods-boycott-20140826.

200 This point is made by Ira Robinson when discussing anti-Zionism in Canada. See Ira Robinson, *A History of Antisemitism in Canada*, Wilfred Laurier University Press, Waterloo, 2015, p. 163.

201 For the breakaway in 2020, see https://www.sajr.co.za/bds-sa-splinters-as-global-body-backs-new-group/. According to *Haaretz* (16 June 2019), BDS 'has arguably been more effective in South Africa than anywhere else in the world'.

202 SA Rochlin Archives, 'Antisemitism Report, South Africa 2013'.

203 See Rebecca Hodes, '"Dubul ijuda/Shoot the Jew" and the Local Architecture of Anti-Semitism', *Daily Maverick*, 12 September 2013. BDS-SA director, Muhammed Desai, defended the song, which he equated with 'Kill the Boer' sung at funerals at the height of the struggle against apartheid. See SA Rochlin Archives, 'Antisemitism Report, South Africa 2013'.

204 https://www.sajbd.org/media/antisemitism-levels-in-south-africa-greatly-over-stated. In January 2022 the Muslim twins Brandon-Lee and Tony-Lee Thulsie were found guilty by the Johannesburg High Court of trying to join Islamic State in Syria and conspiring to attack Shia, Jewish and foreign targets in South Africa.

205 *South African Jewish Report*, 31 January 2020.

206 For Jewish concerns, see Graham, *The Jews in South Africa in 2019*, p. 10.

207 SA Rochlin Archives, 'Antisemitism Report, South Africa 2021'; Tali Feinberg, 'SA Jews Face Vitriolic Antisemitism Online', *South African Jewish Report*, 28 May – 4 June 2021 and 'No Ceasefire in SA Antisemitism', *South African Jewish Report*, 3–10 June 2021.

208 See Feinberg, 'SA Jews Face Vitriolic Antisemitism Online', *South African Jewish Report*, 27 May 2021. For an examination of social media at the time

of these clashes, see Rousset, Maluleke and Mendelsohn, *The Dynamics of Racism, Antisemitism and Xenophobia on Social Media in South Africa: A Report*, pp. 84–105.

209 See Ben Cohen, 'Top South African Leader Claims Israel Wants to Conquer African Continent in Conspiracy-Laden Antisemitic Rant', The Algemeiner, 26 May 2021, https://www.algemeiner.com/2021/05/26/top-south-african-leader-claims-israel-wants-to-conquer-african-continent-in-conspiracy-laden-antisemitic-rant/.

210 SA Rochlin Archives, 'Antisemitism Report, 2020'.

211 See, for example, the white supremacist 'History Reviewed' website run by the Johannesburg-based Jan Lamprecht.

212 *South African Jewish Times*, 7 March 1997. The Board has on several occasion used the courts to challenge what it has determined to be hate speech and incitement. Most recently, a restraining order was issued against Jan Lamprecht, the white supremacist and Nazi sympathiser, after he threatened Professor Karen Milner, national vice-chairman of the Board.

Afterthoughts

1 See Hannah Arendt, *The Origins of Totalitarianism*, new edn, Harcourt, New York, 1973 [1951], p. 28.

2 As Robert Miles writes, 'The act of representational exclusion is simultaneously an act of inclusion, whether or not Self is explicitly identified in the discourse'. See Robert Miles, *Racism*, Routledge, London and New York, 1989, p. 39.

3 See Shain, *A Perfect Storm*, chapter 6.

4 See Shain, *The Roots of Antisemitism in South Africa*.

5 See Jonathan Hyslop, 'Why Did Apartheid's Supporters Capitulate?: "Whiteness", Class and Consumption in Urban South Africa 1985–1995', *Society in Transition*, vol. 31, no. 1, 2000, pp. 36–7.

6 This 'kernel of truth' notion has been succinctly raised by Peter Pulzer when reflecting on the German and Austrian experience. See Peter Pulzer, *The Rise of Political Antisemitism in Germany and Austria*, rev. edn, Peter Halban Publishers, London, 1988, pp. 14–15. It also informs Fritz Stern's understanding of late nineteenth-century German antisemitism. See Fritz Stern, *Gold and Iron: Bismarck, Bleichröder and the Building of the German Empire*, Vintage Books, Random House, New York, 1979, p. xix.

7 Fantasies or 'chimerical stereotypes' have no 'kernel of truth', notes Langmuir. See Langmuir, *Towards a Definition of Antisemitism*, p. 306.

8 See Stephen Eric Bonner, 'Conspiracy Then and Now: History, Politics, and the Anti-Semitic Imagination', in Richard Landes and Steven T Katz (eds), *The Paranoid Apocalypse: A Hundred Year Retrospective on the Protocols of the Elders of Zion*, New York University Press, New York, 2012, pp. 220–1.

9 As noted by Richard Hofstadter, this was not paranoia in a clinical sense. It was rather paranoia reflected in 'the curious leap in imagination that is always made at some critical point in the recital of events'. See Hofstadter, *The Paranoid Style in American Politics and Other Essays*, pp. 3–4 and 37. Hofstadter understands paranoia as a protective mechanism ignited by panic generated by the fear of threatening impersonal forces.
10 See David Nirenberg, *Anti-Judaism: The Western Tradition*, WW Norton, New York, 2013, p. 466.
11 *Muslim Views*, August 2014.
12 For a hostile domestic site, see 'History Reviewed', http://historyreviewed.best/index.php/2020/12/. Established by Zimbabwean-born Jan Lamprecht, this white supremacist/nationalist site specialises in attacks on the South African government, white nationalist struggles, Holocaust denial, and global and South African Jewry.
13 Wistrich, *A Lethal Obsession*, p. 600.
14 Zionism was referred to by Isaiah Berlin as 'the last child of the European Risorgimento'. See Isaiah Berlin, 'Jewish Slavery and Emancipation', in Henry Hardy (ed.), *The Power of Ideas*, Pimlico, London, 2001.
15 Hermann Giliomee, 'Manipulating the Past', in Rainer Erkens and John Kane-Berman (eds), *Political Correctness in South Africa*, South African Institute of Race Relations, Johannesburg, 2000, pp. 93–4. Of course, race is not obliterated as a collective tool for redress and the issue is played out in daily politics.
16 For the intellectual origins of this anti-Zionist worldview, see Milton Shain, 'The Roots of Anti-Zionism in South Africa and the Delegitimization of Israel', in Alvin H Rosenfeld (ed.), *Anti-Zionism and Antisemitism: The Dynamics of Delegitimization*, Indiana University Press, Bloomington, 2019.
17 See Jean and John Comaroff, 'Reflections on Liberalism, Postculturalism and ID-ology: Citizenship and Difference in South Africa', *Social Identities*, vol. 9, no. 4, 2003, p. 445. This hostility to ethnic identity has gradually dissipated and today there is a greater tolerance for cultural diversity (anticipated in the 1996 Constitution) despite parallel indications of an emergent racial nationalism.
18 Interview: Archbishop Desmond Tutu, in Hoffman and Fischer, *The Jews in South Africa*, p. 15.
19 This is classically illustrated in the call to boycott Jewish business because of ties to Israel by Africa4Palestine. See 'Call for Boycotts against Jewish Businesses Alarming – SAJBD', Politicsweb, 10 June 2021, https://www.politicsweb.co.za/politics/calls-for-boycotts-on-jewish-business-alarming--sa.
20 Dr Neo Mnumzana: Interview, in Hoffman and Fischer, *The Jews in South Africa*, p. 71. It would be fair to state that similar sentiments are shared by the ANC's alliance partners, COSATU and the SACP. In Mnumzana's

comments we see evidence of a 'Third Worldist' and leftist anti-Zionism that in time has morphed into an ideational package – a shorthand signal for hatred of Western imperialism and its infelicities.

21   As noted earlier, Muslims identified with the notion of *Nakba* at the time of the Israeli War of Independence in 1948 and shared in the humiliation of Arab defeats at the hands of Israeli forces.

22   These progressives appear to be aware only of successful Jews in the West and oblivious to the historical oppression of Jews of eastern Europe and Arab lands.

23   See Gizela C Lebzelter, *Political Anti-Semitism in England, 1918–1939*, Macmillan, London, 1978, pp. 2 and 22–3.

24   See Beamish's evidence in Mark Lazarus, *The Challenge*, Mercantile Press, Port Elizabeth, 1935, pp. 77–97.

25   See Muhammed Haron, 'The Formation of Religious Networks between the Muslim Heartlands and the South African Muslims', *BOLESWA: Journal of Theology, Religion and Philosophy*, vol. 1, no. 3, 2007. In particular, the seemingly well-funded BDS movement makes sophisticated use of electronic media.

26   Einat Wilf, 'South African Danger', *Yediot Achronot*, 23 November 2013.

27   Ironically, left and right often cooperate closely. This was sharply on display in 2006 when the Iranian regime (under presidential patronage) hosted a Holocaust denial conference in Tehran which included David Duke (a good friend of the radical white right in South Africa), as well as the German-Australian denier Fredrick Töben and the French denier Robert Faurisson. See Wistrich, *A Lethal Obsession*, pp. 649–50.

28   Fred Halliday, *Islam and the Myth of Confrontation*, IB Tauris, London, 2003, p. 5.

29   See Irina Filatova and Apollon Davidson, '"We the South African Bolsheviks": The Russian Revolution and South Africa', *Journal of Contemporary History*, vol. 52, no. 4, 2017, p. 951, n. 72.

30   See Daniel Pipes, *Conspiracy: How the Paranoid Style Flourishes and Where It Comes From*, Simon and Schuster, New York, 1997, pp. 21, 82–3, 174–88.

31   It needs to be noted that Lenin was not an antisemite, but the communist critique of 'monopoly capitalism' often descended into classical Jew-hatred.

32   Bryan Cheyette, 'Hilaire Belloc and the "Marconi Scandal", 1900–1914: A Reassessment of the Interactionist Model of Racist Hatred', *Immigrants and Minorities*, vol. 8, nos. 1 and 2, March 1989. For the deep roots of anti-Judaism in global culture, see Nirenberg, *Anti-Judaism*.

33   See Irving Abella, 'Antisemitism in Canada in the Interwar Years', in Moses Rischin (ed.), *The Jews of North America*, Wayne State University Press, Detroit, 1987; and Allison Down, 'The Struggle for Self-Determination: A Comparative Study of Ethnicity and Nationalism among the Québecois and

Notes

the Afrikaners', MA dissertation, University of Stellenbosch, 1999.

34 See, for example Shmuel Almog, *Nationalism and Antisemitism in Modern Europe, 1815–1945*, Pergamon Press, Oxford, 1990; and Götz Aly, *Europe against the Jews, 1880–1945*, Metropolitan Books, New York, 2020.

35 See Milton Shain, 'Ethnonationalism, Anti-Semitism, and Identity Politics: The North American and South African Experiences', in Sander L Gilman and Milton Shain (eds), *Jewries at the Frontier: Accommodation, Identity, Conflict*, University of Illinois Press, Urbana, IL, 1999.

36 The Bill of Rights states that the government may not discriminate directly or indirectly against any individual based on religion; in addition, no one may deny members of a religious group either the right to practise their religion or to form, join, or maintain religious associations with other members of that group.

37 Hansard, 4 August 1998.

38 See SA Rochlin Archives, 'An Open Letter of Apology', Dawood Khan to South African Jewish Board of Deputies 7 April 1993: South African Jewish Board of Deputies, National Executive Council, Minutes of the Meeting, 23 May 1993.

39 At the same time there are interesting indications of emerging identity politics.

40 Ebrahim Rasool: Interview in Hoffman and Fischer, *The Jews in South Africa*, p. 115.

41 Farid Esack: Interview in Hoffman and Fischer, *The Jews in South Africa*, p. 126.

42 Taj Hargey: Interview in Hoffman and Fischer, *The Jews in South Africa*, p. 155.

43 See *The Citizen*, 13 December 1982; and https://en.wikipedia.org/wiki/Ahmed_Deedat. The IPCI was reportedly funded by the Bin Laden family in Saudi Arabia. See *The Mercury*, 26 September 1998; and *Sunday Times*, 9 September 2001.

44 See Esack, *Qur'an, Liberation and Pluralism*, p. 218. For Deedat on Israel, see Ahmed Deedat, *Arabs and Israel: Conflict or Conciliation?*, Islamic Propagation Centre International, Durban, 1989.

45 This was again evident in a talk show on Power FM during Operation Guardian of the Walls in 2021. Several callers made malevolent comments about Jewish domination and explicitly supported these comments with allusions to *The Protocols of the Elders of Zion*. See *South African Jewish Report*, 17–24 June 2021.

46 For a recent study of divisions among Muslims in Cape Town, see Tore Refslund Hamming, 'Diffusion of Islamic Discourse: Saudi and Iranian Influence in Lagos and Cape Town', SciencesPo, Institut d'Études Politiques de Paris, Paris School of International Affairs, Master's in International Security, 2014.

47 See Moosa, 'Islam in South Africa'. Deobandi and conservative Sunni traditions also gained ground in the new South Africa – energised (without regard for the Islamic worldview) by the legalisation of abortion, prostitution and pornography after 1994. A plethora of Islamic schools (madrasas) have been established, while more Muslim women are covering their faces and more Muslims in general are observing dietary laws than in the past. Some Muslim families have even eschewed television.

48 The full range of Muslim radio stations have devoted time to promoting the Palestinian cause and have hosted international speakers. See Haron, 'The South African Muslims Making (Air) Waves during the Period of Transformation', p. 137.

49 See Farid Esack: Interview in Hoffman and Fischer, *The Jews in South Africa*, p. 128.

50 See Mark Orkin, *Predicting Xenophobic Attitudes: Statistical Path Models of Objective and Subjective Factors*, Gauteng Region-City Observatory (GCRO), September 2019.

51 Jewish leaders do, however, recognise a widespread hostility towards Israel which they believe is fuelled – at least to some extent – by the ANC.

52 For all that, a large proportion of Jews surveyed in 2019 expressed concern about anti-Zionism and antisemitism. See Graham, *The Jews in South Africa in 2019*, pp. 9–10.

53 See Pew Global Attitudes Project: Spring 2007 Survey of 47 Publics, p. 96, http:www.pewglobal.org/files/pdf/256topline.pdf.

54 See Richard Evans, *In Defence of History*, Granta Books, London, 1997, pp. 61–2; and Paul Kennedy, *The Rise and Fall of Great Powers: Economic Change and Military Conflict from 1500 to 2000*, Random House, New York, 1987.

55 See Andrei S. Markovits, 'Peter Pulzer's Writing on Political Anti-Semitism and the Jewish Question in Germany and Austria: An Assessment', in Henning Tewes and Jonathan Wright (eds), *Liberalism, Anti-Semitism, and Democracy: Essays in Honour of Peter Pulzer*, Oxford University Press, Oxford, 2004, p. 58.

56 Trevor-Roper, 'The Phenomenon of Fascism', p. 23.

Index

A

Abdication of the White Man, The 96
Abrahams, Chief Rabbi Israel 6
Ackerman, Raymond 121
Action Moral Standards 77
African Muslim Party 126
African National Congress *see* ANC
African Resistance Movement (ARM) 34
Afrikaans Teachers' Association 11
Afrikaner Christian Nationalism 8
Afrikaner elite 8
Afrikaner nationalism 11, 25, 28, 82, 103, 107, 110, 164
Afrikaner Volkswag 95, 111
Afrikaner Weerstandsbeweging *see* AWB
Afrikaner, Die 72, 75, 77, 83, 86, 92–94, 98, 130
Afrikanerdom 45
Aksie Red Blank Suid-Afrika (ARBSA) 109
Albertyn, Christiaan Fick 33
Aliens Act 2
ANC 32, 129, 132–134, 143–144, 148, 151, 153, 158–159, 164, 166, 168
  banning 34
  unbanning 115
Anglo-Afrikaner Bond 80–81
Anglo-Boer War (1899–1902) 51, 59, 62, 73, 93, 97, 111, 114, 128, 149, 160–162

anti-Jewish stereotypes 46, 52, 121–122, 152, 156, 168
anti-apartheid
  activist 16, 45, 143
  boycotts 32
  movement 41, 87
  stance 42
anti-communist 15, 21, 23, 25–26, 34, 36, 61, 67–68
Anti-Defamation League (ADL) 55, 57
anti-Jewish 132, 149
  activism 50
  caricatures 146
  commentary 33, 63
  conspiracy 63, 129, 157
  extremists 4, 116
  fantasies 72, 79, 96, 127–128, 153
  fantasists 92
  hatred 125
  hostility 47, 156, 162
  incidents 81, 115–116, 122, 152
  material 55, 63
  motifs 116, 166
  oratory 21–22, 54
  pamphlets 4, 70, 91
  policies 4
  propaganda 55, 70–71
  rhetoric 10
  sentiment 122, 156, 164
  tropes 65, 131, 133, 152, 166

219

Anti-Kommunistiese Aksiekommissie *see* Antikom 23
anti-Nationalist activists 30
anti-Zionist 68, 81, 125, 132–134, 137, 140, 142, 144–145, 149, 151, 157, 161, 165–166
Antikom 23–24, 36, 79, 93
Antikom 37–39
antisemitism 47, 57, 70–71, 82, 101, 107, 114, 117, 125, 131–134, 149–153, 156–157, 162–167
programmatic 131, 155
apartheid 5, 7–8, 13, 20, 41, 67, 87, 94, 102, 111–112, 121–122, 134, 139, 144, 160
antisemitism in 120
classification 158
grand 6, 99, 120
ideology 3
leaders 17
legislation 32
lexicon 45
opposition to 42, 45, 138, 157
order 19, 115
policy 16, 31, 70, 80, 82
project 3, 8, 157–158
racial 23
regime 115, 141, 147–148, 151, 157, 161
state 50, 132–133, 137, 146, 165
struggle against 47, 132, 159
apartheid government 126
apartheid Israel 125, 127, 133, 145, 151
Arafat, Yasser 132, 142, 144, 166
Aryan Bookstore 55–57
AWB 80–82, 88, 100, 102–111, 113–116, 157
Azanian People's Organisation (AZAPO) 121, 137

B

Band of Brothers *see* Broederbond
Banks, Peter 127
Barromi, Joel 47
Battersby, James Larratt 6
Bawa, Ahmed 124–125
Beeld 18, 44, 77, 102

Behind the News: A Southern African Bulletin 66–67, 86, 94, 96, 98
Ben-Gurion, David 42, 44, 47
Benson, Ivor 36, 66–68, 72, 77, 86, 96–98, 103, 106, 109, 149, 161
Birth of a Community, The 6
black African proletariat 2
Black Consciousness Movement 87, 136
Blanke Volkstaat Party (BVP) 108
Blanke Werkersparty 50
Blankebevrydingsbeweging (BBB) 111–114
bloedvreemdelinge 7
Blueprint for Blackout 11
Boerestaat Party 112–113
Bolshevik Jews 20
Bolshevik Revolution 50, 98, 149
Bolshevism 21–22, 38, 62, 65, 72
Boomerang 64, 69
Boonzaier, Daniël Cornelis 51
Botha, Pieter Willem 82, 94, 99–100, 108
Boycott, Divestment and Sanctions (BDS) 124, 151, 161
Bremer, Karl 23
British imperialism 32
Broederbond 2, 7, 9, 17, 81, 86–87, 100, 102, 111
Brown, Sydney Eustace Denys (SED) 29–30, 36, 48, 64, 71–72, 75–78, 86, 94, 103, 149, 161
Bureau for State Security 45, 102
Burger, Die 4, 9, 26–27, 39, 43
Butz, Arthur R 75, 92, 130
Buxbaum, Stuart 120

C

Call of Islam 138, 140
Calvinist principles 12, 88
Candour League 68–69
Cape Town Holocaust Centre 130, 150
capitalism 32, 41, 47, 51, 54, 79, 98, 122, 136, 142, 161–162
Carter, Gwendolen Margaret 8–9
Carto, Willis 129
Chalmers, William (Bill) 79–80
Chesterton, Arthur Kenneth 35, 37, 64, 68

Index

Christian anti-Semitism 103
Christian National Education *see* CNE
Christian-National philosophy 11
CNE 10–12, 18, 43, 90
Cobden, Michael 69
Coetzee, Barzillai (Blaar) 42
Cold War 22, 26–28, 33, 41, 67, 70
Common Sense 57, 63, 73
communism 16, 19–28, 32, 35–42, 45, 57, 59, 61–65, 68–70, 74, 149, 157
  international 75, 79
Communist Danger in South Africa, The 23
Communist Party of South Africa *see* CPSA 20, 22, 27–28, 32
Congress of South African Trade Unions *see* COSATU
Congress of the People 28, 32
conscience clause 12–14, 18
Conservative Party (CP) 99–101, 115
Conspiracy of Truth, The 79–80
conspiratorial discourse 2
Constitution of South African 1996 122, 127, 159, 164
Cooper, Saths 121–122
COSATU 115, 124, 134, 150–151, 164, 168
cosmological struggle 147, 149
Cotton, Richard 73–74
Covid-19 pandemic 123, 153
CPSA 20, 22, 27–28, 32

D

Dagbreek en Sondagnuus 19, 35, 40, 73
Dapper Boodskapper, Die 55
Davis, Adolf 11
De Klerk, Frederik Willem 34, 100, 115, 139
De Lille, Patricia 127
De Wet Nel, Michel Christiaan 30
De Wet, Quartus 37
Defiance Campaign 32
Democratic Alliance (DA) 126–127
Did Six Million Die? The Truth at Last 75, 78, 130
Diederichs, Nicolaas Johannes 15, 17, 20
Dispossessed Majority, The 93
Dlamini, Mcebo 125

Dönges, Theophilus Ebenhaezer (Eben) 43
Duarte, Jessie 153
Durban University of Technology (DUT) 124–125
Dutch Reformed Churches 8, 11

E

eastern European Jews 2, 4
Economic Freedom Fighters (EFF) 125
Edelstein, Melville 120
Education League 11
Eichmann Is Not Guilty 73
En Mammon het gesê: Laat ons geld maak 127
English-medium schools 12
eugenicist 67
and nativist concerns 2
European fascism 2, 54

F

fantasists 50, 65, 70, 72, 86, 92, 108, 115, 128, 161
Federasie van Afrikaner Kultuurverenigings (FAK) 9–11
Fick, Marthinus 12, 14
Freedom Charter 33, 158

G

Gamieldien,147 Mogamat Faaik 147
Garment Workers' Union 20
geldmag 10
General Synod of the NGK 38
Gereformeerde Kerk (Dopper) 8
German Democratic Republic 56
German-Jewish refugees 2, 62
Gesuiwerde Nasionale Party (GNP) 2–4, 21, 54, 87
God-fearing conservatism 10
Goldmann, Haim 37–38
Goldreich, Arthur 35–36, 40
Goldstone Commission 117
Goodson, Steven Mitford 129
grand apartheid 6, 99, 120
Greyshirt Trial 51, 59, 160
Greyshirts 27, 50, 54, 93, 103, 107
Grobbelaar, Janis 109
Gulf War 140, 142

221

H

Halliday, Fred 161
Hamas 143–145, 152
Hand behind the Scenes, The 63
Haron, Imam Abdullah 125
Hartzenberg Ferdinand (Ferdi) 100–101
Harwood, Richard 56, 75–76, 78, 104, 130
Herenigde Nasionale Party *see also* HNP 3
Herstigte Nasionale Party *see also* HNP 46, 86
Hertzog, James Barry Munnik 3, 45
Hertzog, Johannes Albertus Munnik (Albert) 45–46, 78, 87–88, 96, 98, 102
Hess, Rudolf Walter Richard 71, 101, 114
Heusler, Karl 71
Hillbrow Affair 70–71
Hitler Handbill 147
Hitler, Adolf 25, 54–55, 61–62, 70–77, 80–81, 93, 101, 113, 123–125, 160, 162, 164
Hitler memorial institutes 6
Hitler was right, Jews are communists 115–116
HNP 3–6, 25, 46, 69, 74–75, 78, 81–83, 87–88, 93, 96, 98–99, 102–103, 107, 128, 130, 157
Hoax of the Twentieth Century, The 75, 92, 130
Hobson, John Atkinson 97, 161–162
Hoernlé Memorial Lecture 6
Hofmeyr, Jan Hendrik 4, 6, 26
Hofstadter, Richard 1, 49–50
Hoggenheimer cartoon 9–10, 47, 51, 97–98, 156
Holm, Erik 9
Holocaust 5, 59, 73–77, 80–81, 83, 95–96, 101, 113, 123, 125, 145, 153
  denial 72, 74, 78, 92–93, 96, 127–128, 130, 146, 149–150, 157, 166
  denial literature 75, 96
  deniers 56, 75, 92–93, 98, 105, 128–129, 160
Hoofstad 74, 87, 101

I

Illuminati 79, 98, 127, 130
Inside the South African Reserve Bank: Its Origins and Secrets Exposed 129
Institute for Christian National Education (ICNO) 9–11
Institute of Race Relations 6
international monetary Zionism 108
Isaac and Jessie Kaplan Centre for Jewish Studies and Research 131
Isacowitz, Jock 25, 28
Islamic Mujahideen Foundation 141
Islamic resurgence 134–136
Islamic Unity Convention (IUC) 130, 140
Israel Question 42

J

Jagarnath, Vashna 125
Jameson Raid of 1895-6 51
Jansen, Ernest George 30
Jew-baiting 4, 10, 19, 52, 86
Jew-hatred 9, 55, 116–117, 122–126, 129, 131–132, 134, 151–153, 156, 158–160, 165
Jewish 2
  activists 2
  domination 2, 94
  emancipation 8
  perfidy 95
  problem 86, 130, 167
  question 1–6, 25–27, 30, 47, 55, 70, 88, 91, 93, 101, 114–115, 132, 155–156, 160
  stereotypes 121
  subversion 42, 44–45, 47–48, 97
Jewish Board of Deputies 16, 32, 56, 68, 91–92, 110, 116, 125–126, 142, 146, 150
Jews of South Africa: A History, The 31
Jews, views of 120, 131
jingos 25, 30

K

Kappiekommando 100, 109
Katzew Henry 4
Kerk van die Skepper 112–114

Kerkbode, Die 39, 44, 75, 87–88
Klassen, Bernhardt (Ben) 112, 114
Kleist, Bruno Peter 56, 69
Ku Klux Klan 56, 80–81, 117

L

Last Trek, The 8
League of Gentiles 29
Leibbrandt, Sidney Robey 9
Lemeer, Karl 4
Leveson, Marcia 121
Lewsen, Phyllis 10
Liberal Party 25, 28, 36
liberalism 8, 16, 19–21, 26, 28, 30, 32, 36, 40–42, 44–45, 87, 111, 157
Lilla, Mark 1
Loock, JH 10
Louw, Eric Hendrik 4, 9, 23, 42, 62

M

Macmillan, Maurice Harold 34
Mafeje, Archibald (Archie) 16
Maimane, Mmusi 127
Malan, Daniël François 2–6, 8–9, 15, 17, 19, 21–23, 25–26, 32, 50, 52, 54–55, 57, 61,
Mandela, Nelson Rolihlahla 35, 113, 115–116, 123, 128, 132–133, 143–144, 166
Manichaean
   fantasies 134
   Struggle 147, 149
   worldview 58
Mantashe, Gwede 151
Marais, Jacob Albertus (Jaap) 46, 98
Maritz, Manie 54, 127
Marx, Karl 39, 126
Marxism 25, 111
Marxist communism 96
Masuku, Bongani 124
Mein Kampf 25
Melville, Stephen 37
Mossad 143, 147
Mulder, Cornelius Petrus (Connie) 12, 42, 101, 109
Muller, Lourens 16–19, 32, 45–46
multiculturalism 8, 164

multi-nationalism 86
multiracialism 67
Muslim Students Association (MSA) 136, 138
Muslim Views 130, 135, 140, 142, 147
Muslim Youth Movement (MYM) 135–138
Mussolini, Benito Amilcare Andrea 3, 70
My lewe en strewe 127
myth of the Holocaust 95

N

Nasionale Pers 33
Natal Witness 33
National Conservative Party (NCP) 101, 109
National Council Against Communism 38, 40
National Democratic Party (NDP) 69
National Education Policy Act 12
National Front of South Africa 81
National Intelligence Agency 1 27
National Party 4–10, 12–14, 16–18, 26–28, 32–34, 45–46, 87–91, 94, 98–103, 107, 109, 143–144, 157
National Union of South African Students *see* NUSAS
nativist categories 3
nativist movement 29
Natte, Neels 30–31
Nazism 2, 162
Nederduitsch Hervormde Kerk 8–9, 103–104
Nederduitse Gereformeerde Kerk *see* NGK
neo-Calvinism 87, 163
neo-Calvinist Afrikaners 163
neo-Calvinist culture 10
neo-Calvinist ethos and ethic 10
neo-Calvinist exclusivism 157
neo-Calvinist intellectuals 7
neo-Calvinist values 17
neo-Kuyperianism 3
neo-Nazis 52, 55–56, 69–70, 72, 161
New Era 30
New World Order (NWO) 71, 130, 145
NGK 8, 12–13, 17–18, 21, 23, 25–26,

39, 54, 79, 87, 90–91
non-Christians 13, 85, 89
non-whites 18, 22, 31, 99, 120
Nordicism 3
Norval, Aletta 21, 86
NS Boerenasie 54–55, 58, 81–82
Nuremberg Trials of 1945–6 52, 72, 75
NUSAS 16–18, 34–35, 40, 45
Nuwe Orde (New Order) 3, 54, 160

O

OB 2, 22–23, 25–26, 82
Odal Clan 80–82
Oggendblad 101
one settler, one bullet 140
Oosterlig, Die 35, 39, 42
Operation Cast Lead 124, 150
Oppenheimer, Harry Frederick 10, 41, 65, 108–109, 113, 122, 143, 148
Ossewabrandwag *see also* OB 2, 5, 54, 160

P

Palestine Liberation Organisation *see* PLO
Palestinian Islamic Resistance Movement *see* Hamas
Pan Africanist Congress (PAC) 34, 115, 140
Patterson, Sheila 8
People Against Gangsterism and Drugs (PAGAD) 143
Petersen, Sebastian Sebbi 123
Phahlamohlaka, Thabo Elias 123
Pirow, Oswald 3, 54, 63, 160
PLO 132–133, 136–137, 142, 144, 166
political Zionism 30, 39, 64, 94, 96
Politics of Inequality, The 8
Portuguese colonialism 87
Potchefstroomse Universiteitskollege vir Christelike Hoër Onderwys 12
Potter, Sidney Barnett 60–61
privileged white minority 9
pro-Nazi 3, 9, 25, 74
Progressive Federal Party (PFP) 33
Progressive Youth Alliance (PYA) 124
Protocols of the Elders of Zion, The 4, 36, 50, 55, 59, 79–80, 98, 127–129, 146–147, 160, 162, 166, 167

Purified National Party 2

Q

Qibla 136–140–144, 167
Quota Act of 1930 2, 4
Qwelane, Jon 119, 124, 129

R

Rabin, Yitzhak 142, 144
racial segregation 25
radical right 2, 19, 22, 27, 41, 68, 82, 86, 92, 102–103, 111, 113, 115–116, 160–161
radical white right 2, 4, 52, 71–74, 76, 78–79, 82, 88, 100, 102, 107, 117, 128
Rand Afrikaans University (RAU) 13
Rand Daily Mail 44, 67, 69, 80, 83, 104, 112
Rapp, AJ 130
Rapportryers 102
Rasool, Ebrahim 138, 165
red peril 21, 28, 39
Reich Party 56, 69
Richard, Dirk Gysbert 19, 40
right-wing antisemitic actions 121
right-wing organisation 104, 109, 111–112
    Afrikaner Volkswag 95, 111
    Aksie Red Blank Suid-Afrika (ARBSA) 109
    AWB 80–82, 88, 100, 102–111, 113–116, 157
    Stallard Foundation 112
Rise and Fall of Great Powers 168
Rivonia trial 35, 37, 97, 114, 128, 156
Rivonia Unmasked: The South African State's Case against Nelson Mandela 128
Robertson, Wilmot 93
Roeder, Manfred 80
Roman Catholic Church 89, 163
Roosevelt, Franklin Delano 75
Rudman, Raymond Kirsch 49, 52–59, 61, 63, 69–70, 72, 74, 81, 103, 106, 111, 149, 161
Russian Revolution of 1917 39, 75, 97

Index

S

SABC 9, 36, 42, 67, 69, 76–77, 79–80, 90, 93
Sachs, Emil Solomon (Solly) 20
SACP 28, 97, 114–115, 132, 134, 168
Saron, Gustav (Gus) 9, 31–32, 36, 44, 68
Sauer Commission of 1947 7
Schmidt, Rudolf 81
Schoeman, Barend Jacobus (Ben) 47
Schoeman, Johan 52, 58–64, 72–73, 149, 161
Scholtz, Gert Daniël 32
Schumann, Theodor Eberhardt Werner 95–96
Schwarz, Harry Heinz 91, 100–101
Second World War 33, 48, 52, 61, 67, 72–75, 96, 104, 111, 128, 149
separate development 5, 40
Sharpeville 34, 88
Shimoni, Gideon 11
Six Day War in 1967 46–47, 135
Six Million Did Die: The Truth Shall Prevail 76, 92
Six Million Swindle, The 130
Skorzeny, Otto Johann Anton 70
Smuts, Jan Christian 5, 9, 20, 23, 27, 52, 54, 61
social
    distance 120
    interests 1
    reality 1
    snobbery 3
Sons of South Africa 29–30, 64
South African Broadcasting Corporation *see* SABC
South African Bureau of Racial Affairs (SABRA) 9
South African Communist Party (SACP) *see also* CPSA 28, 34
South African Communist Party *see* SACP
South African Jewish Board of Deputies 6, 27, 57, 127, 167
South African Jewish Report 145
South African Jewish Times 38–40
South African National Front (SANF) 81

South African Observer 30, 33, 35, 37, 41, 46, 48, 64–65, 75–76, 78, 8–86, 94–95
South African Zionist Federation 121, 150
Soviet communism 39, 64
Soweto 120, 125
Soweto uprising of 1976 87
Springbok Legion 25–26, 28
Stäglich, Wilhelm 92
Stallard Foundation 112
State of Israel 5, 97–98, 140, 149, 159
Stofberg, Louis 46
Stoker, Hendrik Gerhardus 7
Strijdom, Johannes Gerhardus (Hans) 10, 23, 32, 37, 50
struggle against apartheid 47, 132, 159
Strydom, Lauritz 128
Student Representative Council (SRC) 25, 81, 124–125
Sunday Express 18
Sunday Times 63, 80–81, 103
Sunday Tribune 78, 107
Suppression of Communism Act of 1950 27
Suttner, Raymond 45
Suzman, Arthur 91–92
Suzman, Helen 33, 46
Swart, Charles Robberts (Blackie) 15, 26, 28, 36

T

Terre'Blanche, Eugène Ney 99, 102, 105–111, 114–117
transformation 1, 122, 156
    economic 33, 51
    political 33
    rural 51
    social 51
    university 125
Transvaler, Die 25, 30–31, 38, 42–43, 73, 82, 103
Treason trial 33, 97, 156
Treurnicht, Andries Petrus 87–88, 99–101, 107, 115
tricameral parliament 99
Troskie, GFC 36

U

UCT 16, 25, 131, 135, 137, 142, 145
UDF 115, 137–139
Umkhonto we Sizwe (MK) 34
Union Review 60
United Democratic Front *see* UDF
United Party 3–5, 10, 26, 30, 32–33, 46, 61, 91
University of Cape Town *see* UCT
University of the Witwatersrand *see* Wits
Uys, CJ 32
Uys, Pieter-Dirk 91

V

Vaderland, Die 30, 43, 48, 73–74, 77, 114
Van den Bergh, Hendrik Johan 35, 41, 65
Van Jaarsveld, Floris Albertus (Floors) 106–107
Van Nierop, Petrus 28
Van Rooy, Johannes Cornelis 7
Van Tonder, Robert 112–113
Van Wyk De Vries Commission 13
verkramptes 46, 87, 102
verligtes 46, 87, 102
Verwoerd, Hendrik Frensch 37, 42–43, 45, 58, 64, 113
Viljoen, Gerrit Van Niekerk 13
völkisch 105, 156
    Afrikaner nationalism 2–3, 10, 116, 155, 160
    agenda 20
    intellectuals 19
    mindset 3
    myths and symbols 98
    nationalists 16
    organisations 8
    project 34, 52
    solidarity 88
    thinkers 20
    vocabulary 103
volksfront 108–109, 111
Von Moltke, Johannes von Strauss 27, 50, 160, 162
Vorster, Balthazar Johannes (John) 16, 24, 34–35, 45–47, 65, 71, 78, 80, 82, 88, 91, 102–103, 139
Vorster, Jacobus Daniël (Koot) 24–25, 37–38, 41, 44, 47, 79, 89

W

War in South Africa, The 97
Weichardt, Louis 50, 54, 70, 103, 107
white civilisation 3, 26
white financial wealth 120
white radical right 116, 157, 160
white radical right propaganda 156
white supremacy 61, 87, 101–102
Willem ('Wimpie') de Klerk 82
Wilmer, Brendon 109
Wit Kommando 81
Wits 10, 16, 25, 81, 125, 137, 142, 145, 151
Wolpe, Harold 35–36, 40
World Aryan Union (WAU) 55
World at War, The 76, 78, 83
World Conference Against Racism, Racial Discrimination, Xenophobia and Related Intolerance (WCAR) 145–146
World Trade Centre in Kempton Park 116

Z

Zaki, Yaqub 130, 149
Zille, Helen 112, 127
Zionism 44, 54, 57, 59, 64–65, 67, 70, 78, 85, 94, 98, 103, 119, 129, 132–137, 139, 142, 167
    is apartheid 144
    is racism 79, 133, 136, 145, 166
    political 30, 39, 64, 94, 96
Zionist manipulation 97, 139
Zionist Record 4, 9
Zuma, Jacob Gedleyihlekisa 124, 158

Also by Milton Shain

A Perfect Storm: Antisemitism in South Africa, 1930-1948, 2015.

Holocaust Scholarship: Personal Trajectories and Professional Interpretations (edited with Christopher R Browning, Susannah Heschel, Michael R Marrus), 2015.

The Jews in South Africa: An Illustrated History (with Richard Mendelsohn), 2008 and updated edition 2014.

Zakor v'Makor: Place and Displacement in Jewish History and Memory (edited with David Cesarani and Tony Kushner), 2009.

Opposing Voices: Liberalism and Opposition in South Africa Today, (editor), 2006.

Memories Realities and Dreams: Aspects of the South African Jewish Experience, (co-editor with Richard Mendelsohn), 2002.

Looking Back: Jews in the Struggle for Democracy and Human Rights in South Africa, (with Albie Sachs, Adrienne Folb, Jon Weinberg, Jon Berndt, Barry Feinberg, André Odendaal), 2001.

Israel: Culture, Religion and Society 1948–1998, (co-editor with Stuart A. Cohen), 2000.

Jewries at the Frontier: Accommodation, Identity and Conflict, (co-editor with Sander L Gilman), 1999.

Antisemitism, 1998.

The Roots of Antisemitism in South Africa, 1994.

Jewry and Cape Society: The Origins and Activities of the Jewish Board of Deputies for the Cape Colony, 1983.

www.ingramcontent.com/pod-product-compliance
Lightning Source LLC
Chambersburg PA
CBHW031425150426
43191CB00006B/406